Learning Perl on Win32 Systems

The Perl Series

Advanced Perl Programming
Learning Perl
Learning Perl on Win32 Systems
Perl 5 Desktop Reference
Programming Perl

Also by O'Reilly

Mastering Regular Expressions
CGI Programming on the World Wide Web
Web Client Programming with Perl

Learning Perl on Win32 Systems

Randal L. Schwartz, Erik Olson, and
Tom Christiansen

O'REILLY™

Cambridge · Köln · Paris · Sebastopol · Tokyo

Learning Perl on Win32 Systems

by Randal L. Schwartz, Erik Olson, and Tom Christiansen

Published by O'Reilly & Associates, Inc., 101 Morris Street, Sebastopol, CA 95472.

Editor: Robert Denn

Production Editor: Jane Ellin

Printing History:

August 1997:   First Edition

ISBN: 1-56592-324-3   [9/97]

Table of Contents

Foreword to the First Edition of Learning Perl

Attention, class! Attention! Thank you.

Greetings, aspiring magicians. I hope your summer vacations were enjoyable, if too short. Allow me to be the first to welcome you to the College of Wizardry and, more particularly, to this introductory class in the Magic of Perl. I am not your regular instructor, but Professor Schwartz was unavoidably delayed, and has asked me, as the creator of Perl, to step in today and give a few introductory remarks.

Let's see now. Where to begin? How many of you are taking this course as freshmen? I see. Hmmm, I've seen worse in my days. Occasionally. *Very* occasionally.

Eh? That was a joke. Really! Ah well. No sense of humor, these freshmen.

Well now, what shall I talk about? There are, of course, any number of things I *could* talk about. I could take the egotistical approach and talk about myself, elucidating all those quirks of genetics and upbringing that brought me to the place of creating Perl, as well as making a fool of myself in general. That might be entertaining, at least to me.

Or I could talk instead about Professor Schwartz, without whose ongoing efforts the world of Perl would be much impoverished, up to and including the fact that this course of instruction wouldn't exist.

That might be enlightening, though I have the feeling you'll know more of Professor Schwartz by the end of this course than I do.

Or, putting aside all this personal puffery, I could simply talk about Perl itself, which is, after all, the subject of this course.

Or is it? Hmmm ...

When the curriculum committee discussed this course, it reached the conclusion that this class isn't so much about Perl as it is about you! This shouldn't be too surprising, because Perl is itself also about you—at least in the abstract. Perl was created for someone like you, by someone like you, with the collaboration of many other someones like you. The Magic of Perl was sewn together, stitch by stitch and swatch by swatch, around the rather peculiar shape of your psyche. If you think Perl is a bit odd, perhaps that's why.

Some computer scientists (the reductionists, in particular) would like to deny it, but people have funny-shaped minds. Mental geography is not linear, and cannot be mapped onto a flat surface without severe distortion. But for the last score years or so, computer reductionists have been first bowing down at the Temple of Orthogonality, then rising up to preach their ideas of ascetic rectitude to any who would listen.

Their fervent but misguided desire was simply to squash your mind to fit their mindset, to smush your patterns of thought into some sort of Hyperdimensional Flatland. It's a joyless existence, being smushed.

Nevertheless, your native common sense has shown through in spots. You and your conceptual ancestors have transcended the dreary landscape to compose many lovely computer incantations. (Some of which, at times, actually did what you wanted them to.) The most blessed of these incantations were canonized as Standards, because they managed to tap into something mystical and magical, performing the miracle of Doing What You Expect.

What nobody noticed in all the excitement was that the computer reductionists were still busily trying to smush your minds flat, albeit on a slightly higher plane of existence. The decree, therefore, went out (I'm sure you've heard of it) that computer incantations were only allowed to perform one miracle apiece. "Do one thing and do it well" was the rallying cry, and with one stroke, shell programmers were condemned to a life of muttering and counting beads on strings (which in these latter days have come to be known as pipelines).

This was when I made my small contribution to saving the world. I was rolling some of those very beads around in my fingers one day and pondering the hopelessness (and haplessness) of my existence, when it occurred to me that it might be interesting to melt down some of those mystical beads and see what would happen to their Magic if I made a single, slightly larger bead out of them. So I fired up the old Bunsen burner, picked out some of my favorite beads, and let them melt together however they would. And lo! the new Magic was more powerful than the sum of its parts and parcels.

That's odd, thought I. Why should it be, that the Sedulous Bead of Regular Expressions, when bonded together with the Shellacious Bead of Gnostic Interpolation, and the Awkward Bead of Simple Data Typology, should produce more Magic, pound for pound, than they do when strung out on strings? I said to myself, could it be that the beads can exchange power with each other because they no longer have to commune with each other through that skinny little string? Could the pipeline be holding back the flow of information, much as wine doth resist flowing through the neck of Doctor von Neumann's famous bottle?

This demanded (of me) more scrutiny (of it).

So I melted that larger bead together with a few more of my favorite beads, and the same thing happened, only more so. It was practically a combinatorial explosion of potential incantations: the Basic Bead of Output Formats and the Lispery Bead of Dynamic Scoping bonded themselves with the C-rationalized Bead of Operators Galore, and together they put forth a brilliant pulse of power that spread to thousands of machines throughout the entire civilized world. That message cost the net hundreds if not thousands of dollars to send everywhere. Obviously I was either onto something, or on something.

I then gathered my courage about me and showed my new magical bead to some of you, and you then began to give me your favorite beads to add in as well. The Magic grew yet more powerful, as yet more synergy was imbued in the silly thing. It was as if the Computational Elementals summoned by each bead were cooperating on your behalf to solve your problems for you. Why the sudden peace on earth and good will toward mentality? Perhaps it was because the beads were your favorite beads? Perhaps it was because I'm just a good bead picker?

Perhaps I just got lucky.

Whatever, the magical bead eventually grew into this rather odd-looking Amulet you see before you today. See it glitter, almost like a pearl.

That was another joke. Really! I assure you! Ah well. I was a freshman once too...

The Amulet isn't exactly beautiful though—in fact, up close it still looks like a bunch of beads melted together. Well, all right, I admit it. It's downright ugly. But never mind that. It's the Magic that counts. Speaking of Magic, look who just walked in the door! My good buddy Merlyn, er, I should say, Professor Schwartz, is here just in the nick of time to begin telling you how to perform miracles with this little Amulet, if you're willing to learn the proper mysterious incantations. And you're in good hands—I must admit that there's no one better at muttering mysterious incantations than Professor Schwartz. Eh, Merlyn?

Anyway, to sum up. What you'll need most is courage. It is not an easy path that you've set your foot upon. You're learning a new language—a language full of strange runes and ancient chants, some easy and some difficult, many of which sound familiar, and some of which don't. You may be tempted to become discouraged and quit. But think you upon this: consider how long it took you to learn your own native tongue. Was it worth it? I think so. And have you finished learning it? I think not. Then do not expect to learn all the mysteries of Perl in a moment, as though you were consuming a mere peanut, or an olive. Rather, think of it as though you were consuming, say, a banana. Consider how this works. You do not wait to enjoy the banana until after you have eaten the whole thing. No, of course not. You enjoy each bite as you take it. And each bite motivates you to take the next bite, and the next.

So then, speaking now of the fruit of Merlyn's labors, I would urge you to enjoy this, um, course. The fruit course, of course. Ahem, that was a joke too. Ah well.

Here then, Professor, I present to you your new class. They seem to have no sense of humor whatsoever, but I expect you'll manage somehow.

Class, I present to you Professor Randal L. Schwartz, Doctor of Syntax, Wizard at Large, and of course, Just Another Perl Hacker. He has my blessings, just as you have my blessings. May you Learn Perl. May you do Good Magic with Perl. And above all, may you have Lots of Fun with Perl. So be it!

So do it!

Larry Wall
September, 1993

Foreword to the Present Edition

I hope you enjoy using Perl on Win32 and are as enthralled as I was when I first experienced Perl. Easy tasks were easy and hard tasks were possible—cool! While at hip communications inc., I started using the Perl 4 port developed in part by Clark Williams from Intergraph and Dean Troyer from Honeywell. Seeing the need for a Win32 port of Perl 5, I convinced Microsoft to fund the core port, Automation support, additional administrative modules, and an ISAPI plug in. After leaving hip communications inc. and taking Perl for Win32 with me, I started ActiveWare Internet Corp. and developed PerlScript, again with Microsoft funding. Responding to the demand for commercial Perl-related products and services, my development partner, Doug Lankshear, and I founded ActiveSTATE tool corporation where we are striving to balance freeware and commercial software development efforts.

As the operator of the perl-win32-* mailing lists, I am very relieved with the release of this book. There is finally a definitive, introductory reference for Perl on Win32 systems. Most of the Perl books that I have seen have a UNIX slant that can be very confusing to the uninitiated. I now have somewhere to send the aspiring but confused Win32 Perl developer.

Unlike UNIX systems, which typically come with several powerful scripting tools, Windows systems are shipped without one (I don't count batch files or <gasp> BASIC in the "powerful" category). Fortunately Perl is freely available for Win32 systems to help you create scripting solutions for everything from repetitive system administration tasks to building powerful, dynamic web sites. Perl for Win32 gives you access to the Registry, event logs, ODBC databases, and any Automation Object so that you can glue together all the components you need to solve the task at hand.

If you are experienced with Perl on UNIX platforms, this book will help you become familiar with the unique features of Perl for Win32. Either as a novice or experienced programmer, whether you are a System Administrator, Web Master, or Power User, you will be brought up to speed and ready to use Perl to solve real problems on Win32 systems. You will also be poised to take advantage of all the cool stuff coming for Perl. Some of these technologies are: tools to make it easier to develop and manage Perl modules, graphical development environments; enhanced Automation capabilities and performance; as well as solid compiler, multithread, and Unicode support.

I am excited about Perl and its future—I hope you are too.

Dick Hardt
July 1997

Preface

What This Book Is About

This book is a gentle introduction to Perl. By the time you've gone through this book, you'll have touched on the majority of the most common operations and language idioms found in most Perl programs.

This book is not intended as a comprehensive guide to Perl—on the contrary, in order to keep the book from being yet another comprehensive reference guide, we've been selective about covering the things you are most likely to use early in your Perl hacking career. For more information, check out the voluminous and readily available Perl reference material. For obvious reasons, we recommend highly the companion volume to this book, *Programming Perl*, Second Edition, published by O'Reilly & Associates.

This book is based on the second edition of *Learning Perl*. We have removed some things that are not applicable to Perl programmers on Windows NT systems, and have added coverage of other things that are special to Windows NT. A wealth of Perl extensions for the Windows platforms exist; we have introduced some of the most important of these extensions, but we have again been selective in doing so.

Each chapter ends with a series of exercises to help you practice what you have just read. If you read at a typical pace, and do all of the exercises, you should be able to get through each chapter in about 2 or 3 hours, and finish the book in 40 or 50 hours.

We'd Like to Hear from You

We have tested and verified all of the information in this book to the best of our ability, but you may find that features have changed (or even that we have made mistakes!). Please let us know about any errors you find, as well as your suggestions for future editions, by writing to:

> O'Reilly & Associates, Inc.
> 101 Morris Street
> Sebastopol, CA 95472
> 1-800-998-9938 (in US or Canada)
> 1-707-829-0515 (international/local)
> 1-707-829-0104 (FAX)

You can also send us messages electronically. To be put on the mailing list or request a catalog, send email to:

> *info@oreilly.com* (via the Internet)

To ask technical questions or comment on the book, send email to:

> *bookquestions@oreilly.com* (via the Internet)

Conventions

The following typographic conventions are used in this book:

Italic
> is used for filenames and command names. It is also used to highlight comments in command examples, and to define new terms when they first appear in the text.

`Constant Width`
> is used in examples to show the text that you enter literally, and in regular text to show operators, variables, and the output from commands or programs.

`Constant Bold`
> is used in examples to show the user's actual input at the terminal.

`Constant Italic`
> is used in examples to show variables for which a context-specific substitution should be made. The variable `filename`, for example, would be replaced by some actual filename.

Footnotes
> are used to attach parenthetical notes which you *should not* read on your first reading of this book. Sometimes, lies are presented to simplify the discussion, and a footnote restores the lie to truth. Often, the material in the footnote will be advanced information that is not discussed anywhere else in the book.

Exercises

The exercises in this book are available electronically by FTP and FTPMAIL. Use FTP if you are directly on the Internet. Use FTPMAIL if you are not on the Internet but can send and receive electronic mail to Internet sites. (This includes CompuServe users.)

FTP

If you have an Internet connection (permanent or dialup), the easiest way to use FTP is via your web browser or favorite FTP client. To get the examples, simply point your browser to:

ftp://ftp.oreilly.com/published/oreilly/nutshell/learning_perlnt/examples.zip

If you don't have a web browser, you can use the command-line FTP client included with Windows NT (or Windows 95).

```
% ftp ftp.oreilly.com
Connected to ftp.oreilly.com.
220 ftp.oreilly.com FTP server (Version 6.34 Thu Oct 22 14:32:01 EDT 1992)
ready.
Name (ftp.oreilly.com:username): anonymous
331 Guest login ok, send e-mail address as password.
Password: username@hostname            Use your username and host here
230 Guest login ok, access restrictions apply.
ftp> cd /published/oreilly/nutshell/learning_perlnt
250 CWD command successful.
ftp> get README
200 PORT command successful.
150 Opening ASCII mode data connection for README (xxxx bytes).
226 Transfer complete.
local: README remote: README
xxxx bytes received in xxx seconds (xxx Kbytes/s)
ftp> binary
200 Type set to I.
ftp> get examples.zip
200 PORT command successful.
150 Opening BINARY mode data connection for examples.zip (xxxx bytes).
226 Transfer complete. local: exercises remote: exercises
xxxx bytes received in xxx seconds (xxx Kbytes/s)
ftp> quit
221 Goodbye.
%
```

FTPMAIL

FTPMAIL is a mail server available to anyone who can send electronic mail to, and receive electronic mail from, Internet sites. Any company or service provider that allows email connections to the Internet can access FTPMAIL.

You send mail to *ftpmail@online.oreilly.com*. In the message body, give the FTP commands you want to run. The server will run anonymous FTP for you, and mail the files back to you. To get a complete help file, send a message with no subject and the single word "help" in the body. The following is an example mail message that gets the examples. This command sends you a listing of the files in the selected directory and the requested example files. The listing is useful if you are interested in a later version of the examples.

```
Subject:
reply-to username@hostname         (Message Body) Where you want files mailed
open
cd /published/oreilly/nutshell/learning_perlnt
dir
get README
mode binary
uuencode
get examples.zip
quit
```

A signature at the end of the message is acceptable as long as it appears after "quit."

Acknowledgments for First Edition

First, I wholeheartedly thank Chick Webb and Taos Mountain Software (in Silicon Valley). The folks at TMS offered me an opportunity to write an introductory Perl course for them (with substantial assistance from Chick), and a chance to present their course a few times. From that experience, I gained the motivation and resources to write and repeatedly present a new course of my own, from which this book is derived. Without them, I don't think I'd be doing this, and I wish them continued success at marketing their course. (And if they're looking for a good text for a revision of their course, I just may have a suggestion...)

Thanks also to the reviewers: Perl Godfather Larry Wall (of course), Larry Kistler (Director of Education, Pyramid), fellow Perl trainer Tom Christiansen, the students of the *Learning Perl* classes I taught at Intel and Pyramid, and—from O'Reilly & Associates—Tanya Herlick, Lar Kaufman, Lenny Muellner, Linda Mui, and Andy Oram.

This book was created and edited entirely on my personal Apple Macintosh Powerbook (well, actually a series of them—the 140, 160, and now the 520c models). More often than not, I was away from my office while writing—sometimes in a park, sometimes in a hotel, sometimes waiting for the weather to clear so I could continue to snow-ski, but most often in restaurants. In fact, I wrote a substantial portion of this book at the Beaverton McMenamin's just down the road from my house. The McM's chain of brewpubs make and serve the finest microbrew and best cheesecake and greasiest sandwiches in my hometown area. I consumed many pints of ale and pieces of cheesecake in this ideal work environment, while my Powerbook swallowed many kilowatt hours of electricity at their four tables with power outlets. For the electricity, and the generous hospitality and courtesy (and rent-free booth-office space), I thank the exceptional staff at the Beaverton McM's. I also hacked some early work on the book at the Beaverton Chili's Restaurant, to which I am also grateful. (But they didn't have any outlets near the bar, so I switched when I found McM's, to save the wear and tear on my batteries.)

Thanks also to "the Net" (especially the subscribers to *comp.lang.perl.**) for their continued support of Larry and me, and their unending curiosity about getting Perl to work for them.

Further thanks to the O'Reilly & Associates folks who made this book happen, including Clairemarie Fisher O'Leary, who copyedited the book and managed the production with invaluable help from Kismet McDonough, Mike Sierra, and Stephen Spainhour; and Edie Freedman who designed the cover and the internal format. Thanks, also, to Tim O'Reilly, for Taoistically being.

And especially, a huge personal thanks to my friend Steve Talbott, who guided me through every step of the way (especially suggesting the stroll at the end of the first chapter). His editorial criticisms were always right on, and his incessant talent for beating me over the head ever so gently allowed me to make this book a piece of art with which I'm extremely pleased.

As always, a special thank you to both Lyle and Jack, for teaching me nearly everything I know about writing.

And finally, an immeasurable thank you to my friend and partner, Larry Wall, for giving Perl to us all in the first place.

> A one L Randal wrote a book,
> A two L llama for the look,
> But to whom we owe it all
> Is the three L Larry Wall!

Randal L. Schwartz

Acknowledgments for the Second Edition

I'd like to thank Larry Wall for writing Perl, the Perl Porters for their continued maintenance efforts, and the entire Perl community for their helpfulnesss toward one another.

Thanks also to Jon Orwant, Nate Torkington, and Larry Wall for reviewing the CGI chapter.

Tom Christiansen

Acknowledgments for the Win32 Edition

First, thanks to Robert Denn for his expert editorial guidance. Thanks also to the technical reviewers for the Win32 edition of this book for their comments and observations: Dick Hardt, Jon Udell, Jon Forrest, Mike McMillan, and Eric Pearce. They all provided valuable feedback, and even offered lots of suggestions that unfortunately didn't get applied to the final version due to scheduling constraints.

Thanks to the folks, both at ActiveState and the Perl Porters, who have made a Win32 version of Perl possible.

Thanks also to Randal Schwartz and Tom Christiansen for the version of *Learning Perl* upon which this book is based, and for their comments on this version.

Thanks to the folks at O'Reilly & Associates who either helped with the manuscript or offered suggestions, including Tim O'Reilly, Mike Sierra, who provided Tools support, Jane Ellin, the production editor, John Files, Peter Fell, Mary Anne Weeks Mayo, and Sheryl Avruch for quality control, Seth Maislin for the index, Nancy Priest for the interior design, Edie Freedman for the cover, Robert Romano and Chris Reilley for the figures, and Madeleine Newell for freelance support.

Thanks also to my extremely understanding employers at Axiom Technologies, who let me practically live in their offices during a hectic schedule, and who provided moral support and easy targets.

Finally, a huge thanks to my wife, Jodi, and my son, Isaac, for their love, understanding, and support.

Erik Olson

1

Introduction

History of Perl

Perl is a language designed for people who need to get things done. Written by the amazing Larry Wall as a kind of glue language to tie together all of the loose ends of everyday computing life, Perl is a tool for leveraging the skills and tools that you already have. Perl has become an indispensable boon to Windows NT webmasters, power users, administrators, and programmers who have discovered how much easier it is to get their work done when Perl is doing some of it for them.

Do you know a little about C? Then you probably already know a lot about Perl. In fact, if you have used any programming or scripting language before, you might be surprised at how familiar Perl looks. Perl is not only an easy language to use, but also makes great use of your existing tools and solutions.

Perl is an easy language, but it's also a rich language, offering lots of functionality right out of the box. You'll be surprised at how much you can do with just a little bit of Perl code. Often, rewriting a small scrap of Perl wizardry requires hundreds of lines of C. Some languages that let you do a lot with a little don't let you do a whole lot. Perl not only lets you do a lot, it lets you do so with minimal effort. And if you run into something that you can't do in Perl, you'll find most likely that Perl will cooperate quite nicely with whatever you do have to do it in.

For many addicts, Perl is more than a language, it's an entire culture. For many folks, Perl was an indispensable part of their UNIX toolkits that they took with them to new environments. As a result, Perl grew, and became even more general and more powerful. What was once just an exceptional text-processing language that bound UNIX programs together has become a widespread language that seems to bind much of the Internet together. Perl is now used to create web pages, read Usenet news, do system adminstration and systems programming, write network clients and servers, and much more.

The three chief virtues of a Perl programmer (indeed, of any programmer) are sometimes said to be laziness, impatience, and hubris. Although these may seem like undesirable qualities at first blush (just ask your SO), there's more to this than there appears to be.

Laziness is the quality that makes you take great efforts to reduce the overall amount of work that you have to do. Lazy programmers are apt to develop reusable and general solutions that can be used in more than one place, and are more apt to document what they do, so that they don't have to ever waste time or torture their brains figuring it out again.

Impatient programmers get angry whenever they have to do anything that the computer could be doing for them. Hence, they develop programs that anticipate their needs and solve problems for them, so that they can do less (there's that laziness again) while accomplishing more.

Finally, hubris is that quality which makes programmers write programs that they want other people to see (and be able to maintain). Hubris is also a quality that promotes innovation: if you think that you have a better way and you're not afraid to prove it, you're often right.

Odd ideas for a culture, perhaps, but effective ones. Here's another tenet of the Perl way: "There's more than one way to do it." What this means is that Perl programmers are a results-oriented lot. They're likely to applaud any tool that gets the job done, regardless of whether or not the code looks like something they would have written. Another side effect of this tenet that particularly endears itself to Win32 Perl programmers is that Perl is highly portable. Although ready-made scripts that you find on the Net may use existing UNIX tools or UNIX system calls that aren't portable to the Windows environment (this scenario has led Win32 programmers to say, "There's more than one way to do it, and it's a good thing, because most of the ways don't work"), you can nearly always find a way to make them work (and nobody will make fun of you if your solution is perhaps somewhat less than elegant).

True to this philosophy, Perl stands for either Practical Extraction and Report Language or Pathologically Eclectic Rubbish Lister (both derivations are sanctioned by the Perl community). Perl for Win32 sprang into existence when Microsoft commissioned ActiveState Tool Corporation (formerly Hip Communications) to do a port for inclusion in the Windows NT Resource Kit. ActiveState is still improving Perl for Win32, extending it with functionality specific to the Win32 platforms, and incorporating the best and most appropriate new features as they are added to the core Perl distribution.

You'll find that Perl for Win32 uses some of the coolest and most compelling technologies available to Windows programmers including OLE automation, ODBC database connectivity, ActiveX scripting, and much more. The source code for Perl (including Perl for Win32) is freely available and freely redistributable. If you want to extend Perl to provide additional features, or embed the interpreter in your own application, you can easily do so.

You'll also find that the Perl community believes in (and practices) information and code sharing. There is an archive network (called the CPAN, for Comprehensive Perl Archive Network), where you can find thousands of existing Perl programs and code fragments.

In addition to a vast body of high quality pre-written code, Perl excels at rapid application development. Part of this is due to the powerful qualities of language that let you do lots of work with a few statements—another part is due to the Perl development tools themselves.

Perl is an interpreted language, but it might work a little bit differently from other interpreted languages that you've used. Perl is actually both a compiler and an interpreter. When you invoke the Perl interpreter on a Perl script file, the file is first compiled and optimized, then efficiently executed. Not only does this allow for efficient runtime execution, it also promotes a quick development cycle, in which you can quickly make changes and rerun your script without going through a long compile and link cycle.

In spite of Perl's relatively free syntax, you can easily develop correct Perl programs. Not only is there a Perl debugger, but the compiler itself will issue informative warnings when you're treading on thin ice. Furthermore, the interpreter doesn't execute unless the program compiles completely. This feature saves you from the common interpreted-language nightmare in which the first half of your program works and does something to a file, and then the second half doesn't.

Purpose of Perl

Well, you've made it through the Perl hype. You might be wondering why you'd ever use Perl. This section provides a couple of ideas.

You can use Perl for World Wide Web (WWW) programming. You've probably heard that Perl has become a sort of *lingua franca* for the Web (actually, you may have heard that statement for more than one language, but we'll say it again here). Perl cannot only be used as a CGI language (for which there are wonderful modules available), but it can be used as an ISAPI extension (an in-process extension to your web server), or even as an ActiveX scripting language. You can also use Perl to validate HTML syntax, to verify that web hyperlinks are still correct, and to fetch URLs from the Internet.

You can use Perl for many system administration chores. Not only will Perl let you manipulate the Registry, the Event Log, and Windows NT user account information, it's also the best tool going for processing log files of nearly any format.

You can use Perl to drive your favorite word processor or spreadsheet using OLE Automation. You can use the freely available Win32::ODBC module or Active Data Objects (ADO) to access your favorite local or enterprise database.

You can use Perl to retrieve (and filter) your email and Usenet news. You can use Perl to send email, interact with FTP and HTTP servers, and be a client for nearly any other type of Internet server you can dream up.

You can use Perl to process textual or numerical data, to prototype projects, to do quick search and replace functions in text files, to drive the execution of a sequence of commands, and much, much more.

In short, Perl can do zillions of thing to help you do your job faster and get back to doing things that are fun (many of which you can also use Perl to do). And along the way, you might find that the journey itself can be a lot of fun.

Like any language, Perl can be "write only"; it's possible to write programs that are impossible to read. But with proper care, you can avoid this common accusation. Yes, sometimes Perl looks like line noise to the uninitiated, but to the seasoned Perl programmer, it looks like checksummed line noise with a mission in life. If you follow the guidelines of this book, your programs should be easy to read and easy to maintain, but they probably won't win any obfuscated Perl contests.

Availability

Unless you have had the good fortune of having a system administrator install Perl on your workstation, you will need to obtain and install a copy yourself.

Perl is distributed under the GNU Public License,* which says something like, "you can distribute binaries of Perl only if you make the source code available at no cost, and if you modify Perl, you have to distribute the source to your modifications as well." And that's essentially free. You can get the source to Perl for the cost of a few megabytes over a wire.

At the time of this writing, there are two Perl distributions that run on Windows NT and Windows 95. There is the ActiveState port of Perl, called Perl for Win32,

---

* Or the slightly more liberal Artistic License, found in the distribution sources.

and starting with Perl 5.004, the standard Perl distribution includes support for Win32 systems. The two versions are largely compatible, with some of the Perl 5.004 code being based on the ActiveState port, but there are some differences. The programs and examples presented in this tutorial have been tested on both systems; when a distribution requires different code, we point that fact out. The architects of both distibutions have announced their intention to merge the distributions, but they have not yet announced a time frame for that to happen.

ActiveState Perl for Win32

The canonical source for the ActiveState Perl for Win32 distribution at the time of this writing is at *http://www.activestate.com*. You can also find the source and binaries for the Perl for Win32 distribution at CPAN. To use the CPAN archives, visit *http://www.perl.com/CPAN* for a mirror site close to you. The CPAN site will also provide the source distribution for the UNIX version of Perl and precompiled binaries for other platforms. If you're absolutely stumped, write *bookques-tions@ora.com* and say "Where can I get Perl?!?!"

Perl for Win32 comes in a variety of flavors, in both source and binary distributions. Unless you have access to a C++ compiler,* you'll probably want to get the binary distribution that contains the Perl executables and libraries, pre-built and ready to use. You might also want to grab the source distribution for reference purposes, if you're familiar with C/C++.

You can choose from one of several different binary distributions: there's a standalone version of the Perl interpreter (Perl for Win32), a version for use as an ISAPI† extension with ISAPI compliant Web servers (PerlIS), and an ActiveX scripting version (PerlScript). If you choose either the ISAPI or the PerlScript version, you will still need the standalone version of the interpreter, because it contains the Perl libraries, documentation, and example files. Binary distributions exist for both DEC Alpha and Intel versions of Windows NT. At the time of this writing, the current release version of Perl for Win32 is based on Perl 5.003, and the build number is 306.

The standalone version of Perl for Win32 is easy to install; the distribution comes as a self-extracting executable. Just run the executable, select the directory to install into, and run the installation script as prompted by the installer. You'll probably need to re-logon (in Windows NT) or reboot (in Windows 95) to your workstation because the installation changes the PATH environment variable.

---

* The Perl for Win32 distribution currently includes makefiles only for the Microsoft Visual C++ compiler.

† For more on ISAPI and PerlIS, see Chapter 18, *CGI Programming*.

The Perl for Win32 distribution includes the Perl interpreter, the standard Perl libraries (useful collections of code that aren't part of the core language), and a number of Win32 extension modules. The Win32 extension modules either extend Perl to provide additional functionality for Win32 platforms or they provide functionality that is present in UNIX versions of Perl, but which is unimplemented or otherwise missing in Win32 versions. The distribution also includes help documentation (in HTML format) and example scripts that demonstrate the various features of Perl and the Win32 extensions.

Currently, if you're interested in either the ISAPI version of Perl, or PerlScript, you need to get the ActiveState distribution, because neither of these tools works with the standard distribution. Also, if you don't have convenient access to either the Microsoft or Borland C++ compilers, you'll definitely want to grab the binary ActiveState distibution.

Standard Perl Distribution

The standard Perl distribution can be found at *http://www.perl.com/CPAN/* and compiles out of the box for several different platforms, including Windows NT. As we write this, the standard distribution is only available in source form; the binary distribution on CPAN is the ActiveState port. This scenario is likely to change by the time you are reading this, so you'll want to visit CPAN to investigate your options.

The source distribution of Perl 5.004 requires either the Microsoft Visual C++ compiler (versions 2.0 - 5.0) or the Borland C++ compiler (version 5.x). After you get the distribution, you should start with the *readme.win32* file, which contains detailed instructions for building, testing, and installing the distribution.

Briefly, here's what you need to do to build and install the distribution (this example assumes you're using the Microsoft compiler, but using the Borland C++ compiler should be quite similar, except that you'll need to get the *dmake* make utility; see *readme.win32* for details).

Extract the distribution using some utility that supports *gzip* and *tar* files, as well as long filenames. There are ports of both GNU *gzip* and *tar* available for the various Win32 platforms (you can find both at the Virtually UN*X site at *www.itribe.net/virtunix* or several other places on the Net), and these will work quite nicely. Alternatively, you might try one of the graphical zip archive programs (we recommend *WinZip* at *www.winzip.com*).

Assuming you're using *gzip* and *tar*, execute the following (you might need to adjust the filename):

```
> gzip -dc perl5.004_01.tar.gz | tar xf -
```

If you're using *WinZip* or some other utility, make sure that you preserve the directory structure.

Next, edit the makefile (*Makefile*) in the *win32* subdirectory of the distribution and make sure that you're happy with the values for the install drive and directory.

Then, execute the following commands from the *win32* subdirectory of the distribution to build, test, and install the distribution. This assumes that you have the proper environment variables (LIB, INCLUDE, etc) set up for your compiler (this assumes *nmake* is your make utility).

```
> nmake          (Build all of Perl)
> nmake test     (Test your distribution)
> nmake install  (Install to the target dir. in the Makefile)
```

Assuming everything is built correctly, you just need to add the *bin* subdirectory of the installation target directory to your path. For example, if you installed the Perl distribution to *c:\Perl*, you'll want to add *c:\Perl\bin* to your path.

Finally, restart your machine to get the environment changes, and you're ready to go. We strongly recommend getting the *libwin32* package from CPAN, and installing it as well. We'll be discussing several of the extensions provided by *libwin32* throughout this book (the ActiveState distribution includes most of these extensions already). Installation of *libwin32* is easy. Simply download and extract the file, and then execute the following commands from the directory to which you extracted the files:

```
> perl Makefile.PL
> nmake
> nmake test
> nmake install
```

Windows NT and Windows 95

A word of warning is probably in order here: Windows 95 users can expect significantly different functionality from their Perl distribution than Windows NT users. For various reasons, some of the Win32 modules don't work on Windows 95. The functionality required to implement them may be missing on Windows 95, or bugs in Windows 95 may prevent them from working correctly. We'll explore some of the specifics in later chapters, but for now remember that some of the examples and concepts presented in this book require Windows NT.

Support

Perl is the child of Larry Wall, and is still being coddled by him. Bug reports and requests for enhancements generally get fixed in later releases, but he is under no obligation to do anything with them. Nevertheless, Larry really does enjoy hearing from all of us, and does truly like to see Perl be useful to the world at large. Direct email generally gets a response (even if it is merely his email answering machine), and sometimes a personal response. These days, Larry is actually acting as an architect to the "Perl 5 Porters" group, a bunch of very clever people that have had a lot to do with the last few Perl releases. If Larry got hit by a bus, everyone would be very sad for a long time, but Perl would still continue to mature under the direction of this group.

You will probably find that your best bet for support comes from the global online Perl community, accessible via the Usenet newsgroup *comp.lang.perl.misc*. If you are emailable to the Internet, but not amenable to Usenet, you can also wire yourself into this group by sending a request to *perl-users-request@cs.orst.edu*, which will reach a human who can connect you to a two-way email gateway into the group, and give you guidelines on how the group works.

When you subscribe to the newsgroup, you'll find roughly 50 to 200 postings a day (at the time of this writing) on all manner of subjects from beginner questions to complicated porting issues and interface problems, and even a fairly large program or two.

The newsgroup is almost constantly monitored by many Perl experts. Most of the time, your question gets answered within minutes of your news article reaching a major Usenet hub. Just try getting *that* level of support from your favorite software vendor for free! Larry himself reads the group as time permits, and has been known to interject authoritative articles to end bickering or clarify a point. After all, without Usenet, there probably wouldn't have been a place to easily announce Perl to the world.

In addition to the newsgroup, you should also be reading the Perl documentation which comes with the Perl distribution. Another authoritative source is the *Programming Perl* Nutshell Handbook, by Larry Wall, Tom Christiansen, and Randal L. Schwartz (O'Reilly & Associates, 1996). *Programming Perl* is known as "The Camel Book" because of the animal on its cover. The Camel Book contains the complete reference information, some tutorial stuff, and a bunch of miscellaneous information about Perl in a nicely bound form.

The Frequently Asked Questions (FAQ) list for Perl is a great source of answers for common questions that arise about Perl. The FAQ is available in the *perlfaq* documentation page as of the 5.004 release of Perl, is posted periodically to the moderated *comp.lang.perl.announce* newsgroup, and can also be found on any CPAN mirror under the *doc/FAQs* directory.

Finally, for specific issues concerning Perl for Win32, a trio of mailing lists is available: Perl-Win32-Users, Perl-Win32-Porters, and Perl-Win32-Announce. Perl-Win32-

Users[*] is for general questions on installation and usage. This list has moderate traffic at times and can be a valuable resource for Perl-for-Win32 users. The Perl-Win32-Porters list is for development and porting issues only. Please do not ask installation or usage questions of this list. The Perl-Win32-Announce list is for announcements of new builds, bugs, or issues, and is a read-only list. The traffic is very light, and if you're serious about Perl for Win32, you probably want to subscribe to this list.

To subscribe to any of the Perl-for-Win32 lists, send a message to *ListManager@ActiveState.com* with the message `SUBSCRIBE Perl-Win32-Users` (or whichever list you're interested in) in the *body* of the message.

Even though the Perl community is largely a helpful and collaborative group, they do expect you to do your homework before asking questions. You should always search the applicable FAQs *before* posting your question to the Usenet or a mailing list. You can find the Perl-for-Win32 FAQ at *http://www.endcontsw.com/people/evangelo/Perl_for_Win32_FAQ.html*, or by searching around at the ActiveState site (*http://www.activestate.com*). You can find the general Perl FAQs at any CPAN site (try the */doc/FAQs*) directory.

Basic Concepts

A Perl program is a bunch of Perl statements and definitions thrown into a file. You can execute the file by invoking the Perl interpreter with the script name as an argument. You will often see a line

```
#!/usr/bin/perl
```

as the first line of a Perl script. This line is a bit of magic employed by UNIX-like operating systems to automatically execute interpreted languages with the correct command interpreter. This line is called a *shebang* line due to the first two characters: # is sometimes called sharp, and ! is sometimes called bang. This line normally won't work for Perl-for-Win32 users,[†] although it doesn't hurt anything since Perl sees lines beginning with # as comments.

The invocation examples that follow assume that you have invoked the Windows NT command interpreter (*cmd.exe*) and are typing into a console window. You can run Perl scripts from the Explorer or the File Manager (assuming that you've associated the script extension with the Perl interpreter) by double-clicking on the

---

[*] This list has a history of down time. If it seems to be down for a few days, try resubscribing or wait a while. It usually starts working again.

[†] However, there are Win32 ports of UNIX shells (e.g., *tcsh*, *ksh*, and *bash*) that do understand shebang lines. If you're using one of these shells, you can use shebang lines by specifying the path to your Perl interpreter.

script icon to launch it. Throughout this book, we're going to be discussing standard output and input streams; these are generally assumed to be your console window.

We recommend naming scripts with a *.plx* extension. Traditionally, Perl modules have a *.pm* extension, and Perl libraries have a *.pl* extension. The ActiveState installer prompts you to associate *.pl* with the interpreter.

You can always execute a script by calling the Perl interpreter with the script as an argument:

```
> perl myscript.plx
```

You can also associate files with the *.plx* extension (or another of your choosing) with the Perl interpreter, so that executing

```
> myscript.plx
```

will correctly invoke the Perl interpreter and execute your script. This step is normally done for you by the ActiveState installation script[*] for the *.pl* extension, but if you wish to change the extension or if you've got the standard distribution, you can do this step manually. If you're using Windows NT 4.0 (or greater), the following commands will do the trick (use the full path to your interpreter):

```
> assoc .plx=Perl
> ftype Perl=c:\myperl\bin\perl.exe %1 %*
```

If you can't bear the thought of typing the extension every time you execute a Perl script, you can set the *PATHEXT* environment variable so that it includes Perl scripts. For example:

```
> set PATHEXT=%PATHEXT%;.PLX
```

This setting will let you type

```
> myscript
```

without including the file extension. Take care when setting *PATHEXT* permanently—it also includes executable file types like *.COM*, *.EXE*, *.BAT*, and *.CMD*. If you inadvertently lose those extensions, you'll have difficulty invoking applications and script files.

Perl is mostly a free-format language like C—whitespace between tokens (elements of the program, like `print` or `+`) is optional, unless two tokens placed together can be mistaken for another token, in which case whitespace of some kind is mandatory. (Whitespace consists of spaces, tabs, newlines, returns, or

---

[*] This statement is not true if you're using Windows 95, in which case you'll have to do the whole thing manually. From an Explorer window, go to View/Options/File Types and add a new type with the *.pl* extension and the path to the Perl interpreter.

formfeeds.) A few constructs require a certain kind of whitespace in a certain place, but they'll be pointed out when we get to them. You can assume that the kind and amount of whitespace between tokens is otherwise arbitrary.

Although many interesting Perl programs can be written on one line, typically a Perl program is indented much like a C program, with nested parts of statements indented more than the surrounding parts. You'll see plenty of examples showing a typical indentation style throughout this book.

Just like a batch file, a Perl program consists of all of the Perl statements of the file taken collectively as one big routine to execute. Perl has no concept of a "main" routine as in C.

Perl comments are single-line comments (like REM in a batch file or // in a C++ or Java file). Anything from an unquoted pound sign (#) to the end-of-line is a comment. There are no C-like multiline comments.

Unlike the command shell, the Perl interpreter completely parses and compiles the program before executing any of it. This means that you can never get a syntax error from a program once the program has started, and that the whitespace and comments simply disappear and won't slow the program down. In fact, this compilation phase ensures the rapid execution of Perl operations once execution starts, and provides additional motivation for dropping C as a systems utility language merely on the grounds that C is compiled.

This compilation does take time—it's inefficient to have a voluminous Perl program that does one small quick task (out of many potential tasks) and then exits, because the run-time for the program will be dwarfed by the compile time.

So, Perl is like a compiler and an interpreter. It's a compiler because the program is completely read and parsed before the first statement is executed. It's an interpreter because no object code sits around filling up disk space. In some ways, it's the best of both worlds. Admittedly, a caching of the compiled object code between invocations, or even translation into native machine code, would be nice. A working version of such a compiler already exists, and is currently scheduled to be bundled into the 5.005 release. See the Perl FAQ for the current status.

Documentation

Throughout this book, we'll refer to the documentation included with the Perl distributions. The ActiveState port comes with documentation in HTML format; you can find it in the */docs* subdirectory of the distribution. When we refer to the documentation, we'll just refer to the base name of the file without the extension. For example, if we refer to *perlfunc*, we really mean */docs/Perl/perlfunc.html*. Win32 specific documentation is located in the */docs/Perl-Win32* subdirectory, so a reference to *win32ext* really refers to */docs/Perl-Win32/win32ext.html*.

If you have the standard 5.004 distribution, you can use the *perldoc* command from the command line. *perldoc* is a batch file wrapper around a Perl script, found in the */bin* directory of the distribution. *perldoc* lets you view documentation pages or module documentation by invoking it as follows:

```
> perldoc perlfunc
```

perldoc extracts the documentation from the Perl POD (plain old documentation) format found in the */pod* subdirectory of the distribution. If all else fails, you can just read the pod files with your favorite text editor.

A Stroll Through Perl

We begin our journey through Perl by taking a little stroll. This stroll presents a number of different features by hacking on a small application. The explanations here are extremely brief—each subject area is discussed in *much* greater detail later in this book. But this little stroll should give you a quick taste for the language, and you can decide if you really want to finish this book instead of reading some more Usenet news or running off to the ski slopes.

The "Hello, world" Program

Let's look at a little program that actually *does* something. Here is your basic "Hello, world" program (use any text editor to type it in):

```
print ("Hello, world!\n");
```

This single line is the entire program. The built-in function `print` starts it off, and in this case has just one argument, a C-like text string. Within this string, the character combination \n stands for a newline character, just as it does in C. The `print` statement is terminated by a semicolon (`;`). As in Pascal or C, all simple statements in Perl are terminated by a semicolon.*

When you invoke this program, the Perl interpreter parses the entire program and then executes the compiled form. The first and only operation is the execution of the `print` function, which sends any arguments to the standard output. After the program has completed, the Perl process exits, returning a successful exit code to the parent process.

Soon, you'll see Perl programs in which `print` and other functions are sometimes called with parentheses, and sometimes called without them. The rule is simple: in Perl, parentheses for built-in functions are never required nor forbidden. Their use can help or hinder clarity, so use your own judgment.

---

* The semicolon can be omitted when the statement is the last statement of a block, file, or `eval`.

Asking Questions and Remembering the Result

Let's add a bit more sophistication. The `Hello, world` greeting is a touch cold and inflexible. Let's have the program call you by your name. To do this, we need a place to hold the name, a way to ask for the name, and a way to get a response.

One kind of place to hold values (like a name) is a *scalar variable*. For this program, we'll use the scalar variable `$name` to hold your name. In Chapter 2, *Scalar Data*, we'll go into more detail about what these variables can hold, and what you can do with them. For now, assume that you can hold a single number or string (sequence of characters) in a scalar variable.

The program needs to ask for the name. To do that, we need a way to prompt and a way to accept input. The previous program showed us how to prompt: use the `print` function. And the way to get a line from the terminal is with the `<STDIN>` construct, which (as we're using it here) grabs one line of input. We assign this input to the `$name` variable. This gives us the following program:

```
print "What is your name? ";
$name = <STDIN>;
```

The value of `$name` at this point has a terminating newline (`Erik` comes in as `Erik\n`). To get rid of the newline, we use the `chomp()` function, which takes a scalar variable as its sole argument and removes the trailing newline, if present, from the string:

```
chomp $name;
```

Now, all we need to do is say `Hello,` followed by the value of the `$name` variable, which we can do by embedding the variable inside the quoted string:

```
print "Hello, $name!\n";
```

Putting it all together, we get:

```
print "What is your name? ";
$name = <STDIN>;
chomp $name;
print "Hello, $name!\n";
```

Adding Choices

Now, let's say we have a special greeting for Erik, but want an ordinary greeting for anyone else. To do this, we need to compare the name that was entered with the string `Erik`, and if they are identical, do something special. Let's add a C-like *if-then-else* branch and a comparison to the program:

```
print "What is your name? ";
$name = <STDIN>;
chomp $name;
```

```
if ($name eq "Erik") {
  print "Hello, Erik! How good of you to be here!\n";
} else {
  print "Hello, $name!\n"; # ordinary greeting
}
```

The **eq** operator compares two strings. If they are equal (character for character, and of the same length), the result is true. (No comparable operator* exists in C or C++.)

The **if** statement selects which *block* of statements (between matching curly braces) is executed—if the expression is true, it's the first block, otherwise it's the second block.

Guessing the Secret Word

Well, now that we have the name, let's have the person running the program guess a secret word. For everyone except Erik, we'll have the program repeatedly ask for guesses until the person guesses properly. First the program, and then an explanation:

```
$secretword = "gecko"; # the secret word
print "What is your name? ";
$name = <STDIN>;
chomp $name;
if ($name eq "Erik") {
    print "Hello, Erik! How good of you to be here!\n";
} else {
    print "Hello, $name!\n"; # ordinary greeting
    print "What is the secret word? ";
    $guess = <STDIN>;
    chomp $guess;
    while ($guess ne $secretword) {
        print "Wrong, try again. What is the secret word? ";
        $guess = <STDIN>;
        chomp $guess;
    }
}
```

First, we define the secret word by putting it into another scalar variable, **$secretword**. After the greeting, the (non-Erik) person is asked (with another **print**) for the guess. The guess is compared with the secret word using the **ne** operator, which returns true if the strings are not equal (**ne** is the logical opposite of the **eq** operator). The result of the comparison controls a **while** loop, which executes the block as long as the comparison is true.

---

* Well, OK, there's a standard C **library** function. But that's not an operator.

Of course, this program is not very secure, because anyone who is tired of guessing can merely interrupt the program and get back to the prompt, or even look at the source to determine the word. But, we weren't trying to write a security system, just an example for this book.

More than One Secret Word

Let's see how we can modify this program to allow more than one valid secret word. Using what we've already seen, we could compare the guess repeatedly against a series of good answers stored in separate scalar variables. However, such a list would be hard to modify or read in from a file or compute based on the day of the week.

A better solution is to store all of the possible answers in a data structure called a *list*, or (preferably) an *array*. Each *element* of the array is a separate scalar variable that can be independently set or accessed. The entire array can also be given a value in one fell swoop. We can assign a value to the entire array named `@words` so that it contains three possible good passwords:

```
@words = ("camel","gecko","alpaca");
```

Array variable names begin with @, so they are distinct from scalar variable names. Another way to write this so that we don't have to put all those quotemarks there is with the qw() syntax, like so:

```
@words = qw(camel gecko alpaca);
```

These mean exactly the same thing; the **qw** makes it as if we had quoted each of three strings.

After the array is assigned, we can access each element by using a subscript reference (subscripts start at zero). So, `$words[0]` is `camel`, `$words[1]` is `gecko`, and `$words[2]` is `alpaca`. The subscript can be an expression as well, so if we set `$i` to 2, then `$words[$i]` is `alpaca`. (Subscript references start with $ rather than @, because they refer to a single element of the array rather than the whole array.) Going back to our previous example:

```
@words = qw(camel gecko alpaca);
print "What is your name? ";
$name = <STDIN>;
chomp $name;
if ($name eq "Erik") {
    print "Hello, Erik! How good of you to be here!\n";
} else {
    print "Hello, $name!\n"; # ordinary greeting
    print "What is the secret word? ";
    $guess = <STDIN>;
    chomp ($guess);
    $i = 0; # try this word first
```

```
    $correct = "maybe"; # is the guess correct or not?
    while ($correct eq "maybe") { # keep checking til we know
        if ($words[$i] eq $guess) { # right?
            $correct = "yes"; # yes!
    } elsif ($i < 2) { # more words to look at?
        $i = $i + 1; # look at the next word next time
    } else { # no more words, must be bad
        print "Wrong, try again. What is the secret word?";
        $guess = <STDIN>;
        chomp ($guess);
        $i = 0; # start checking at the first word again
    }
    } # end of while not correct
} # end of "not Erik"
```

You'll notice we're using the scalar variable `$correct` to indicate that we are either still looking for a good password, or that we've found one.

This program also shows the `elsif` block of the `if-then-else` statement. This exact construct is not present in all programming languages—it's an abbreviation of the `else` block together with a new `if` condition, but it does not nest inside yet another pair of curly braces. It's a very Perl-like thing to compare a set of conditions in a cascaded `if-elsif-elsif-elsif-else` chain. Perl doesn't really have the equivalent of C's `switch` or Pascal's `case` statement, although you can build one yourself without too much trouble. See Chapter 2 of *Programming Perl* or the *perlsyn* documentation for details.

Giving Each Person a Different Secret Word

In the previous program, any person who comes along could guess any of the three words and be successful. If we want the secret word to be different for each person, we'll need a table that matches people with words. Table 1-1 does just this.

Table 1-1. Matching Persons to Secret Words

Person	Secret Word
Fred	camel
Barney	gecko
Betty	alpaca
Wilma	alpaca

Notice that both Betty and Wilma have the same secret word. This is fine.

The easiest way to store such a table in Perl is with a *hash*. Each element of the hash holds a separate scalar value (just like the other type of array), but each hash is referenced by a *key*, which can be any scalar value (any string or number, including noninteger and negative values). To create a hash called `%words` (notice the use of %, rather than @) with the keys and values given in Table 1-1, we assign a value to %words (much as we did earlier with the array):

```
%words = qw(
   fred    camel
   barney  gecko
   betty   alpaca
   wilma   alpaca
);
```

Each pair of values in the list represents one key and its corresponding value in the hash. Note that we broke this assignment over many lines without any sort of line continuation character. We could do so because whitespace is generally insignificant in a Perl program.

To find the secret word for Betty, we need to use Betty as the key in a reference to the hash %words, via some expression such as $words{"betty"}. The value of this reference is alpaca, similar to what we had before with the other array. Also, as before, the key can be any expression, so setting $person to betty and evaluating $words{$person} gives alpaca as well.

Putting all this together, we get a program like this:

```
%words = qw(
    fred      camel
    barney    gecko
    betty     alpaca
    wilma     alpaca
);
print "What is your name? ";
$name = <STDIN>;
chomp ($name);
if ($name eq "Erik") {
    print "Hello, Erik! How good of you to be here!\n";
} else {
    print "Hello, $name!\n"; # ordinary greeting
    $secretword = $words{$name}; # get the secret word
    print "What is the secret word? ";
    $guess = <STDIN>;
    chomp ($guess);
    while ($guess ne $secretword) {
        print "Wrong, try again. What is the secret word? ";
        $guess = <STDIN>;
        chomp ($guess);
    }
}
```

Note the lookup of the secret word. If the name is not found, the value of `$secretword` will be an empty string,* which we can then check for if we want to define a default secret word for everyone else. Here's how that process looks:

```
[... rest of program deleted ...]
  $secretword = $words{$name}; # get the secret word
  if ($secretword eq "") { # oops, not found
      $secretword = "groucho"; # sure, why a duck?
  }
  print "What is the secret word? ";
[... rest of program deleted ...]
```

Handling Varying Input Formats

If we enter `Erik Olson` or `erik` rather than `Erik`, we're lumped in with the rest of the users, because the `eq` comparison requires an exact equality. Let's look at one way to handle that.

Suppose we wanted to look for any string that began with `Erik`, rather than just a string that was equal to `Erik`. We could do this with a regular expression: a template that defines a collection of strings that match. The regular expression in Perl that matches any string that begins with `Erik` is `^Erik`. To match this against the string in `$name`, we use the match operator as follows:

```
if ($name =~ /^Erik/) {
    ## yes, it matches
} else {
    ## no, it doesn't
}
```

Note that the regular expression is delimited by slashes. Within the slashes, spaces and other whitespace are significant, just as they are within strings.

This addition almost meets our needs, but it doesn't handle selecting `erik` or rejecting `eriko`. To accept `erik`, we add the *ignore-case* option, a small `i` appended after the closing slash. To reject `eriko`, we add a *word boundary* special marker in the form of `\b` in the regular expression. This ensures that the character following the first `k` in the regular expression is not another letter. The addition also changes the regular expression to be `/^erik\b/i`, which means "`erik` at the beginning of the string, no letter or digit following, and OK to be in either case."

When this is added to the rest of the program, the final version looks like this:

```
%words = qw(
    fred    camel
```

---

* Well, OK, the value is really the `undef` value, but it looks like an empty string to the `eq` operator. You'd get a warning about this value if you used `-w` on the command line, which is why we omitted it here.

```
        barney  gecko
        betty   alpaca
        wilma   alpaca
);
print "What is your name? ";
$name = <STDIN>;
chomp ($name);
if ($name =~ /^erik\b/i) {
    print "Hello, Erik! How good of you to be here!\n";
} else {
    print "Hello, $name!\n"; # ordinary greeting
    $secretword = $words{$name}; # get the secret word
    if ($secretword eq "") { # oops, not found
        $secretword = "groucho"; # sure, why a duck?
    }
    print "What is the secret word? ";
    $guess = <STDIN>;
    chomp ($guess);
    while ($guess ne $secretword) {
        print "Wrong, try again. What is the secret word? ";
        $guess = <STDIN>;
        chomp ($guess);
    }
}
```

As you can see, the program is a far cry from the simple `Hello world`, but it's still very small and workable, and does quite a bit for being so short. This is The Perl Way.

Perl provides nearly every regular expression feature imaginable. In addition, the way Perl handles string matching is about the fastest on the planet, so you don't lose performance. String matching in Perl often compares favorably to hand-coded C programs written specifically for the same purpose.

Making It Fair for the Rest

So, now we can enter `Erik` or `erik` or `Erik Olson`, but what about everyone else? Barney still has to say exactly `barney` (not even `barney` followed by a space).

To be fair to Barney, we need to grab the first word of whatever's entered, and then convert it to lowercase *before* we look up the name in the table. We do this with two operators: the *substitute* operator, which finds a regular expression and replaces it with a string, and the *translate* operator, which puts the string in lowercase.

First, we discuss the substitute operator. We want to take the contents of `$name`, find the first nonword character, and zap everything from there to the end of the string. `/\W.*/` is the regular expression we are looking for—the `\W` stands for a nonword character (something besides a letter, digit, or underscore), and `.*`

represents any characters from that point to the end of the line. Now, to zap these characters, we need to take whatever part of the string matches this regular expression and replace it with nothing:

```
$name =~ s/\W.*//;
```

We're using the same =~ operator that we did before, but now on the right we have a substitute operator: the letter s followed by a slash-delimited regular expression and string. (The string in this example is the empty string between the second and third slashes.) This operator looks and acts very much like the substitution command of various editors.

Now, to get whatever's left into lowercase, we translate the string using the `tr` operator.* This operation takes a list of characters to find, and another list of characters with which to replace them. For our example, to put the contents of $name in lowercase, we use:

```
$name =~ tr/A-Z/a-z/;
```

The slashes delimit the searched-for and replacement character lists. The dash between A and Z stands for all the characters in between, so we have two lists that each contain 26 characters. When the `tr` operator finds a character from the string in the first list, the character is then replaced with the corresponding character in the second list. So, all uppercase A's become lowercase a's, and so on.†

Putting everything together results in the following:

```
%words = qw(
    fred    camel
    barney  gecko
    betty   alpaca
    wilma   alpaca
);
print "What is your name? ";
$name = <STDIN>;
chomp ($name);
$original_name = $name; #save for greeting
$name =~ s/\W.*//; # get rid of everything after first word
$name =~ tr/A-Z/a-z/; # lowercase everything
if ($name eq "erik") { # ok to compare this way now
    print "Hello, Erik! How good of you to be here!\n";
} else {
    print "Hello, $original_name!\n"; # ordinary greeting
    $secretword = $words{$name}; # get the secret word
    if ($secretword eq "") { # oops, not found
        $secretword = "groucho"; # sure, why a duck?
```

---

* This method doesn't work for characters with accent marks, although the uc function would.

† Experts will note that we could have also constructed something like `s/(\S*).*/\L$1/` to do this processing in one fell swoop, but experts probably won't be reading this section.

```
        }
        print "What is the secret word? ";
        $guess = <STDIN>;
        chomp ($guess);
        while ($guess ne $secretword) {
            print "Wrong, try again. What is the secret word? ";
            $guess = <STDIN>;
            chomp ($guess);
        }
    }
```

Notice how the regular expression match for **Erik** became a simple comparison again. After all, both **Erik Olson** and **Erik** become **erik** after the substitution and translation. And everyone else gets a fair ride, because **Fred** and **Fred Flintstone** both become **fred**, **Barney Rubble** and **Barney, the little guy** become **barney**, and so on.

With just a few statements, we've made the program much more user friendly. You'll find that expressing complicated string manipulation with a few keystrokes is one of Perl's many strong points.

However, hacking away at the name so that we could compare it and look it up in the table destroyed the name that was entered. So, before the program hacks on the name, it saves it in `$original_name`. (Like C symbols, Perl variable names consist of letters, digits, and underscores and can be of nearly unlimited length.) We can then make references to `$original_name` later.

Perl has many ways to monitor and mangle strings. You'll find out about most of them in Chapters 7, *Regular Expressions*, and 15, *Other Data Transformation*.

Making It a Bit More Modular

Now that we've added so much to the code, we have to scan through many detailed lines in order to get the overall flow of the program. What we need is to separate the high-level logic (asking for a name, looping based on entered secret words) from the details (comparing a secret word to a known good word). We might do this for clarity, or maybe because one person is writing the high-level part and another is writing (or has already written) the detailed parts.

Perl provides *subroutines* that have *parameters* and *return values*. A subroutine is defined once in a program, and can be invoked repeatedly from within any expression.

For our small-but-rapidly-growing program, let's create a subroutine called **good_ word** that takes a name and a guessed word, and returns *true* if the word is correct, and *false* if not. The definition of such a subroutine looks like this:

```
sub good_word {
    my($somename,$someguess) = @_; # name the parameters
```

```
    $somename =~ s/\W.*//; # get rid of everything after first word
    $somename =~ tr/A-Z/a-z/; # lowercase everything
    if ($somename eq "erik") { # should not need to guess
        return 1; # return value is true
    } elsif (($words{$somename} || "groucho") eq $someguess) {
        return 1; # return value is true
    } else {
        return 0; # return value is false
    }
}
```

First, the definition of a subroutine consists of the reserved word **sub**, followed by the subroutine name, followed by a block of code (delimited by curly braces). These definitions can go anywhere in the program file, but most people put them at the end.

The first line within this particular definition is an assignment that copies the values of the two parameters of this subroutine into two local variables named `$somename` and `$someguess`. (The **my()** defines the two variables as private to the enclosing block—in this case, the entire subroutine—and the parameters are initially in a special local array called **@_**.)

The next two lines clean up the name, just like in the previous version of the program.

The `if-elsif-else` statement decides whether the guessed word (`$some-guess`) is correct for the name (`$somename`). **Erik** should not make it into this subroutine, but even if it does, whatever word was guessed is OK.

A `return` statement can be used to make the subroutine immediately return to its caller with the supplied value. In the absence of an explicit `return` statement, the last expression evaluated in a subroutine is the return value. We'll see how the return value is used after we finish describing the subroutine definition.

The test for the `elsif` part looks a little complicated—let's break it apart:

```
($words{$somename} || "groucho") eq $someguess
```

The first thing inside the parentheses is our familiar hash lookup, yielding some value from **%words** based on a key of `$somename`. The operator between that value and the string `groucho` is the `||` (logical-or) operator similar to that used in C. If the lookup from the hash has a value (meaning that the key `$somename` was in the hash), the value of the expression is that value. If the key could not be found, the string `groucho` is used instead. This step is a very Perl-like thing to do—specify some expression, and then provide a default value using `||` in case the expression turns out to be false.

In any case, whether it's a value from the hash, or the default value groucho, we compare it to whatever was guessed. If the comparison is true, we return 1; otherwise, we return 0.

So, expressed as a rule, if the name is erik, or the guess matches the lookup in %words based on the name (with a default of groucho if not found), then the subroutine returns 1; otherwise, it returns 0.

Now, let's integrate all these additions with the rest of the program:

```
%words = qw(
    fred    camel
    barney  gecko
    betty   alpaca
    wilma   alpaca
);
print "What is your name? ";
$name = <STDIN>;
chomp ($name);
if ($name =~ /^erik\b/i) { # back to the other way :-)
    print "Hello, Erik! How good of you to be here!\n";
} else {
    print "Hello, $name!\n"; # ordinary greeting
    print "What is the secret word? ";
    $guess = <STDIN>;
    chomp ($guess);
  while (! good_word($name,$guess)) {
    print "Wrong, try again. What is the secret word? ";
    $guess = <STDIN>;
    chomp $guess;
  }
}
[... insert definition of good_word() here ...]
```

Notice that we've gone back to the regular expression to check for Erik, because now the main program does not have to pull apart the first name and convert it to lowercase.

The big difference is the while loop containing good_word. Here, we see an invocation of the subroutine passing two parameters, $name and $guess. Within the subroutine, the value of $somename is set from the first parameter, in this case $name. Likewise, $someguess is set from the second parameter, $guess.

The value returned by the subroutine (either 1 or 0, recalling the definition given earlier) is logically inverted with the prefix ! (logical not) operator. As in C, this operator returns true if the expression following is false, and vice versa. The result of this negation controls the while loop. You can read this as "while it's not a good word..." Many well-written Perl programs read very much like English, provided you take a few liberties with either Perl or English. (But you certainly won't win a Pulitzer that way.)

Note that the subroutine assumes that the value of the **%words** hash is set by the main program.

Such a cavalier approach to global variables doesn't scale very well, of course. Generally speaking, variables not created with **my** are global to the whole program, while those **my** creates last only until the block in which they were declared exits. Don't worry; Perl does in fact support a rich variety of other kinds of variables, including those private to a file (or package), as well as variables private to a function that retain their values between invocations (which is what we could really use here). However, at this stage in your Perl education, explaining these variables would only complicate your life. When you're ready for such information, check out what *Programming Perl* has to say about scoping, subroutines, modules, and objects. Or, see the online documentation in the *perlsub*, *perlmod*, *perlobj*, and *perltoot* documentation.

Moving the Secret Word List into a Separate File

Suppose we wanted to share the secret word list among three programs. If we store the word list as we have done already, we will need to change all three programs when Betty decides that her secret word should be **swine** rather than **alpaca**. This change can get to be a hassle, especially considering how often Betty is likely to change her mind.

So, let's put the word list into a file, and then read the file to get the word list into the program. To do so, we need to create an I/O channel called a *filehandle*. Your Perl program automatically gets three filehandles called **STDIN**, **STDOUT**, and **STDERR**, corresponding to the three standard I/O channels in many programming environments. We've already been using the **STDIN** handle to read data from the person running the program. Now, we just have to get another handle attached to a file of our own choice.

Here's a small chunk of code to do that:

```
sub init_words {
    open (WORDSLIST, "wordslist");
    while (defined ($name = <WORDSLIST>) {
        chomp ($name);
        $word = <WORDSLIST>;
        chomp ($word);
        $words{$name} = $word;
    }
    close (WORDSLIST);
}
```

We're putting this code into a subroutine so that we can keep the main part of the program uncluttered. This organization also means that at a later time (hint: after a few more revisions in this stroll), we can change where the word list is stored, or even the format of the list.

The arbitrarily chosen format of the word list is one item per line, with names and words alternating. So, for our current database, we'd have something like this:

```
fred
camel
barney
gecko
betty
alpaca
wilma
alpaca
```

The **open** function creates a filehandle named WORDSLIST by associating it with a file named **wordslist** in the current directory. Note that the filehandle doesn't have a funny character in front of it as do the three variable types. Also, filehandles are generally uppercase—although they aren't required to be—for reasons detailed later.

The **while** loop reads lines from the **wordslist** file (via the WORDSLIST file-handle) one line at a time. Each line is stored into the $name variable. When end-of-file is reached, the value returned by the <WORDSLIST> operation is the empty string,* which looks false to the **while** loop, and terminates it. That's how we get out at the end.

If you were running with the -w option, you would have to check that the return value read in was actually **defined**. The empty string returned by the <WORDSLIST> operation isn't merely empty—it's **undef** again. The **defined** function is how you test for **undef** when this matters. In the case of reading lines from a file, you'd test as shown:

```
while ( defined ($name = <WORDSLIST>) ) {
```

But if you were being that careful, you'd probably also have checked to make sure that **open** returned a true value. You know, that's probably not a bad idea either. The built-in **die** function is frequently used to exit the program with an error message in case something goes wrong. We'll see an example of this function in the next revision of the program.

On the other hand, the normal case is that we've read a line (including the newline) into $name. First, off comes the newline using the **chomp** function. Then, we have to read the next line to get the secret word, holding it in the $word variable. This variable also gets the newline hacked off.

The final line of the **while** loop puts $word into %words with a key of $name, so that the rest of the program can access it later.

---

* Well, technically the value is **undef** again, but empty string is close enough for this discussion.

After the file has been read, the filehandle can be recycled with the `close` function. (Filehandles are automatically closed anyway when the program exits, but we're trying to be tidy. If we were *really* tidy, we'd even check for a true return value from `close` in case the disk partition which held the file went south, its network filesystem became unreachable, or a similar catastrophe occurred. Yes, these things really do happen. Murphy will always be with us.)

This subroutine definition can go after or before the other one. And, we invoke the subroutine instead of setting `%words` in the beginning of the program. Therefore, you could wrap up all of this as follows:

```
init_words();
print "What is your name? ";
$name = <STDIN>;
chomp ($name);
if ($name =~ /^erik\b/i) { # back to the other way :-)
    print "Hello, Erik! How good of you to be here!\n";
} else {
    print "Hello, $name!\n"; # ordinary greeting
    print "What is the secret word? ";
    $guess = <STDIN>;
    chomp ($guess);
    while (! good_word($name,$guess)) {
        print "Wrong, try again. What is the secret word? ";
        $guess = <STDIN>;
        chomp ($guess);
    }
}
## subroutines from here down
sub init_words {
    open (WORDSLIST,"wordslist") ||
            die "can't open wordlist:$!";
    while (defined ($name = <WORDSLIST>)) {
        chomp ($name);
        $word = <WORDSLIST>;
        chomp ($word);
        $words{$name} = $word;
    }
    close (WORDSLIST);
}
sub good_word {
    my($somename,$someguess) = @_; # name the parameters
    $somename =~ s/\W.*//; # delete everything after first word
    $somename =~ tr/A-Z/a-z/; # lowercase everything
    if ($somename eq "erik") { # should not need to guess
        return 1; # return value is true
    } elsif (($words{$somename} || "groucho") eq $someguess) {
        return 1; # return value is true
    } else {
        return 0; # return value is false
    }
}
```

Now our program is starting to look full-grown. Notice the first executable line is an invocation of `init_words()`. The return value is not used in a further calculation, which is good because we didn't return anything remarkable. In this case, a true value is guaranteed (the value 1, in particular), because if the `close` had failed, the `die` would have printed a message to our STDERR error and exited the program. The `die` function is fully explained in Chapter 10, *Filehandles and File Tests,* but because the return values of anything that might fail must be checked, we'll get into the habit of using the function right from the start. The $! variable (also explained in Chapter 10) contains the system error message explaining why the system call failed.

The `open` function is also used to open files for output, or open programs as files (demonstrated shortly). The full scoop on `open` comes much later in this book, however, in Chapter 10.

Ensuring a Modest Amount of Security

"That secret word list has got to change at least once a week!" cries the Chief Director of Secret Word Lists. Well, we can't force the list to be different, but we can at least issue a warning if the secret word list has not been modified in more than a week.

The best place for handling this warning is the `init_words()` subroutine— we're already looking at the file there. The Perl operator `-M` returns the age in days since a file or filehandle has last been modified, so we just need to see whether this value is greater than seven for the `WORDSLIST` filehandle:

```perl
sub init_words {
    open (WORDSLIST,"wordslist") ||
            die "can't open wordlist:$!";
    if (-M WORDSLIST > 7.0) { # comply with bureaucratic policy
        die "Sorry, the wordslist is older than seven days.";
    }
    while (defined ($name = <WORDSLIST>)) {
        chomp ($name);
        $word = <WORDSLIST>;
        chomp ($word);
        $words{$name} = $word;
    }
    close (WORDSLIST) || die "couldn't close wordlist: $!";
}
```

The value of `-M WORDSLIST` is compared to seven, and if the value is greater, bingo, we've violated policy.

The rest of the program remains unchanged, so in the interest of saving a few trees, we won't repeat it here.

Besides getting the age of a file, we can also find out its size, access time, and everything else that an operating system maintains about a file. More information about this feature appears in Chapter 10.

Warning Someone When Things Go Astray

We really ought to know when someone guesses incorrectly so that we can watch for break-in attempts. If we were using a UNIX system, we would probably use the *mail* command to send an email message to someone about the failed attempt. However, on a Windows workstation, no standard *mail** command exists, so we're going to log failures to a file.† We need only do a little work to accomplish this task. We'll add a new subroutine and modify only the good_ word() subroutine (thanks to modularity), because we have all the information we need:

```
sub good_word {
    my($somename,$someguess) = @_; # name the parameters
    $somename =~ s/\W.*//; # get rid of stuff after first word
    $somename =~ tr/A-Z/a-z/; # lowercase everything
    if ($somename eq "erik") { # should not need to guess
        return 1; # return value is true
    } elsif (($words{$somename}||"groucho") eq $someguess) {
        return 1; # return value is true
    } else {
        log_failure($somename, $someguess);
        return 0; # return value is false
    }
}

sub log_failure {
    my($somename,$someguess) = @_; # name the parameters
    open(LOG, ">>failures.log") || die "failures.log: $!";
    print LOG "bad news: $somename guessed $someguess\n";
    close (LOG)  || die "can't close failures.log: $!";
}
```

Notice the **open**, which has a redirection symbol (>>) in the filename. This symbol is a special indication that we are appending to a file. The next statement, a **print**, shows that a filehandle between the **print** keyword and the values to be printed selects that filehandle for output, rather than STDOUT.‡ This means that the message will be written to the output file that we've opened. Finally, we close the filehandle.

---

* Perl for Win32 programmers will encounter this *mail* comand issue frequently in scripts that they find on the Net. The solution is to use one of a number of readily available command-line mailers, or to use Perl's network interface to talk to an SMTP server directly.

† We could also use the Win32::EventLog module to log our warnings to the Windows NT Event Log.

‡ Well, technically, the currently selected filehandle. That's covered much later, though.

Many Secret Word Files in the Current Directory

Let's change the definition of the secret word filename slightly. Instead of just the file named `wordslist`, let's look for anything in the current directory that ends in `.sec`. At the command prompt, we say:

```
> dir /B *.sec
```

to get a brief listing of all of these names. As you'll see in a moment, Perl uses a similar wildcard name syntax.

Pulling out the `init_words()` definition again:

```
sub init_words {
    while (defined ($filename = glob("*.sec")) ) {
        open (WORDSLIST, $filename) ||
                die "can't open $filename:$!";
        if (-M WORDSLIST <= 7.0) {
            while (defined ($name = <WORDSLIST>) {
                chomp ($name);
                $word = <WORDSLIST>;
                chomp ($word);
                $words{$name} = $word;
            }
        }
        close (WORDSLIST) || die "couldn't close $filename: $!";
    }
}
```

First, I've wrapped a new `while` loop around the bulk of the routine from the previous version. The new thing here is the `glob` function. This is called a *filename glob** for historical reasons. The function works much like `<STDIN>`, in that each time it is accessed, it returns the next value: successive filenames that match the pattern, in this case `*.sec`. When there are no additional filenames to be returned, the filename glob returns an empty string.† In Perl on Windows systems, filename globbing‡ is implemented by means of another program, called *PerlGlob.exe*, which must be somewhere in your search path (this should usually be the case, because *PerlGlob.exe* is installed in the same directory as your Perl interpreter by default).

---

* Glob might be a new word to Win32 programmers. We'll talk much more about globbing in Chapter 12, *Directory Access*.

† Yeah, yeah, `undef` again.

‡ If you're using the ISAPI version of Perl, you'll have better luck if you avoid file globbing altogether and use the following equivalent technique:

```
opendir(DIR, '.');
@files = grep(/\.sec/, readdir(DIR));
closedir DIR;
```

This method leaves you with a list (`@files`) of all filenames in the current directory that contain the `.sec` pattern. We'll provide more information on this later.

So, if the current directory contains `fred.sec` and `barney.sec`, then `$file-name` is `barney.sec` on the first pass through the `while` loop (the names come out in alphabetically sorted order). On the second pass, `$filename` is `fred.sec`. And there is no third pass because the glob returns an empty string the third time it is called, perceived by the `while` loop to be a false, causing an exit from the subroutine.

Within the `while` loop, we open the file and verify that it is recent enough (less than seven days since the last modification). For the recent-enough files, we scan through as before.

Note that if there are no files that match `*.sec` and are less than seven days old, the subroutine will exit without having set any secret words into the `%words` array. In such a case, everyone must use the word `groucho`. Oh well. (For *real* code, we would have added some check on the number of entries in `%words` before returning, and `die`'d if the check wasn't good. See the `keys` function when we get to hashes in Chapter 5, *Hashes.*)

Listing the Secret Words

Well, the Chief Director of Secret Word Lists wants a report of all the secret words currently in use, and how old they are. If we set aside the secret word program for a moment, we'll have time to write a reporting program for the Director.

First, let's get all of the secret words, by stealing some code from the `init_words()` subroutine:

```
while ( defined ($filename = glob("*.sec")) ) {
    open (WORDSLIST, $filename) ||
            die "can't open $filename: $!";
    if (-M WORDSLIST <= 7.0) {
        while (defined ($name = <WORDSLIST>) {
            chomp ($name);
            $word = <WORDSLIST>;
            chomp ($word);
            ### new stuff will go here
        }
    }
    close (WORDSLIST) || die "couldn't close $filename: $!";
}
```

At the point marked "new stuff will go here," we know three things: the name of the file (`$filename`), someone's name (`$name`), and that person's secret word (`$word`). Here's a place to use Perl's report generating tools. We define a format somewhere in the program (usually near the end, like a subroutine):

```
format STDOUT =
@<<<<<<<<<<<<<<< @<<<<<<<<< @<<<<<<<<<<<
$filename, $name, $word
.
```

The format definition begins with `format STDOUT =`, and ends with a single period. The other two lines comprise the format itself. The first line of this format is a *field definition line* that specifies the number, length, and type of the fields. For this format, we have three fields. The line following a field definition line is always a *field value line*. The value line gives a list of expressions that will be evaluated when this format is used, and the results of those expressions will be plugged into the fields defined in the previous line.

We invoke this format with the **write** function, as shown:

```
while ( defined($filename = glob("*.sec")) ) {
    open (WORDSLIST, $filename) ||
            die "can't open $filename: $!";
    if (-M WORDSLIST <= 7.0) {
        while (defined ($name = <WORDSLIST>) {
            chomp ($name);
            $word = <WORDSLIST>;
            chomp ($word);
            write; # invoke format STDOUT to STDOUT
        }
    }
    close (WORDSLIST) || die "couldn't close $filename: $!";
}
format STDOUT =
@<<<<<<<<<<<<<< @<<<<<<<<< @<<<<<<<<<<<
$filename, $name, $word
.
```

When the format is invoked, Perl evaluates the field expressions and generates a line that it sends to the **STDOUT** filehandle. Because **write** is invoked once each time through the loop, we'll get a series of lines with text in columns, one line for each secret word entry.

Hmm. We haven't labeled the columns. That's easy enough. We just need to add a top-of-page format, as shown:

```
format STDOUT_TOP =
Page @<<
$%

Filename          Name       Word
================ ========== ============
.
```

This format is named **STDOUT_TOP**, and will be used initially at the first invocation of the **STDOUT** format, and again every time 60 lines of output to **STDOUT** have been generated. These column headings line up with the columns from the **STDOUT** format, so everything comes out tidy.

The first line of this format shows some constant text (**Page**) along with a three-character field definition. The following line is a field value line, which in this case has one expression. This expression is the $$ variable,* which holds the number of pages printed—a very useful value in top-of-page formats.

The third line of the format is blank. Because this line does not contain any fields, the line following it is not a field value line. This blank line is copied directly to the output, creating a blank line between the page number and the column headers below.

The last two lines of the format also contain no fields, so they are copied as-is, directly to the output. So this format generates four lines, one of which has a part that changes from page to page.

Just tack this definition onto the previous program to get it to work. Perl notices the top-of-page format automatically.

Perl also has fields that are centered or right justified, and supports a *filled paragraph area* as well. More on these features when we get to formats in Chapter 11, *Formats*.

Making Those Old Word Lists More Noticeable

As we are scanning through the `*.sec` files in the current directory, we may find files that are too old. So far, we are simply skipping over those files. Let's go one step more—we'll rename them to `*.sec.old` so that a directory listing will quickly show us which files are too old, simply by name.

Here's how the **init_words()** subroutine looks with this modification:

```
sub init_words {
    while ( defined($filename = glob("*.sec")) ) {
        open (WORDSLIST, $filename) ||
                die "can't open $filename: $!";
        if (-M WORDSLIST <= 7.0) {
            while (defined ($name = <WORDSLIST>) {
                chomp ($name);
                $word = <WORDSLIST>;
                chomp ($word);
                $words{$name} = $word;
            }
        } else { # rename the file so it gets noticed
            rename ($filename,"$filename.old");
        }
        close (WORDSLIST) ||
                die "couldn't close $filename: $!";
    }
}
```

---

* More mnemonic aliases for these predefined scalar variables are available via the English module, which provides English names for Perl's special variables.

Notice the new **else** part of the file age check. If the file is older than seven days, it gets renamed with the **rename** function. This function takes two parameters, renaming the file named by the first parameter to the name given in the second parameter.

Perl has a complete range of file manipulation operators—nearly anything you can do to a file from a C program, you can also do from Perl.

Maintaining a Last-Good-Guess Database

Let's keep track of when the most recent correct guess has been made for each user. One data structure that might seem to work at first glance is a hash. For example, the statement:

```
$last_good{$name} = time;
```

assigns the current time in internal format (some large integer above 800 million, incrementing one number per second) to an element of **%last_good** that has the name for a key. Over time, this method would seem to give us a database indicating the most recent time the secret word was guessed properly for each of the users who had invoked the program.

But, the hash doesn't have an existence between invocations of the program. Each time the program is invoked, a new hash is formed, so at most, we create a one-element hash and then immediately forget it when the program exits.

The **dbmopen** function[*] maps a hash out into a disk file (actually a pair of disk files) known as a DBM. It's used like this:

```
dbmopen (%last_good,"lastdb",0666) ||
                 die "can't dbmopen lastdb: $!";
$last_good{$name} = time;
dbmclose (%last_good) || die "can't dbmclose lastdb: $!";
```

The first statement performs the mapping, using the disk filenames of `lastdb.dir` and `lastdb.pag` (these names are the normal names for a DBM called `lastdb`). Showing Perl's UNIX heritage, **dbmopen** takes an octal file permission mask as the third argument. Although all Windows filesystems support file attributes of some sort, they are largely incompatible with the UNIX filesystem scheme used by Perl. The UNIX file permissions used for these two files, if the files must be created (as they will the first time through), is `0666`. This mode means that anyone can read or write the files. This mode is usually the one that you want to use when working with files with read/write attributes.[†]

---

[*] On a specific database, use the more low-level `tie` function, as detailed in Chapters 5 and 7 of *Programming Perl*, or in the *perltie* documentation.

[†] The Win32::File module provides additional features for setting file attributes. We'll discuss those features in more detail in Chapter 13, *File and Directory Manipulation.*

The Perl file permission value is composed of a series of bits with read, write, and execute privileges for the user, the user's group, and everyone else. Traditionally, FAT filesystems only keep track of read and write privileges for the user, along with a few other tidbits of information, like whether the file is a hidden or a system file. We'll discuss file permissions and attributes in detail in Chapter 13, *File and Directory Manipulation*. For now, just trust us that you want to use 0666 for creating DBM files.

The second statement shows that we use this mapped hash just like a normal hash. However, creating or updating an element of the hash automatically updates the disk files that form the DBM. And, when the hash is later accessed, the values within the hash come directly from the disk image. This gives the hash a life beyond the current invocation of the program—a persistence of its own.

The third statement disconnects the hash from the DBM, much like a file close operation.

You can insert these three statements just ahead of the subroutine definitions.

Although the inserted statements maintain the database adequately (and even create the database initially), we don't have any way of examining the information yet. To do so, we can create a separate little program that looks something like this:

```
dbmopen (%last_good,"lastdb",0666) ||
                die "can't dbmopen lastdb: $!";
foreach $name (sort keys %last_good) {
    $when = $last_good{$name};
    $hours = (time - $when) / 3600; # compute hours ago
    write;
}

format STDOUT =
User @<<<<<<<<<<<: last correct guess was @<<< hours ago.
$name, $hours
```

We've got a few new operations here: a foreach loop, sorting a list, and getting the keys of an hash.

First, the keys function takes a hash name as an argument and returns a list of all the keys of that hash in some unspecified order. For the %words hash defined earlier, the result is something like fred, barney, betty, wilma, in some unspecified order. For the %last_good hash, the result will be a list of all users who have guessed their own secret word successfully.

The sort function sorts the list alphabetically (just like passing a text file through the *sort* command). This function makes sure that the list processed by the foreach statement is always in alphabetical order.

The Perl `foreach` statement takes a list of values and assigns each one in turn to a scalar variable (here, `$name`), executing the body of the loop (a block) once for each value. So, for five names in the `%last_good` list, we get five passes through the loop, with `$name` being a different value each time.

The body of the `foreach` loop loads up a couple of variables used within the `STDOUT` format, and then invokes the format. Note that we figure out the age of the entry by subtracting the stored system time (in the array) from the current time (as returned by `time`), and then divide that by 3600 (to convert seconds to hours).

Perl also provides easy ways to create and maintain text-oriented databases and fixed-length-record databases. These databases are described in Chapter 17, *Database Manipulation*.

The Final Programs

Here are the programs from this stroll in their final form so that you can play with them.

First, the "say hello" program:

```
init_words();
print "What is your name? ";
$name = <STDIN>;
chomp ($name);
if ($name =~ /^erik\b/i) { # back to the other way :-)
    print "Hello, Erik! How good of you to be here!\n";
} else {
    print "Hello, $name!\n"; # ordinary greeting
    print "What is the secret word? ";
    $guess = <STDIN>;
     chomp ($guess);
     while (! good_word($name,$guess)) {
        print "Wrong, try again. What is the secret word? ";
        $guess = <STDIN>;
        chomp ($guess);
    }
}
dbmopen (%last_good,"lastdb",0666) ||
            die "can't dbmopen lastdb: $!";
$last_good{$name} = time;
dbmclose (%last_good) || die "can't dbmclose lastdb: $!";
sub init_words {
    while ( defined($filename = glob("*.sec")) ) {
        open (WORDSLIST, $filename) ||
            die "can't open $filename: $!";
        if (-M WORDSLIST <= 7.0) {
            while (defined ($name = <WORDSLIST>) {
                chomp ($name);
                $word = <WORDSLIST>;
```

```
                        chomp ($word);
                        $words{$name} = $word;
                }
        } else { # rename the file so it gets noticed
            rename ($filename,"$filename.old");
        }
         close (WORDSLIST) ||
                    die "couldn't close $filename: $!";
    }
}
sub good_word {
  my($somename,$someguess) = @_; # name the parameters
  $somename =~ s/\W.*//; # delete everything after first word
  $somename =~ tr/A-Z/a-z/; # lowercase everything
  if ($somename eq "erik") { # should not need to guess
    return 1; # return value is true
  } elsif (($words{$somename} || "groucho") eq $someguess) {
    return 1; # return value is true
  } else {
    log_failure($somename,$someguess);
    return 0; # return value is false
  }
}

sub log_failure {
    my($somename,$someguess) = @_; # name the parameters
    open(LOG, ">>failures.log") || die "failures.log: $!";
    print LOG "bad news: $somename guessed $someguess\n";
    close (LOG)  || die "can't close failures.log: $!";
}
```

Next, we have the secret word lister:

```
while ( defined($filename = glob("*.sec")) ) {
    open (WORDSLIST, $filename) ||
                die "can't open $filename: $!";
    if (-M WORDSLIST <= 7.0) {
        while (defined ($name = <WORDSLIST>)) {
            chomp ($name);
            $word = <WORDSLIST>;
             chomp ($word);
              write; # invoke format STDOUT to STDOUT
        }
    }
    close (WORDSLIST) || die "can't close $filename: $!";
}

format STDOUT =
@<<<<<<<<<<<<<< @<<<<<<<< @<<<<<<<<<<
$filename, $name, $word
.

format STDOUT_TOP =
Page @<<
$%
```

```
Filename          Name        Word
================= ========== ============
     .
```

And finally, the last-time-a-word-was-used display program:

```
dbmopen (%last_good,"lastdb",0666) ||
                 die "can't dbmopen lastdb: $!";
foreach $name (sort keys %last_good) {
    $when = $last_good{$name};
    $hours = (time - $when) / 3600; # compute hours ago
    write;
}
dbmclose(%last_good) || die "can't dbmclose lastdb: $!";
format STDOUT =
User @<<<<<<<<<<: last correct guess was @<<< hours ago.
$name, $hours
     .
```

Together with the secret word lists (files named *something*.sec in the current directory) and the database, lastdb.dir and lastdb.pag, you'll have all you need.

Exercises

Normally, each chapter will end with some exercises, for which answers will be found in Appendix A, *Exercise Answers*. For this stroll, the answers have already been given above.

1. Type in the example programs, and get them to work. (You'll need to create the secret word lists as well.) Consult your local Perl guru if you need assistance.

2

Scalar Data

What Is Scalar Data?

A *scalar* is the simplest kind of data that Perl manipulates. A scalar is either a number (like 4 or 3.25e20) or a string of characters (like "hello" or the Gettysburg Address). Although you may think of numbers and strings as very different things, Perl uses them nearly interchangeably, so we'll describe them together.

A scalar value can be acted upon with operators (like plus or concatenate), generally yielding a scalar result. A scalar value can be stored into a scalar variable. Scalars can be read from files and devices and written out as well.

Numbers

Although a scalar is either a number or a string,[*] consider numbers and strings separately for the moment. Numbers first, strings in a minute...

All Numbers Use the Same Format Internally

As you'll see in the next few paragraphs, you can specify both integers (whole numbers, like 17 or 342) and floating-point numbers (real numbers with decimal points, like 3.14, or 1.35 times 10^{25}). But internally, Perl computes only with double-precision floating-point values.[†] This means that there are no *integer*

---

[*] A scalar can also be a reference, but that is an advanced topic.

[†] A "double-precision floating-point value" is whatever the C compiler that compiled Perl used for a `double` declaration.

values internal to Perl; an integer constant in the program is treated as the equivalent floating-point value.* You probably won't notice the conversion (or care much), but you should stop looking for integer operations (as opposed to *floating-point* operations), because there aren't any.

Float Literals

A *literal* is the way a value is represented in the text of the Perl program. You could also call this a *constant* in your program, but we'll use the term literal. Literals are the way in which data is represented *in* the source code of your program as input to the Perl compiler. (Data that is read from or written to files is treated similarly, but not identically.)

Perl accepts the complete set of floating-point literals available to C programmers. Numbers with and without decimal points are allowed (including an optional plus or minus prefix), as well as tacking on a power-of-10 indicator (exponential notation) with E notation (that's e or E). For example:

```
1.25      # about 1 and a quarter
7.25e45   # 7.25 times 10 to the 45th power (a big number)
-6.5e24   # negative 6.5 times 10 to the 24th
          # (a "big" negative number)
-12e-24   # negative 12 times 10 to the -24th
          # (a very small negative number)
-1.2E-23  # another way to say that
```

Integer Literals

Integer literals are also straightforward, as in:

```
12
15
-2004
3485
```

Don't start the number with a 0, because Perl supports octal and hexadecimal (hex) literals. Octal numbers start with a leading 0, and hex numbers start with a leading 0x or 0X.† The hex digits A through F (in either case) represent the conventional digit values of 10 through 15. For example:

```
0377  # 377 octal, same as 255 decimal
-0xff # negative FF hex, same as -255 decimal
```

---

* Unless you use "integer mode," but that is not the default.

† The "leading zero" indicator works only for literals, not for automatic string-to-number conversion. You can convert a data string that looks like an octal or hex value into a number with oct() or hex().

Strings

Strings are sequences of characters (like `hello`). Each character is an 8-bit value from the entire 256-character set (there's nothing special about the NUL character, as in some languages).

The shortest possible string has no characters. The longest string fills all of your available memory (although you wouldn't be able to do much with that). This is in accordance with the principle of "no built-in limits" that Perl follows at every opportunity. Typical strings are printable sequences of letters, digits, and punctuation in the ASCII 32 to ASCII 126 range. However, the ability to have any character from 0 to 255 in a string means that you can create, scan, and manipulate raw binary data as strings—a task with which most other utilities would have great difficulty. (For example, you can patch your operating system by reading it into a Perl string, making the change, and writing the result back out.)

Like numbers, strings have a literal representation (the way you represent the string in a Perl program). Literal strings come in two different flavors: *single-quoted strings* and *double-quoted strings.** Another form that looks rather like these two is the back-quoted string (`like this`). This form isn't so much a literal string as a way to run external commands and get back their output. This form is covered in Chapter 14, *Process Management*.

Single-Quoted Strings

A *single-quoted string* is a sequence of characters enclosed in single quotes. The single quotes are not part of the string itself; they're just there to let Perl identify the beginning and the ending of the string. Any character between the quote marks (including newline characters, if the string continues onto successive lines) is legal inside a string. There are two exceptions: to get a single quote into a single-quoted string, precede it by a backslash; and, to get a backslash into a single-quoted string, precede the backslash by a backslash. In other pictures:

```
'hello'      # five characters: h, e, l, l, o
'don\'t'     # five characters: d, o, n, single quote, t
' '          # the null string (no characters)
'silly\\me'  # silly, followed by backslash, followed by me
'hello\n'    # hello followed by backslash followed by n
'hello
there'       # hello, newline, there (11 characters in all)
```

---

* Perl also has *here* strings, which we'll touch on in Chapter 18, *CGI Programming*.

Note that the \n within a single-quoted string is not interpreted as a newline, but as the two characters backslash and n. (Only when the backslash is followed by another backslash or a single quote does it have special meaning.)

Double-Quoted Strings

A *double-quoted string* acts a lot like a C string. Once again, it's a sequence of characters, although this time enclosed in double quotes. But now the backslash takes on its full power to specify certain control characters, or even any character at all through octal and hex representations. Here are some double-quoted strings:

```
"hello world\n"# hello world, and a newline
"new \007"     # new, space, and the bell character (octal 007)
"coke\tsprite" # a coke, a tab, and a sprite
"c:\\temp"     # c:, backslash, and temp
```

The backslash can precede many different characters to mean different things (typically called a *backslash escape*). The complete list of double-quoted string escapes is given in Table 2-1.

Table 2-1. Double-Quoted String Representations

Construct	Meaning
\n	Newline
\r	Return
\t	Tab
\f	Formfeed
\b	Backspace
\v	Vertical tab
\a	Bell
\e	Escape
\007	Any octal ASCII value (here, 007 = bell)
\x7f	Any hex ASCII value (here, 7f = delete)
\cC	Any "control" character (here, control C)
\\	Backslash
\"	Doublequote
\l	Lowercase next letter
\L	Lowercase all following letters until \E
\u	Uppercase next letter
\U	Uppercase all following letters until \E
\Q	Backslash quote all nonalphanumerics
\E	Terminate \L , \U or \Q

Another feature of double-quoted strings is that they are *variable interpolated*, meaning that scalar and array variables within the strings are replaced with their current values when the strings are used. We haven't formally been introduced to what a variable looks like yet (except in the stroll), so I'll get back to this later.

A quick note here about using DOS/Win32 pathnames in double-quoted strings: while Perl accepts either backslashes or forward slashes in path names, backslashes need to be escaped. So, you need to write one of the following:

```
"c:\\temp"  # use an escaped backslash
"c:/temp"   # use a  Unix-style forward slash
```

If you forget to escape the backslash, you'll end up with strange results:

```
"c:\temp"  # WRONG - this string contains a c:, a TAB, and emp
```

If you're already used to using pathnames in C/C++, this notation will be second nature to you. Otherwise, beware: pathnames seem to bite each and every Perl-for-Win32 programmer from time to time.

Scalar Operators

An operator produces a new value (the *result*) from one or more other values (the *operands*). For example, + is an operator because it takes two numbers (the operands, like 5 and 6), and produces a new value (11, the result).

Perl's operators and expressions are generally a superset of those provided in most other ALGOL/Pascal-like programming languages, such as C or Java. An operator expects either numeric or string operands (or possibly a combination of both). If you provide a string operand where a number is expected, or vice versa, Perl automatically converts the operand using fairly intuitive rules, which will be detailed in the section "Conversion Between Numbers and Strings," later in this chapter.

Operators for Numbers

Perl provides the typical ordinary addition, subtraction, multiplication, and division operators, and so on. For example:

```
2 + 3      # 2 plus 3, or 5
5.1 - 2.   # 5.1 minus 2.4, or approximately 2.7
3 * 12     # 3 times 12 = 36
10.2 / 0.3 # 10.2 divided by 0.3, or approximately 34
10 / 3     # always floating point divide, so approximately 3.333333...
```

Additionally, Perl provides the FORTRAN-like *exponentiation* operator, which many have yearned for in Pascal and C. The operator is represented by the double asterisk, such as 2**3, which is 2 to the power of 3, or 8. (If the result cannot fit into a double-precision floating-point number, such as a negative number to a noninteger exponent, or a large number to a large exponent, you'll get a fatal error.)

Perl also supports a *modulus* operator. The value of the expression 10 % 3 is the remainder when 10 is divided by 3, which is 1. Both values are first reduced to their integer values, so 10.5 % 3.2 is computed as 10 % 3.

The logical comparison operators are <, <=, ==, >=, >, and !=. These operators compare two values numerically, returning a *true* or *false* value. For example, 3 > 2 returns true because three is greater than two, while 5 != 5 returns false because it's not true that 5 is not equal to 5. The definitions of true and false are covered later, but for now, think of the return values as one for true, and zero for false. (These operators are revisited in Table 2-2.)

You may be wondering about the word "approximately" in the code comments at the start of this section. Don't you get *exactly* 2.7 when subtracting 2.4 from 5.1? In math class you do, but on computers you usually don't. Instead, you get an *approximation* that's only accurate to a certain number of decimal places. Computers don't store numbers in the same way a mathematician does. Although there are infinitely many decimal points in them, the computer only has a limited space to store them (usually 64 bits per number). So, just a few of these infinite real numbers can be exactly represented on the computer—the rest are just close.

Comparing the following statements, you'll see what the computer really got as the result of the subtraction (the `printf` function is described in Chapter 6, *Basic I/O*):

```
printf("%.51f\n", 5.1 - 2.4)
# 2.6999999999999997335464740899624302983283996582203125

print(5.1 - 2.4, "\n");
# 2.7
```

Don't worry too much about this: the `print()` function's default format for printing floating-point numbers usually hides such minor representational inaccuracies. If this ends up being a problem, the Math::BigInt and Math::BigFloat object modules provide infinite-precision arithmetic for integers and floating-point numbers at the cost of somewhat slower execution. For details, see Chapter 7 of *Programming Perl* or the online documentation on these modules.

Operators for Strings

String values can be concatenated with the "." operator. (Yes, we are using a single period.) This concatenation does not alter either string, any more than 2+3 alters either 2 or 3. The resulting (longer) string is then available for further computation or to be stored into a variable. For example:

```
"hello" . "world"      # same as "helloworld"
'hello world' . "\n"   # same as "hello world\n"
"fred" . " " . "barney" # same as "fred barney"
```

Note that the concatenation must be explicitly called for with the . operator. You do not merely have to stick the two values close to each other.

Another set of operators for strings are the string comparison operators. These operators are FORTRAN like, as in using lt for less than, and so on. The operators compare the ASCII values of the characters of the strings in the usual fashion. The complete set of comparison operators (for both numbers and strings) is given in Table 2-2.

Table 2-2. Numeric and String Comparison Operators

Comparison	Numeric	String
Equal	==	eq
Not equal	!=	ne
Less than	<	lt
Greater than	>	gt
Less than or equal to	<=	le
Greater than or equal to	>=	ge

You may wonder why there are separate operators for numbers and strings, if numbers and strings are automatically converted back and forth. Consider the two values 7 and 30. If compared as numbers, 7 is obviously less than 30, but if compared as strings, the string "30" comes *before* the string "7" (because the ASCII value for 3 is less than the value for 7), and hence is less. Perl always requires you to specify the proper type of comparison, whether it be numeric or string.

Still another string operator is the *string repetition* operator, consisting of the single lowercase letter **x**. This operator takes its left operand (a string), and makes as many concatenated copies of that string as indicated by its right operand (a number). For example:

```
"fred" x 3         # is "fredfredfred"
"barney" x (4+1)   # is "barney" x 5, or
                   # "barneybarneybarneybarneybarney"
(3+2) x 4          # is 5 x 4, or really "5" x 4, which is "5555"
```

That last example is worth spelling out slowly. The parentheses on (3+2) force this part of the expression to be evaluated first, yielding five. (The parentheses here are working as in standard math.) But the string repetition operator wants a string for a left operand, so the number 5 is converted to the string "5" (using rules described in detail later), a one-character string. This new string is then copied four times, yielding the four-character string 5555. If we had reversed the order of the operands, we would have made five copies of the string 4, yielding 44444. This shows that string repetition is not commutative.

If necessary, the copy count (the right operand) is first truncated to an integer value (4.8 becomes 4) before being used. A copy count of less than 1 results in an empty (zero-length) string.

Operator Precedence and Associativity

Operator precedence defines how to resolve the ambiguous case in which two operators are trying to operate on three operands. For example, in the expression 2+3*4, do we perform the addition first or the multiplication first? If we did the addition first, we'd get 5*4, or 20. But if we did the multiplication first (as we were taught in math class), we'd get 2+12, or 14. Fortunately, Perl chooses the common mathematical definition, performing the multiplication first. Because of this, we say multiplication has a *higher precedence* than addition.

You can override the order defined by precedence using parentheses. Anything in parentheses is completely computed before the operator outside of the parentheses is applied (just like you learned in your math class). So if I really want the addition before the multiplication, I can say (2+3)*4, yielding 20. Also, if I wanted to demonstrate that multiplication is performed before addition, I could add a decorative but functionless set of parentheses in 2+(3*4).

While precedence is intuitive for addition and multiplication,* we start running into problems when faced with, say, string concatenation compared with exponentiation. You can resolve this by consulting the official, accept-no-substitutes Perl operator precedence chart, shown in Table 2-3. (Note that some of the operators have not yet been described, and in fact, may not even appear anywhere in this book, but don't let that fact scare you away from reading about them.) Operators also found in C have the same precedence as in C).

Table 2-3. Associativity and Precedence of Operators

Associativity	Operator
Left	The "list" operators (leftward)
Left	-> (method call, dereference)
Nonassociative	++ -- (autoincrement, autodecrement)
Right	** (exponentiation)
Right	! ~ \ + - (logical not, bit not, reference operator, unary plus, unary minus)

---

* Asssuming you recall your high school algebra class. If not, simply use parentheses to improve clarity.

Table 2-3. Associativity and Precedence of Operators (continued)

Associativity	Operator
Left	=~ !~ (matches, doesn't match)
Left	* / % x (multiply, divide, modulus, string replicate)
Left	+ - . (add, subtract, string concatenate)
Nonassociative	Named unary operators (like chomp)
Left	& (bit and)
Left	| ^ (bit or, bit xor)
Left	&& (logical and)
Left	|| (logical or)
Nonassociative	.. ... (noninclusive and inclusive range)
Right	?: (if then else)
Right	= += -= *=, etc. (assignment and binary assignment)
Left	, => (comma and comma arrow)
Nonassociative	List operators (rightward)
Right	not (logical not)
Left	and (logical and)
Left	or xor (logical or, logical xor)

In Table 2-3, any given operator has higher precedence than those listed below it, and lower precedence than all of the operators listed above it.

Operators at the same precedence level resolve according to rules of *associativity*. Just like precedence, associativity resolves the order of operations when two operators of the same precedence compete for three operands:

```
2 ** 3 ** 4    # 2 ** (3 ** 4), or 2 ** 81, or approx 2.41e24
72 / 12 / 3    # (72 / 12) / 3, or 6/3, or 2
30 / 6 * 3     # (30/6)*3, or 15
```

In the first case, the ** operator has right associativity, so the parentheses are implied on the right. Comparatively, the * and / operators have left associativity, yielding a set of implied parentheses on the left.

Conversion Between Numbers and Strings

If you use a string value as an operand for a numeric operator (say, +), Perl automatically converts the string to its equivalent numeric value, as if you had entered it as a decimal floating-point value.[*] Trailing nonnumerics and leading whitespaces are politely and quietly ignored, so "123.45fred" (with a leading

---

[*] Hex and octal values are not supported in this automatic conversion. Use hex and oct to interpret hex and octal values.

space) converts to `123.45` with nary a warning.* At the extreme, something that *isn't* a number at all converts to zero without warning (such as the string `fred` used as a number).

Likewise, if you give a numeric value when a string value is needed (for the string concatenate operator, for example), the numeric value is expanded into whatever string would have been printed for that number. For example, if you want to concatenate an X followed by the results of 4 multiplied by 5, you can say this simply as:

```
"X" . (4 * 5) # same as "X" . 20, or "X20"
```

(Remember that the parentheses force `4*5` to be computed first, before considering the string concatenation operator.)

In other words, you don't really have to worry about whether you have a number or a string (most of the time). Perl performs all the conversions for you.

Scalar Variables

A variable is a name for a container that holds one or more values. The name of the variable is constant throughout the program, but the value or values contained in that variable typically change over and over again throughout the execution of the program.

A scalar variable holds a single scalar value (representing a number, a string, or a reference). Scalar variable names begin with a dollar sign followed by a letter, and then possibly more letters, or digits, or underscores.† Upper- and lowercase letters are distinct: the variable $A is a different variable from $a. And all of the letters, digits, and underscores are significant, so:

```
$a_very_long_variable_that_ends_in_1
```

is different from:

```
$a_very_long_variable_that_ends_in_2
```

You should generally select variable names that mean something regarding the value of the variable. For example, $xyz123 is probably not very descriptive, but $line_length is.

---

* Unless you turn on the -w option from the command line. which you should really always do for safety's sake.

† Limited to 255 characters, however. We hope that suffices.

Scalar Operators and Functions

The most common operation on a scalar variable is *assignment*, which is the way to give a value to a variable. The Perl assignment operator is the equal sign (as in C or FORTRAN), which takes a variable name on the left side and gives it the value of the expression on the right, like so:

```
$a = 17;     # give $a the value of 17
$b = $a + 3; # give $b the current value of $a plus 3 (20)
$b = $b * 2; # give $b the value of $b multiplied by 2 (40)
```

Notice that the last line uses the $b variable twice: once to get its value (on the right side of the =), and once to define where to put the computed expression (on the left side of the =). This is legal, safe, and in fact, rather common. In fact, the practice is so common that we'll see in a minute that we can write this expression using a convenient shorthand.

You may have noticed that scalar variables are always specified with the leading $. In batch files, Java, or C, you don't need the $ at all. If you bounce back and forth a lot, you'll find yourself typing the wrong things occasionally. This is expected. (Our solution was to stop writing batch files and C programs, but that may not work for you.)

You may use a scalar assignment as a value as well as an operation, as in C. In other words, $a=3 has a value, just as $a+3 has a value. The value is the value assigned, so the value of $a=3 is 3. Although this usage may seem odd at first glance, using an assignment as a value is useful if you wish to assign an intermediate value in an expression to a variable, or if you simply wish to copy the same value to more than one variable. For example:

```
$b = 4 + ($a = 3);     # assign 3 to $a, then add 4 to that
                       # resulting in $b getting 7
$d = ($c = 5);         # copy 5 into $c, and then also into $d
$d = $c = 5;           # the same thing without parentheses
```

That last example works because assignment is right-associative.

Binary Assignment Operators

Expressions like $a = $a + 5 (in which the same variable appears on both sides of an assignment) occur so frequently that Perl has a shorthand for the operation of *altering a variable*: the *binary assignment operator*. Nearly all binary operators that compute a value have a corresponding binary assignment form with an appended equal sign. For example, the following two lines are equivalent:

```
$a = $a + 5; # without the binary assignment operator
$a += 5;     # with the binary assignment operator
```

And so are these:

```
$b = $b * 3;
$b *= 3;
```

In each case, the operator causes the existing value of the variable to be altered in some way, not simply overwriting the value with the result of some new expression.

Another common assignment operator is the string concatenate operator:

```
$str = $str . " ";   # append a space to $str
$str .= " ";         # same thing with assignment operator
```

Nearly all binary operators are valid in this way. For example, a *raise to the power of* operator is written as **=**. So, `$a **= 3` means "raise the number in `$a` to the third power, placing the result back in `$a`."

Like the simple assignment operator, each of these operators has a value as well: the new value of the variable. For example:

```
$a = 3;
$b = ($a += 4); # $a and $b are both now 7
```

Autoincrement and Autodecrement

As if it weren't already easy enough to add one to `$a` by saying `$a += 1`, Perl goes one step further and shortens even this method. The `++` operator (called the *autoincrement* operator) adds one to its operand, and returns the incremented value, like so:

```
$a += 1;    # with assignment operator
++$a;       # with prefix autoincrement
$d = 17;
$e = ++$d; # $e and $d are both 18 now
```

Here, the `++` operator is being used as a *prefix* operator—that is, the operator appears to the left of its operand. You may also use the autoincrement in a *suffix* form (to the right of its operand). In this case, the result of the expression is the old value of the variable *before* the variable is incremented. For example:

```
$c = 17;
$d = $c++; # $d is 17, but $c is now 18
```

Because the value of the operand changes, the operand must be a real scalar variable, not just an expression. You cannot say `++16` to get 17, nor can you say `++($a+$b)` to somehow get one more than the sum of `$a` and `$b`.

The autodecrement operator (--) is similar to the autoincrement operator, but subtracts one rather than adding one. Like the autoincrement operator, the auto-decrement operator has a prefix and suffix form. For example:

```
$x = 12;
--$x; # $x is now 11
$y = $x--; # $y is 11, and $x is now 10
```

The autoincrement and autodecrement operators also work on floating-point values. So autoincrementing a variable with the value 4.2 yields 5.2 as expected.*

The chop() and chomp() Functions

A useful built-in function is chop(). This prefix function takes a single argument within its parentheses—the name of a scalar variable—and removes the last character from the string value of that variable. For example:

```
$x = "hello world";
chop($x); # $x is now "hello worl"
```

Note that the value of the argument is altered here, hence the requirement for a scalar variable, rather than simply a scalar value. It would not make sense, for example, to write chop('suey') to change it to 'sue', because there is no place in which to save the value. Besides, you could have just written 'sue' instead.

The value returned is the discarded character (the letter d in world above). As a result, the following code is probably wrong:

```
$x = chop($x);  # WRONG: replaces $x with its last character
chop($x);       # RIGHT: as above, removes the last character
```

If you give chop() an empty string, it does nothing, returns nothing, and doesn't raise an error or even whimper a bit.† Most operations in Perl have sensible boundary conditions; in other words, you can use them right up to the edges (and beyond), frequently without complaint. Some have argued that this is one of Perl's fundamental flaws, while others write screaming programs without having to worry about the fringes. You decide which camp you wish to join.

When you chop a string that has already been chopped, another character disappears off into "bit heaven." For example:

```
$a = "hello world\n";
chop $a; # $a is now "hello world"
chop $a; # oops! $a is now "hello worl"
```

---

* Autoincrement even works on strings. See *Programming Perl* or *perlop* for related information.

† Unless you are using the sanity-saving -w switch.

If you're not sure whether the variable has a newline on the end, you can use the slightly safer `chomp()` function, which removes only a newline character,* like so:

```
$a = "hello world\n";
chomp ($a); # $a is now "hello world"
chomp ($a); # aha! no change in $a
```

Interpolation of Scalars into Strings

When a string literal is double quoted, it is subject to *variable interpolation* (besides being checked for backslash escapes). This means that the string is scanned for possible scalar variable† names—namely, a dollar sign followed by letters, digits, and underscores. When a variable reference is found, it is replaced with its current value (or an empty string if the variable has not yet been assigned a value). For example:

```
$a = "fred";
$b = "some text $a";          # $b is now "some text fred"
$c = "no such variable $what"; # $c is "no such variable "
```

The text that replaces the variable is not rescanned; even if there are dollar signs in the replaced value, no further replacement occurs:

```
$x = '$fred';  # literally a dollar sign followed by "fred"
$y = "hey $x"; # value is 'hey $fred': no double substitution
```

To prevent the substitution of a variable with its value, you must either alter that part of the string so that it appears in single quotes, or precede the dollar sign with a backslash, which turns off the dollar sign's special significance:

```
$fred    = 'hi';
$barney  = "a test of " . '$fred';# literally: 'a test of $fred'
$barney2 = "a test of \$fred";    # same thing
```

The variable name will be the longest possible variable name that makes sense at that part of the string. This can be a problem if you want to follow the replaced value immediately with some constant text that begins with a letter, digit, or underscore. As Perl scans for variable names, it would consider those characters to be additional name characters, and this result is not what you want. Perl provides a delimiter for the variable name. Simply enclose the *name* of the variable in a pair of curly braces. Or, you can end that part of the string and start another part of the string with a concatenation operator:

```
$fred = "pay"; $fredday = "wrong!";
$barney = "It's $fredday";              # not payday, but "It's wrong!"
```

---

* Or whatever the input record separator $\ is set to.

† The string is actually scanned for array variables as well, but we won't know about those until Chapter 3, *Arrays and List Data*.

```
$barney = "It's ${fred}day";          # now, $barney gets "It's payday"
$barney2 = "It's $fred"."day";        # another way to do it
$barney3 = "It's " . $fred . "day";   # and another way
```

You can use the case-shifting string escapes to alter the case of letters that are brought in with variable interpolation.* For example:

```
$bigfred = "\Ufred";                            # $bigfred is "FRED"
$fred = "fred"; $bigfred = "\U$fred";           # same thing
$capfred = "\u$fred";                           # $capfred is "Fred"
$barney = "\LBARNEY";                           # $barney is now "barney"
$capbarney = "\u\LBARNEY";                      # $capbarney is now "Barney"
$bigbarney = "BARNEY"; $capbarney = "\u\L$bigbarney"; # same
```

As you can see, the case-shifting string escapes are remembered within a string until they are used, so even though the first letter of **BARNEY** doesn't follow the \u, it remains uppercase because of the \u.

The term *variable interpolation* is often used interchangeably with *double-quote interpolation*, because strings that are double quoted are subject to variable interpolation. So too, are backquoted strings, as described in Chapter 14.

<STDIN> as a Scalar Value

At this point, if you're a typical code hacker, you're probably wondering how to get a value into a Perl program. Here's the simplest way. Each time you use <STDIN> in a place where a scalar value is expected, Perl reads the next complete text line from *standard input* (up to the first newline), and uses that string as the value of <STDIN>. Standard input can mean many things, but unless you do something odd, it means the command console that invoked your program. If there's nothing waiting to be read (typically the case, unless you type ahead a complete line), the Perl program will stop and wait for you to enter some characters followed by a newline (return).

The string value of <STDIN> typically has a newline on the end of it. Most often, you'll want to get rid of that newline right away (there's a big difference between hello and hello\n). It is at this point that our friend, the chomp() function, comes to the rescue. A typical input sequence goes something like this:

```
$a = <STDIN>; # get the text
chomp($a);    # get rid of that pesky newline
```

A common abbreviation for these two lines is:

```
chomp($a = <STDIN>);
```

---

* You may find the uc, ucfirst, lc, and lcfirst operators easier to use.

The assignment inside the parentheses continues to refer to $a, even after it has been given a value with <STDIN>. Thus, the chomp() function is working on $a. (This is true in general about the assignment operator—an assignment expression can be used wherever a variable is needed, and the actions refer to the variable on the left side of the equal sign.)

Output with print

So, we get things in with <STDIN>. How do we get things out? With the print() function. This function takes the values within its parentheses and puts them out without any embellishment onto *standard output*. Once again, unless you've done something odd, this will be your command console. For example:

```
print("hello world\n"); # say hello world, followed by newline
print "hello world\n";   # same thing
```

Note that the second example shows the form of print() without parentheses. In fact, many of the operators that look like functions also have a syntactic form that works without the parentheses. Whether or not to use the parentheses is mostly a matter of style and typing agility, although there are a few cases where you'll need the parentheses to remove ambiguity.

We'll see that you can actually give print a *list* of values, in the "Using print for Normal Output" section of Chapter 6, *Basic I/O*, but we haven't talked about lists yet, so we'll put that discussion off until later.

The Undefined Value

What happens if you use a scalar variable before you give it a value? Nothing serious, and definitely nothing fatal. Variables have the undef value before they are first assigned. This value looks like a zero when used as a number, or the zero-length empty string when used as a string. You will get a warning when running under Perl's -w switch, though, which is a good way to catch programming errors.

Many operators return undef when the arguments are out of range or don't make sense. If you don't do anything special, you'll get a zero or a null string without major consequences. In practice, this scenario is hardly a problem.

One operation we've seen that returns undef under certain circumstances is <STDIN>. Normally, this returns the next line that was read; however, if there are no more lines to read, (such as when you type CTRL-Z at the terminal, or when a file has no more data), <STDIN> returns undef as a value. In Chapter 6, we'll see how to test for this and take special action when there is no more data available to read.

Exercises

See Appendix A for answers.

1. Write a program that computes the circumference of a circle with a radius of
   12.5. The circumference is 2π times the radius, or about 2 times 3.141592654.

2. Modify the program from the previous exercise to prompt for and accept a
   radius from the person running the program.

3. Write a program that prompts for and reads two numbers, and then prints out
   the result of the two numbers multiplied together.

4. Write a program that reads a string and a number, and then prints the string
   the number of times indicated by the number on separate lines. (Hint: use the
   x operator.)

3

Arrays and List Data

What Is a List or Array?

A list is an ordered set of scalar data. An array is a variable that holds a list. Each *element* of the array is a separate scalar variable with an independent scalar value. These values are ordered—that is, they have a particular sequence from the lowest to the highest element.

Arrays can have any number of elements. The smallest array has no elements, while the largest array can fill all of available memory. Once again, this flexibility is in keeping with Perl's philosophy of "no unnecessary limits."

Literal Representation

A *list literal* (the way you represent the value of a list within your program) consists of comma-separated values enclosed in parentheses. These values form the elements of the list. For example:

```
(1,2,3)      # array of three values 1, 2, and 3
("fred",4.5) # two values, "fred" and 4.5
```

The elements of a list are not necessarily constants—they can be expressions that will be evaluated newly each time the literal is used. For example:

```
($a, 17)      # two values: the current value of $a, and 17
($b+$c,$d+$e) # two values
```

The empty list (one of no elements) is represented by an empty pair of parentheses:

```
() # the empty list (zero elements)
```

An item of the list literal can include the *list constructor function*, indicated by two scalar values separated by two consecutive periods. This function creates a list of values starting at the left scalar value and continuing up through the right scalar value, incrementing by one at each value. For example:

```
(1..5)       # same as (1, 2, 3, 4, 5)
(1.2..5.2)   # same as (1.2, 2.2, 3.2, 4.2, 5.2)
(2..6,10,12) # same as (2,3,4,5,6,10,12)
($a..$b)     # range determined by current values of $a and $b
```

Having the right scalar less than the left scalar results in an empty list; you can't count down by switching the order of the values. If the final value is not a whole number of steps above the initial value, the list stops just before the next value would have been outside the range:

```
(1.3..6.1) # same as (1.3,2.3,3.3,4.3,5.3)
```

List literals with lots of short text strings start to look pretty noisy with all the quotes and commas:

```
@a = ("fred","barney","betty","wilma"); # ugh!
```

Fortunately, Perl has a shortcut: the "quote-word" syntax, which creates a list from the nonwhitespace parts between the parentheses:

```
@a = qw(fred barney betty wilma); # better!
@a = qw(
        fred
        barney
        betty
        wilma
);                                # same thing
```

One use of a list literal is as arguments to the **print()** function introduced earlier. Elements of the list are printed out without any intervening whitespace:

```
print("The answer is ",$a,"\n"); # three element literal array
```

This statement prints "**The answer is**" followed by a space, the value of $a, and a newline. Stay tuned for other uses for list literals.

Variables

An array variable holds a single list value (zero or more scalar values). Array variable names are similar to scalar variable names, differing only in the initial character, which is an at sign (@) rather than a dollar sign ($). For example:

```
@fred # the array variable @fred
```

```
@A_Very_Long_Array_Variable_Name
@A_Very_Long_Array_Variable_Name_that_is_different
```

Note that the array variable `@fred` is unrelated to the scalar variable `$fred`. Perl maintains separate namespaces for different types of things.

The value of an array variable that has not yet been assigned is `()`, the empty list.

An expression can refer to array variables as a whole, or it can examine and modify individual elements of the array.

Array Operators and Functions

Array functions and operators act on entire arrays. Some return a list, which can then either be used as a value for another array function, or assigned into an array variable.

Assignment

Probably the most important array operator is the array assignment operator, which gives an array variable a value. It is an equal sign, just like the scalar assignment operator. Perl determines whether the assignment is a scalar assignment or an array assignment by noticing whether the assignment is to a scalar or an array variable.* For example:

```
@fred = (1,2,3); # The fred array gets a three-element literal
@barney = @fred; # now that is copied to @barney
```

If you assign a scalar value to an array variable, the scalar value becomes the single element of an array:

```
@huh = 1; # 1 is promoted to the list (1) automatically
          # that is, @huh now is (1)
```

An array variable name may appear in a list-literal list. When the value of the list is computed, Perl replaces the array variable name with the current values of the array, like so:

```
@fred = qw(one two);
@barney = (4,5,@fred,6,7);   # @barney becomes
                             # (4,5,"one","two",6,7)
@barney = (8,@barney);       # puts 8 in front of @barney
@barney = (@barney,"last");  # and a "last" at the end
# @barney is now (8,4,5,"one","two",6,7,"last")
```

---

* This applies to scalar or array "lvalues" as well as to simple variables.

Note that the inserted array elements are at the same level as the rest of the literals: a list cannot contain another list as an element.*

If a list literal contains only variable references (not expressions), you can treat the list literal as a variable. In other words, you can use it on the left side of an assignment. Each scalar variable in the list literal takes on the corresponding value from the list on the right side of the assignment. For example:

```
($a,$b,$c) = (1,2,3);     # give 1 to $a, 2 to $b, 3 to $c
($a,$b) = ($b,$a);        # swap $a and $b
($d,@fred) = ($a,$b,$c);  # give $a to $d, and ($b,$c) to @fred
($e,@fred) = @fred;       # remove the first element of @fred to $e
                          # this makes @fred = ($c) and $e = $b
```

If the number of elements you assign does not match the number of variables to hold the values, any excess values (on the right side of the equal sign) are silently discarded, and any excess variables (on the left side of the equal sign) are given the value of **undef**.

An array variable appearing in the array literal list must be last, because the array variable is "greedy" and consumes all remaining values. (Well, you could put other variables after it, but they would just get **undef** values.)

If you assign an array variable to a scalar variable, the number assigned is the *length* of the array, as in:

```
@fred = (4,5,6); # initialize @fred
$a = @fred;      # $a gets 3, the current length of @fred
```

The length is also returned whenever you use an array variable name where a scalar value is needed. (In the section "Scalar and List Context" later in this chapter, we'll see that this method is called using the array name in a *scalar context*.) For example, to get one less than the length of the array, you can use **@fred-1**, because the scalar subtraction operator wants scalars for both of its operands. Notice the following:

```
$a = @fred;   # $a gets the length of @fred
($a) = @fred; # $a gets the first element of @fred
```

The first assignment is a scalar assignment, and so **@fred** is treated as a scalar, yielding its length. The second assignment is an array assignment (even if only one value is wanted), and thus yields the first element of **@fred**, silently discarding all the rest.

---

* Although a *list reference* is permitted as a list element, it's not really a list as a list element. Still, it works out to nearly the same thing, allowing for multidimensional arrays. See Chapter 4 of *Programming Perl* or *perllol* for more details.

The value of an array assignment is itself a list value, and can be cascaded as with scalar assignments. For example:

```
@fred = (@barney = (2,3,4)); # @fred and @barney get (2,3,4)
@fred = @barney = (2,3,4);    # same thing
```

Array Element Access

So far, we've been treating the array as a whole, adding and removing values by doing array assignments. Many useful programs are constructed using arrays without ever accessing any specific array element. However, Perl provides a traditional subscripting operator to access an array element by numeric index.

For the subscripting operator, the array elements are numbered using sequential integers, beginning at 0,[*] and increasing by 1 for each element. The first element of the @fred array is accessed as $fred[0]. Note that the @ on the array name becomes a $ on the element reference. This is because accessing an element of the array identifies a scalar variable (part of the array), which can either be assigned to or have its current value used in an expression, like so:

```
@fred = (7,8,9);
$b = $fred[0]; # give 7 to $b (first element of @fred)
$fred[0] = 5;  # now @fred = (5,8,9)
```

Other elements can be accessed with equal ease, as in:

```
$c = $fred[1];                      # give 8 to $c
$fred[2]++;                         # increment the third element of @fred
$fred[1] += 4;                      # add 4 to the second element
($fred[0],$fred[1]) = ($fred[1],$fred[0]); # swap the first two
```

Accessing a list of elements from the same array (as in the previous example) is called a *slice*, and occurs often enough so that a special representation exists for it:

```
@fred[0,1]                  # same as ($fred[0],$fred[1])
@fred[0,1] = @fred[1,0]     # swap the first two elements
@fred[0,1,2] = @fred[1,1,1] # make all 3 elements like the 2nd
@fred[1,2] = (9,10);        # change the last two values to 9 and 10
```

Note that this slice uses an @ prefix rather than a $. This is because you are creating an array variable by selecting part of the array rather than a scalar variable accessing just one element.

Slices also work on literal lists, or any function that returns a list value:

```
@who = (qw(fred barney betty wilma))[2,3];
# like @x = qw(fred barney betty wilma); @who = @x[2,3];
```

---

[*] You can change the index value of the first element to something else (like 1). However, doing so has drastic effects, will probably confuse people maintaining your code, and might break the routines you take from other people. Thus, we highly recommend that you consider this feature unusable.

The index values in these examples have been literal integers, but the index can also be any expression that returns a number, which is then used to select the appropriate element:

```
@fred = (7,8,9);
$a = 2;
$b = $fred[$a];        # like $fred[2], or the value of 9
$c = $fred[$a-1];      # $c gets $fred[1], or 8
($c) = (7,8,9)[$a-1];  # same thing using slice
```

Perl programs can thus have array accesses similar to many traditional programming languages.

This idea of using an expression for the subscript also works for slices. Remember, however, that the subscript for a slice is a list of values, so the expression is an array expression, rather than a scalar expression. For example:

```
@fred = (7,8,9); # as in previous example
@barney = (2,1,0);
@backfred = @fred[@barney];
# same as @fred[2,1,0], or ($fred[2],$fred[1],$fred[0]), or
# (9,8,7)
```

If you access an array element beyond the ends of the current array (that is, an index of less than 0 or greater than the last element's index), the undef value is returned without warning. For example:

```
@fred = (1,2,3);
$barney = $fred[7]; # $barney is now undef
```

Assigning a value beyond the end of the current array automatically extends the array (giving a value of undef to all intermediate values, if any). For example:

```
@fred = (1,2,3);
$fred[3] = "hi"; # @fred is now (1,2,3,"hi")
$fred[6] = "ho"; # @fred is now (1,2,3,"hi",undef,undef,"ho")
```

Assignment to an array element with a subscript of less than 0 is a fatal error, because it is probably the result of Very Bad Programming Style.

You can use $#fred to get the index value of the last element of @fred. You can even assign to this value to change the apparent length of @fred, making it grow or shrink, but such an assignment is generally unnecessary, because the array grows and shrinks automatically.

A negative subscript on an array counts back from the end. So, another way to get at the last element is with the subscript -1. The second to the last element would be -2, and so on. For example:

```
@fred = ("fred", "wilma", "pebbles", "dino");
print $fred[-1];       # prints "dino"
print $#fred;          # prints 3
print $fred[$#fred];   # prints "dino"
```

The push and pop Functions

One common use of an array is as a stack of information, where new values are added to and removed from the right-hand side of the list. These operations occur often enough to have their own special functions:

```
push(@mylist,$newvalue);  # like @mylist = (@mylist,$newvalue)
$oldvalue = pop(@mylist); # removes the last element of @mylist
```

The pop() function returns **undef** if given an empty list, rather than doing something un-Perl-like such as complaining or generating a warning message.

The push() function also accepts a list of values to be pushed. The values are pushed together onto the end of the list. For example:

```
@mylist = (1,2,3);
push(@mylist,4,5,6); # @mylist = (1,2,3,4,5,6)
```

Note that the first argument must be an array variable name—pushing and popping wouldn't make sense on a literal list.

The shift and unshift Functions

The push and pop functions do things to the "right" side of a list (the portion with the highest subscripts). Similarly, the **unshift** and **shift** functions perform the corresponding actions on the "left" side of a list (the portion with the lowest subscripts). Here are a few examples:

```
unshift(@fred,$a);       # like @fred = ($a,@fred);
unshift(@fred,$a,$b,$c); # like @fred = ($a,$b,$c,@fred);
$x = shift(@fred);       # like ($x,@fred) = @fred;
                         # with some real values
@fred = (5,6,7);
unshift(@fred,2,3,4);    # @fred is now (2,3,4,5,6,7)
$x = shift(@fred);       # $x gets 2, @fred is now (3,4,5,6,7)
```

As with pop(), **shift()** returns **undef** if you give it an empty array variable.

The reverse Function

The **reverse** function reverses the order of the elements of its argument, returning the resulting list. For example:

```
@a = (7,8,9);
@b = reverse(@a);    # gives @b the value of (9,8,7)
@b = reverse(7,8,9); # same thing
```

Note that the argument list is unaltered; the **reverse()** function works on a copy. If you want to reverse an array "in place," you'll need to assign it back into the same variable:

```
@b = reverse(@b); # give @b the reverse of itself
```

The sort Function

The `sort` function takes its arguments, and sorts them as if they were single strings in ascending ASCII order. It returns the sorted list, without altering the original list. For example:

```
@x = sort("small","medium","large");
            # @x gets "large","medium","small"
@y = (1,2,4,8,16,32,64);
@y = sort(@y); # @y gets 1,16,2,32,4,64,8
```

Note that sorting numbers does not happen numerically, but by the string values of each number (1, 16, 2, 32, and so on). In the section "Advanced Sorting," in Chapter 15, *Other Data Transformation*, you'll learn how to sort numerically, in descending order, by the third character of each string, or by any other method that you choose.

The chomp Function

The `chomp` function works on an array variable as well as a scalar variable. Each element of the array has its last newline removed. This function can be handy when you've read a list of lines as separate array elements, and you want to remove a newline from all of the lines at once. For example:

```
@stuff = ("hello\n","world\n","happy days");
chomp(@stuff); # @stuff is now ("hello","world","happy days")
```

Scalar and List Context

As you can see, each operator is designed to operate on some specified combination of scalars or lists, and returns either a scalar or a list. If an operator or function expects an operand to be a scalar, we say that the operand or argument is being evaluated in a *scalar context*. Similarly, if an operand or argument is expected to be a list value, we say that it is being evaluated in a *list context*.

Normally, the context is fairly insignificant. But, sometimes you get a completely different operation depending on whether you are within a scalar or a list context. For example, `@fred` returns the contents of the `@fred` array in a list context, but the length of the same array in a scalar context. These subtleties are mentioned when each operator and function is described.

A scalar value used within an array context is promoted to a single-element array.

<STDIN> as an Array

One previously seen operation that returns a different value in a list context is <STDIN>. As described earlier, <STDIN> returns the next line of input in a scalar context. However, in a list context, it returns *all* of the remaining lines up to the end-of-file. Each line is returned as a separate element of the list. For example:

```
@a = <STDIN>; # read standard input in a list context
```

If the person running the program types three lines, then hits CTRL-Z (to indicate end-of-file), the array ends up with three elements. Each element will be a string that ends in a newline, corresponding to the three newline-terminated lines entered.

Variable Interpolation of Arrays

Like scalars, array values may be interpolated into a double-quoted string. A single element of an array will be replaced by its value, like so:

```
@fred = ("hello","dolly");
$y = 2;
$x = "This is $fred[1]'s place";     # "This is dolly's place"
$x = "This is $fred[$y-1]'s place"; # same thing
```

Note that the index expression is evaluated as an ordinary expression, as if it were outside a string. It is not variable interpolated first.

If you want to follow a simple scalar variable reference with a literal left square bracket, you need to delimit the square bracket so it isn't considered part of the array, as follows:

```
@fred = ("hello","dolly");  # give value to @fred for testing
$fred = "right";
# we are trying to say "this is right[1]"
$x = "this is $fred[1]";     # wrong, gives "this is dolly"
$x = "this is ${fred}[1]";   # right (protected by braces)
$x = "this is $fred"."[1]"; # right (different string)
$x = "this is $fred\[1]";    # right (backslash hides it)
```

Similarly, a list of values from an array variable can be interpolated. The simplest interpolation is an entire array, indicated by giving the array name (including its leading @ character). In this case, the elements are interpolated in sequence with a space character between them, as in:

```
@fred = ("a","bb","ccc",1,2,3);
$all = "Now for @fred here!";
            # $all gets "Now for a bb ccc 1 2 3 here!"
```

You can also select a portion of an array with a slice:

```
@fred = ("a","bb","ccc",1,2,3);
$all = "Now for @fred[2,3] here!";
```

```
                    # $all gets "Now for ccc 1 here!"
     $all = "Now for @fred[@fred[4,5]] here!"; # same thing
```

Once again, you can use any of the quoting mechanisms described earlier if you want to follow an array name reference with a literal left bracket rather than an indexing expression.

Exercises

See Appendix A for answers.

1. Write a program that reads a list of strings on separate lines and prints out the list in reverse order. If you're reading the list from the console, you'll probably need to delimit the end of the list by pressing CTRL-Z.

2. Write a program that reads a number and then a list of strings (all on separate lines), and then prints one of the lines from the list as selected by the number.

3. Write a program that reads a list of strings and then selects and prints a random string from the list. To select a random element of **@somearray**, put

```
     srand;
```

at the beginning of your program (this initializes the random number generator), and then use

```
     rand(@somearray)
```

where you need a random value between 0 and 1 less than the length of **@somearray**.

4

Control Structures

Statement Blocks

A *statement block* is a sequence of statements, enclosed in matching curly braces. It looks like this:

```
{
        first_statement;
        second_statement;
        third_statement;
        ...
        last_statement;
}
```

Perl executes each statement in sequence, from the first to the last. (Later, I'll show you how to alter this execution sequence within a block, but this is good enough for now.)

Syntactically, a block of statements is accepted in place of any single statement, but the reverse is not true.

The final semicolon on the last statement is optional. Thus, you can speak Perl with a C-accent (semicolon present) or Pascal-accent (semicolon absent). To make adding more statements at a later time easier, we usually suggest omitting the semicolon only when the block is all on one line. Contrast these two `if` blocks for examples of the two styles:

```
if ($ready) { $hungry++ }
if ($tired) {
    $sleepy = ($hungry + 1) * 2;
}
```

The if/unless Statement

Next up in order of complexity is the `if` statement. This construct takes a control expression (evaluated for its truth) and a block. It may optionally have an *else* followed by a block as well. In other words, it looks like this:

```
if (some_expression) {
        true_statement_1;
        true_statement_2;
        true_statement_3;
} else {
        false_statement_1;
        false_statement_2;
        false_statement_3;
}
```

(If you're a C or Java hacker, you should note that the curly braces are *required*. This eliminates the need for a "confusing dangling else" rule.)

During execution, Perl evaluates the control expression. If the expression is true, the first block (the `true_statement` statements above) is executed. If the expression is false, the second block (the `false_statement` statements above) is executed instead.

But what constitutes true and false? In Perl, the rules are slightly weird, but they give you the expected results. The control expression is evaluated for a *string* value in scalar context (if it's already a string, no change is made; but if it's a number, it is converted to a string[*]). If this string is either the empty string (with a length of zero) *or* a string consisting of the single character 0 (the digit zero), then the value of the expression is false. Anything else is true automatically. Why such funny rules? Because they facilitate branching on an emptyish versus nonempty string, as well as on a zero versus nonzero number, without having to create two versions of interpreting true and false values. Here are some examples of true and false interpretations:

```
0       # converts to "0", so false
1-1     # computes to 0, then converts to "0", so false
1       # converts to "1", so true
""      # empty string, so false
"1"     # not "" or "0", so true
"00"    # not "" or "0", so true (this one is weird, watch out)
"0.000" # also true for the same reason and warning
undef   # evaluates to "", so false
```

Practically speaking, interpretation of values as true or false is fairly intuitive. Don't let us scare you.

---

[*] Internally, this isn't quite true. But it acts as if this is what it does.

Here's an example of a complete `if` statement:

```
print "how old are you? ";
$a = <STDIN>;
chomp($a);
if ($a < 18) {
        print "So, you're not old enough to vote, eh?\n";
} else {
        print "Old enough!  Cool!  So go vote!\n";
        $voter++; # count the voters for later
}
```

You can omit the **else** block, leaving just a *then* part, as in:

```
print "how old are you? ";
$a = <STDIN>;
chomp($a);
if ($a < 18) {
        print "So, you're not old enough to vote, eh?\n";
}
```

Sometimes, you want to leave off the *then* part and have just an **else** part, because saying "do that if this is false," is more natural than saying "do that if not this is true." Perl handles this case with the **unless** variation:

```
print "how old are you? ";
$a = <STDIN>;
chomp($a);
unless ($a < 18) {
        print "Old enough!  Cool!  So go vote!\n";
        $voter++;
}
```

Replacing `if` with **unless** is in effect saying, "If the control expression is false, do..." (An **unless** can also have an **else**, just like an `if`.)

If you have more than two possible choices, add an **elsif** branch to the `if` statement, like so:

```
if (some_expression_one) {
        one_true_statement_1;
        one_true_statement_2;
        one_true_statement_3;
} elsif (some_expression_two) {
        two_true_statement_1;
        two_true_statement_2;
        two_true_statement_3;
} elsif (some_expression_three) {
        three_true_statement_1;
        three_true_statement_2;
        three_true_statement_3;
} else {
        all_false_statement_1;
        all_false_statement_2;
        all_false_statement_3;
}
```

Each expression (here, *some_expression_one*, *some_expression_two*, and *some_expression_three*) is computed in turn. If an expression is true, the corresponding branch is executed, and all remaining control expressions and corresponding statement blocks are skipped. If all expressions are false, the `else` branch is executed (if there is one). You don't have to have an `else` block, but having one is always a good idea. You may have as many `elsif` branches as you wish.

The while/until Statement

No programming language would be complete without some form of iteration[*] (repeated execution of a block of statements). Perl can iterate using the `while` statement:

```
while (some_expression) {
        statement_1;
        statement_2;
        statement_3;
}
```

To execute this `while` statement, Perl evaluates the control expression (*some_expression* in the example). If its value is true (using Perl's notion of truth), the body of the `while` statement is evaluated once. This step is repeated until the control expression becomes false, at which point Perl goes on to the next statement after the `while loop`. For example:

```
print "how old are you? ";
$a = <STDIN>;
chomp($a);
while ($a > 0) {
        print "At one time, you were $a years old.\n";
        $a--;
}
```

Sometimes it is easier to say "until something is true" rather than "while not this is true." Once again, Perl has the answer. Replacing the `while` with `until` yields the desired effect:

```
until (some_expression) {
        statement_1;
        statement_2;
        statement_3;
}
```

Note that in both the `while` and `until` forms, the body statements will be skipped entirely if the control expression is the termination value to begin with.

---

[*] That's why HTML is not a programming language.

For example, if a user enters an age less than zero for the program fragment above, Perl skips over the body of the loop.

Sometimes the control expression never lets the loop exit. This case is perfectly legal, and sometimes desired, and is thus not considered an error. For example, you might want a loop to repeat as long as you have no error, and then have some error handling code following the loop. You might use this for a program that is meant to run until the system terminates.

The do {} while/until Statement

The `while/until` statement you saw in the previous section tests its condition at the top of every loop, before the loop is entered. If the condition was already false to begin with, the loop won't be executed at all.

But sometimes you don't want to test the condition at the top of the loop. Instead, you want to test it at the bottom. To fill this need, Perl provides the `do {} while` statement, which is just like the regular `while`* statement except that it doesn't test the expression until after executing the loop once. For example:

```
do {
    statement_1;
    statement_2;
    statement_3;
} while (some_expression);
```

Perl executes the statements in the `do` block. When it reaches the end, it evaluates the expression for truth. If the expression is false, the loop is done. If it's true, then the whole block is executed one more time before the expression is once again checked.

As with a normal `while` loop, you can invert the sense of the test by changing `do {} while` to `do {} until`. The expression is still tested at the bottom, but its sense is reversed. For some cases, especially compound ones, this is the more natural way to write the test:

```
$stops = 0;
do {
    $stops++;
    print "Next stop? ";
    chomp($location = <STDIN>);
} until $stops > 5 || $location eq 'home';
```

---

* Well, this statement is not quite true; the loop control directives explained in Chapter 9, *Miscellaneous Control Structures*, don't work for the bottom-testing form.

The for Statement

Another Perl iteration construct is the `for` statement, which looks suspiciously like C's or Java's `for` statement, and works roughly the same way. Here it is:

```
for ( initial_exp; test_exp; re-init_exp ) {
        statement_1;
        statement_2;
        statement_3;
}
```

Unraveled into forms we've seen before, this construct turns out as:

```
initial_exp;
while (test_exp) {
        statement_1;
        statement_2;
        statement_3;
        re-init_exp;
}
```

In either case, the *initial_exp* expression is evaluated first. This expression typically assigns an initial value to an iterator variable, but there are no restrictions on what it can contain; in fact, it may even be empty (doing nothing). Then the *test_exp* expression is evaluated for truth or falsehood. If the value is true, the body is executed, followed by the *re-init_exp* (typically, but not solely, used to increment the iterator). Perl then reevaluates the *test_exp*, repeating as necessary.

This example prints the numbers 1 through 10, each followed by a space:

```
for ($i = 1; $i <= 10; $i++) {
        print "$i ";
}
```

Initially, the variable `$i` is set to 1. Then, this variable is compared with 10, which it is indeed less than or equal to. The body of the loop (the single **print** statement) is executed, and then the re-init expression (the autoincrement expression `$i++`) is executed, changing the value in `$i` to 2. Because this value is still less than or equal to 10, we repeat the process until the last iteration in which the value of 10 in `$i` gets changed to 11. The value is then no longer less than or equal to 10, so the loop exits (with `$i` having a value of 11).

The foreach Statement

Yet another iteration construct is the `foreach` statement. This statement takes a list of values and assigns them one at a time to a scalar variable, executing a block of code with each successive assignment. It looks like this:

```
foreach $i (@some_list) {
        statement_1;
        statement_2;
        statement_3;
}
```

The original value of the scalar variable is automatically restored when the loop exits; another way to say this is that the scalar variable is *local* to the loop.

Here's an example of a `foreach`:

```
@a = (1,2,3,4,5);
foreach $b (reverse @a) {
        print $b;
}
```

This program snippet prints `54321`. Note that the list used by the `foreach` can be an arbitrary list expression, not just an array variable. (This flexibility is typical of all Perl constructs that require a list.)

You can omit the name of the scalar variable, in which case Perl pretends you have specified the `$_` variable name instead. You'll find that the `$_` variable is used as a default for many of Perl's operations, so you can think of it as a scratch area.* (All operations that use `$_` by default can also use a normal scalar variable as well.) For example, the `print` function prints the value of `$_` if no other value is specified, so the following example works like the previous one:

```
@a = (1,2,3,4,5);
foreach (reverse @a) {
        print;
}
```

See how using the implied `$_` variable makes it easier? After you've learned more functions and operators that default to `$_`, this construct will become even more useful. This is one case where the shorter construct is more legible than the longer one.

If the list you are iterating over is made of real variables rather than some function returning a list value, then the variable being used for iteration is in fact an alias for each variable in the list instead of being merely a copy of the values. Consequently, if you change the scalar variable, you are also changing that particular element in the list that the variable is standing in for. For example:

```
@a = (3,5,7,9);
foreach $one (@a) {
        $one *= 3;
    $x = 17;
    @a = (3,5,7,9);
```

---

* Which means you'd better localize it in functions when we learn about them.

```
@b = (10,20,30);
foreach $one (@a, @b, $x) {
$one *= 3;
}
# $x is now 51
# @a is now (9,15,21,27)
# @b is now (30,60,90);
}
# @a is now (9,15,21,27)
```

Notice how altering $one in fact altered each element of @a.

Exercises

See Appendix A for answers.

1. Write a program that asks for the temperature outside, and prints "too hot" if the temperature is above 72, and "too cold" otherwise.

2. Modify the program from the previous exercise so that it prints "too hot" if the temperature is above 75, "too cold" if the temperature is below 68, and "just right!" if it is between 68 and 75.

3. Write a program that reads a list of numbers (on separate lines) until the number 999 is read, and then prints the total of all the numbers added together. (Be sure not to add in the 999!) For example, if you enter 1, 2, 3, and 999, the program should reply with the answer of 6 (1+2+3).

4. Write a program that reads in a list of strings on separate lines and then prints out the list of strings in reverse order—*without* using reverse on the list. (Recall that <STDIN> will read a list of strings on separate lines when used in an array context.)

5. Write a program that prints a table of numbers and their squares from 0 to 32. Try to come up with a way in which you don't need to have all the numbers from 0 to 32 in a list, and then try a way in which you do. (For nice looking output,

   ```
   printf "%5g %8g\n", $a, $b
   ```

   prints $a as a five-column number and $b as an eight-column number.)

5

Hashes

What Is a Hash?

A hash* is like the array that we discussed earlier, in that it is a collection of scalar data, with individual elements selected by some index value. Unlike a list array, the index values of a hash are not small nonnegative integers, but instead are arbitrary scalars. These scalars (called *keys*) are used later to retrieve the values from the array.

The elements of a hash have no particular order. Consider them instead like a deck of filing cards. The top half of each card is the key, and the bottom half is the value. Each time you put a value into the hash, a new card is created. Later when you want to modify the value, you give the key, and Perl finds the right card. So, really, the order of the cards is immaterial. In fact, Perl stores the cards (the key-value pairs) in a special internal order that makes finding a specific card easy, so Perl doesn't have to look through all the pairs to find the right one. You cannot control this order, so don't try.†

Hash Variables

A hash variable name is a percent sign (%) followed by a letter, followed by zero or more letters, digits, and underscores. In other words, the part after the percent is the same as that after scalar and array variable names. And, just as there is no relationship between $fred and @fred, the %fred hash variable is also unrelated to the other two.

---

* In older documentation, hashes were called "associative arrays," but the Perl hackers got tired of a seven-syllable word for such a common item, so we replaced it with a much nicer one-syllable word.

† Actually, modules like *IxHash* and *DB file* do provide some ordering, but at the cost of a performance penalty.

Rather than referencing the entire hash, more commonly you create and access the hash by referring to its elements. Each element of the hash is a separate scalar variable, accessed by a string index, called the key. Elements of the hash `%fred` are thus referenced with `$fred{$key}` where `$key` is any scalar expression. Notice once again that accessing an element of a hash requires different notation than when you access the entire hash.

As with arrays, you create new elements merely by assigning to a hash element:

```
$fred{"aaa"} = "bbb"; # creates key "aaa", value "bbb"
$fred{234.5} = 456.7; # creates key "234.5", value 456.7
```

These two statements create two elements in the hash. Subsequent accesses to the same element (using the same key) return the previously stored value:

```
print $fred{"aaa"}; # prints "bbb"
$fred{234.5} += 3;  # makes it 459.7
```

Referencing an element that does not exist returns the **undef** value, just as with a missing array element or an undefined scalar variable.

Literal Representation of a Hash

You may wish to access the hash as a whole, either to initialize it, or to copy it to another hash. Perl doesn't really have a literal representation for a hash, so instead it unwinds the hash as a list. Each pair of elements in the list (which should always have an even number of elements) defines a key and its corresponding value. This unwound representation can be assigned into another hash, which will then recreate the same hash. In other words:

```
@fred_list = %fred;   # @fred_list gets ("aaa","bbb","234.5",456.7)
%barney = @fred_list; # create %barney like %fred
%barney = %fred;      # a faster way to do the same
%smooth = ("aaa","bbb","234.5",456.7);
                      # create %smooth like %fred, from literal values
```

The order of the key-value pairs is arbitrary in this unwound representation and cannot be controlled. Even if you swap some of the values around and create the hash as a whole, the returned unwound list is still in whatever order Perl has created for efficient access to the individual elements. You should never rely on any particular ordering.

One quick use of this winding and unwinding is to copy a hash value to another hash variable:

```
%copy = %original; # copy from %original to %copy
```

And you can construct a hash with keys and values swapped using the **reverse** operator, which works magically well here:

```
%backwards = reverse %normal;
```

Of course, if **%normal** has two identical values, those will end up as only a single element in **%backwards**, so this swap is best performed only on hashes with unique keys and values.

Hash Functions

Here are some functions for hashes.

The keys Function

The keys(**%hashname**) function yields a list of all the current keys in the hash **%hashname**. In other words, it's like the odd-numbered (first, third, fifth, and so on) elements of the list returned by unwinding **%hashname** in an array context, and in fact, returns them in that order. If there are no elements to the hash, then **keys** returns an empty list.

Here's an example using the hash from the previous examples:

```
$fred{"aaa"} = "bbb";
$fred{234.5} = 456.7;
@list = keys(%fred); # @list gets ("aaa",234.5) or
                     #               (234.5,"aaa")
```

As with all other built-in functions, the parentheses are optional: **keys %fred** is like **keys(%fred)**. For example:

```
foreach $key (keys %fred) { # once for each key of %fred
        print "at $key we have $fred{$key}\n"; # show key and value
}
```

This example also shows that individual hash elements can be interpolated into double-quoted strings. You cannot interpolate the entire hash, however.[*]

In a scalar context, the **keys** function gives the number of elements (key-value pairs) in the hash. For example, you can find out whether a hash is empty:

```
if (keys(%somearray)) { # if keys() not zero:
        ...;            # array is non empty
}
                        # ... or ...
while (keys(%somearray) < 10) {
        ...;            # keep looping while we have less than 10 elements
}
```

In fact, merely using **%somehash** in a scalar context will reveal whether the hash is empty or not:

---

[*] Well, you *can*, using a slice, but we don't talk about slices here.

```
if (%somehash) { # if true, then something's in it
    # do something with it
}
```

The values Function

The `values(%hashname)` function returns a list of all the current values of the %*hashname*, in the same order as the keys returned by the `keys(%hashname)` function. As always, the parentheses are optional. For example:

```
%lastname = ();                   # force %lastname empty
$lastname{"fred"} = "flintstone";
$lastname{"barney"} = "rubble";
@lastnames = values(%lastname); # grab the values
```

At this point, `@lastnames` contains either (``flintstone``, ``rubble``) or (``rubble``, ``flintstone``).

The each Function

To iterate over (that is, examine every element of) an entire hash, use `keys`, looking up each returned key to get the corresponding value. Although this method is frequently used, a more efficient way is to use `each(%hashname)`, which returns a key-value pair as a two-element list. On each evaluation of this function for the same hash, the next successive key-value pair is returned until all the elements have been accessed. When there are no more pairs, `each` returns an empty list.

So, for example, to step through the %`lastname` hash from the previous example, do something like this:

```
while (($first,$last) = each(%lastname)) {
    print "The last name of $first is $last\n";
}
```

Assigning a new value to the entire hash resets the `each` function to the beginning. Adding or deleting elements of the hash is quite likely to confuse `each` (and possibly you as well).

The delete Function

So far, with what you know, you can add elements to a hash, but you cannot remove them (other than by assigning a new value to the entire hash). Perl provides the `delete` function to remove hash elements. The operand of `delete` is a hash reference, just as if you were merely looking at a particular value. Perl removes the key-value pair from the hash. For example:

```
%fred = ("aaa","bbb",234.5,34.56); # give %fred two elements
```

```
delete $fred{"aaa"};
# %fred is now just one key-value pair
```

Hash Slices

Like an array variable (or list literal), a hash can be sliced to access a collection of elements instead of just one element at a time. For example, consider the bowling scores set individually:

```
$score{"fred"} = 205;
$score{"barney"} = 195;
$score{"dino"} = 30;
```

This collection seems rather redundant, and in fact can be shortened to:

```
($score{"fred"},$score{"barney"},$score{"dino"}) =
        (205,195,30);
```

But even these seem redundant. Let's use a *hash slice*:

```
@score{"fred","barney","dino"} = (205,195,30);
```

There. Much shorter. We can use a hash slice with variable interpolation as well:

```
@players = qw(fred barney dino);
print "scores are: @score{@players}\n";
```

Hash slices can also be used to merge a smaller hash into a larger one. In this example, the smaller hash takes precedence in the sense that if there are duplicate keys, the value from the smaller hash is used:

```
%league{keys %score) = values %score;
```

Here, the values of %score are merged into the %league hash. This operation is equivalent to the much slower operation:

```
%league = (%league, %score); # merge %score into %league
```

Exercises

See Appendix A for answers.

1. Write a program that reads in a string, then prints that string and its mapped value according to the mapping presented in Table 5-1.

Table 5-1. Sample Hash Mapping

Input	Output
red	apple
green	leaves
blue	ocean

2. Write a program that reads a series of words with one word per line until end-of-file, then prints a summary of how many times each word was seen. (For extra challenge, sort the words in ascending ASCII order in the output.)

6

Basic I/O

Input from STDIN

Reading from standard input (via the Perl filehandle called STDIN) is easy. We've been doing it already with the <STDIN> construct. Evaluating this in a scalar context gives the next line of input,[*] or undef if there are no more lines, like so:

```
$a = <STDIN>; # read the next line
```

Evaluating in a list context produces all remaining lines as a list: each element is one line, including its terminating newline. We've seen this before, but as a refresher, it might look something like this:

```
@a = <STDIN>;
```

Typically, one thing you want to do is read all lines one at a time and do something with each line. One common way to do this is:

```
while (defined($line_ = <STDIN>)) {
    # process $line here
}
```

As long as a line has been read in, <STDIN> evaluates to a defined value, so the loop continues to execute. When <STDIN> has no more lines to read, it returns undef, terminating the loop.

Reading a scalar value from <STDIN> into $_ and using that value as the controlling expression of a loop (as in the previous example) occurs frequently enough so that Perl has an abbreviation for it. Whenever a loop test consists solely of the

---

[*] Up to a newline, or whatever you've set $/ to.

input operator (something like < . . .>), Perl automatically copies the line that is read into the $_ variable. For example:

```
while (<STDIN>) { # like "while(defined($_ = <STDIN>_)"
        chomp;   # like "chomp($_)"
                 # other operations with $_ here
}
```

Because the $_ variable is the default for many operations, you can save a noticeable amount of typing this way.

Input from the Diamond Operator

Another way to read input is with the diamond operator: <>. This operator works like <STDIN> in that it returns a single line in a scalar context (undef if all the lines have been read) or all remaining lines if used in a list context. However, unlike <STDIN>, the diamond operator gets its data from the file or files specified on the command line that invoked the Perl program. For example, if you have a program named *type.plx*, consisting of:

```
while (<>) {
        print $_;
}
```

and you invoke *type.plx* with:

perl type.plx file1 file2 file3

then the diamond operator reads each line of file1 followed by each line of file2 and file3 in turn, returning undef only when all of the lines have been read. As you can see, *type.plx* works a little like the NT command *type*, sending all the lines of the named files to standard output in sequence. If you don't specify any filenames on the command line, the diamond operator reads from standard input automatically.

Technically, the diamond operator isn't looking literally at the command-line arguments; it works from the @ARGV array. This array is a special array initialized by the Perl interpreter to the command-line arguments. Each command-line argument goes into a separate element of the @ARGV array. You can interpret this list any way you want.* You can even set this array within your program and have the diamond operator work on that new list rather than the command-line arguments, like so:

```
@ARGV = ("aaa","bbb","ccc");
while (<>) { # process files aaa, bbb, and ccc
```

---

* The Perl standard distribution contains routines for parsing the command-line arguments of a Perl program. See *Programming Perl* for more information on the getopt library.

```
                print "this line is: $_";
    }
```

In Chapter 10, *Filehandles and File Tests*, we'll see how to open and close specific filenames at specific times, but the technique detailed here has been used for some of our quick-and-dirty programs.

Output to STDOUT

Perl uses the `print` and `printf` functions to write to standard output. Let's look at how they are used.

Using print for Normal Output

We've already used `print` to display text on standard output. Let's expand on that usage a bit.

The `print` function takes a list of strings and sends each string to standard output in turn, without any intervening or trailing characters added. What might not be obvious is that `print` is really just a function that takes a list of arguments, and returns a value like any other function. In other words:

```
    $a = print("hello ", "world", "\n");
```

would be another way to say `hello world`. The return value of `print` is a true or false value, indicating the success of the print. The print nearly always succeeds, unless you get some I/O error, so `$a` in this case will usually be 1.

Sometimes you'll need to add parentheses to `print` as shown in the example given below, especially when the first thing you want to print starts with a left parenthesis, as in:

```
    print (2+3),"hello";    # wrong! prints 5, ignores "hello"
    print ((2+3),"hello");  # right, prints 5hello
    print 2+3,"hello";      # also right, prints 5hello
```

Using printf for Formatted Output

You may wish to have a little more control over your output than `print` provides. In fact, you may be accustomed to the formatted output of C's `printf` function. Fear not: Perl provides a comparable operation with the same name.

The `printf` function takes a list of arguments (enclosed in optional parentheses, like the `print` function). The first argument is a format control string, defining how to print the remaining arguments. Here's an example:

```
    printf "%15s %5d %10.2f\n", $s, $n, $r;
```

This function prints $s in a 15-character field, then a space, then $n as a decimal integer in a 5-character field, then another space, then $r as a floating-point value with 2 decimal places in a 10-character field, and finally a newline.

Among the many formats supported by Perl's `printf()` and `sprintf()` functions are the following commonly used ones:

%%	Percent sign
%c	Character with the given number
%s	String
%d	Signed integer, in decimal
%u	Unsigned integer, in decimal
%o	Unsigned integer, in octal
%x	Unsigned integer, in hexadecimal
%e	Floating-point number, in scientific notation
%f	Floating-point number, in fixed decimal notation
%g	Floating-point number, in %e or %f notation

Between the percent and the format character, you may place one or more of the following flags:

space	Prefix positive number with a space
+	Prefix positive number with a plus sign
-	Left justify within the field
0	Use zeros, not spaces, to right justify
number	Minimum field width
.number	Precision: digits after decimal point for floating-point number, maximum length for string, minimum length for integer

Exercises

See Appendix A for answers.

1. Write a program that acts like *type*, but reverses the order of the lines from the files specified on the command line, or all the lines from standard input if no files are specified.

2. Modify the program from the previous exercise so that *each* file specified on the command line has its lines individually reversed. (Yes, you can do this with only what's been shown to you so far, even excluding the stroll in Chapter 1.)

3. Write a program that reads a list of strings on separate lines, and prints the strings in a right-justified 20-character column. For example, inputting `hello`, `good-bye` prints `hello` and `good-bye`, right-justified in a 20-character

column. (Be sure your program is actually using a 20-character column, and not a 21-character column. That mistake is common.)

4. Modify the program from the previous exercise to allow the user to select the column width. For example, entering `20`, `hello`, and `good-bye` should do the same thing as the previous program did; but, entering `30`, `hello`, and `good-bye` should justify `hello` and `good-bye` in a 30-character column.

7

Regular Expressions

Concepts About Regular Expressions

A *regular expression* is a pattern—a template—to be *matched* against a string. Matching a regular expression against a string either succeeds or fails. Sometimes, the success or failure may be all you are concerned about. At other times, you will want to take a matched pattern and replace it with another string, parts of which may depend on exactly how and where the regular expression matched.

Regular expressions are used by many programs: editors, search utilities, and word processors. Each program has a different set of (mostly overlapping) template characters. Perl is a semantic superset of all of these tools—any regular expression that can be described in one of these tools can also be written in Perl, but will not necessarily use exactly the same characters.

Simple Uses of Regular Expressions

If we were looking for all lines of a file that contain the string abc, we might use the Windows NT *findstr* command:

```
>findstr abc somefile > results
```

In this case, abc is the regular expression that the *findstr* command tests against each input line. Lines that match are sent to standard output, and end up in the file results because of the command-line redirection.

In Perl, we can speak of the string abc as a regular expression by enclosing the string in slashes:

```
if (/abc/) {
  print $_;
}
```

But what is being tested against the regular expression abc in this case? Why, it's our old friend, the $_ variable! When a regular expression is enclosed in slashes (as above), the $_ variable is tested against the regular expression. If the regular expression matches, the *match* operator returns true. Otherwise, it returns false.

For this example, the $_ variable is presumed to contain some text line and is printed if the line contains the characters abc in sequence anywhere within the line—similar to the *findstr* command above. Unlike the *findstr* command, which is operating on all of the lines of a file, this Perl fragment is looking at just one line. To work on all lines, add a loop, as in:

```
while (<>) {
  if (/abc/) {
    print $_;
  }
}
```

What if we didn't know the number of b's between the a and the c? That is, what if we want to print the line if it contains an a followed by zero or more b's, followed by a c? With *findstr*, we'd say:

>findstr ab*c somefile >results

In Perl, we can say exactly the same thing:

```
while (<>) {
  if (/ab*c/) {
    print $_;
  }
}
```

Just like *findstr*, this loop looks for an a followed by zero or more b's followed by a c.

We'll visit more uses of pattern matching in the section "More on the Matching Operator," later in the chapter, after we talk about all kinds of regular expressions.

Another simple regular expression operator is the *substitute* operator, which replaces the part of a string that matches the regular expression with another string. The substitute operator consists of the letter s, a slash, a regular expression, a slash, a replacement string, and a final slash, looking something like:

```
s/ab*c/def/;
```

The variable (in this case, $_) is matched against the regular expression (ab*c). If the match is successful, the part of the string that matched is discarded and replaced by the replacement string (def). If the match is unsuccessful, nothing happens.

As with the match operator, we'll revisit the myriad options on the substitute operator later, in the section "Substitutions."

Patterns

A regular expression is a pattern. Some parts of the pattern match single characters in the string of a particular type. Other parts of the pattern match multiple characters. First, we'll visit the single-character patterns, and then the multiple-character patterns.

Single-Character Patterns

The simplest and most common pattern-matching character in regular expressions is a single character that matches itself. In other words, putting a letter a in a regular expression requires a corresponding letter a in the string.

The next most common pattern-matching character is the dot ".". This character matches any single character *except* newline (\n). For example, the pattern /a./ matches any two-letter sequence that starts with a and is not a\n.

A pattern-matching *character class* is represented by a pair of open and close square brackets and a list of characters between the brackets. One and only one of these characters must be present at the corresponding part of the string for the pattern to match. For example,

    /[abcde]/

matches a string containing any one of the first five letters of the lowercase alphabet, while

    /[aeiouAEIOU]/

matches any of the five vowels in either lower- or uppercase. If you want to put a right bracket (]) in the list, put a backslash in front of it, or put it as the first character within the list. Ranges of characters (like a through z) can be abbreviated by showing the end points of the range separated by a dash (–); to get a literal dash in the list, precede the dash with a backslash or place it at the end. Here are some other examples:

```
[0123456789] # match any single digit
[0-9]        # same thing
[0-9\-]      # match 0-9, or minus
[a-z0-9]     # match any single lowercase letter or digit
[a-zA-Z0-9_] # match any single letter, digit, or underscore
```

There's also a negated character class, which is the same as a character class, but has a leading up arrow (or caret: ^) immediately after the left bracket. This character class matches any single character that is *not* in the list. For example:

```
[^0-9] # match any single non-digit
[^aeiouAEIOU] # match any single non-vowel
[^\^] # match single character except an up-arrow
```

For your convenience, some common character classes are predefined, as described in Table 7-1.

Table 7-1. Predefined Character Class Abbreviations

Construct	Equivalent Class	Negated Construct	Equivalent Negated Class
\d (a digit)	[0-9]	\D (digits, not!)	[^0-9]
\w (word char)	[a-zA-Z0-9_]	\W (words, not!)	[^a-zA-Z0-9_]
\s (space char)	[\r\t\n\f]	\S (space, not!)	[^ \r\t\n\f]

The \d pattern matches one **digit**. The \w pattern matches one **word character**, although the pattern is really matching any character that is legal in a Perl variable name. The \s pattern matches one **space** (whitespace), defined here as spaces, carriage returns, tabs, line feeds, and form feeds. The uppercase versions match the complements of these classes. Thus, \W matches one character that can't be in an identifier, \S matches one character that is not a whitespace (including letters, punctuation marks, control characters, etc.), and \D matches any single non-digit character.

These abbreviated classes can be used as part of other character classes as well:

```
[\da-fA-F] # match one hex digit
```

Grouping Patterns

The true power of regular expressions comes into play when you can say "one or more of these" or "up to five of those." Let's talk about how these cases are handled.

Sequence

The first (and probably most obvious) grouping pattern is *sequence*. In using this pattern, Perl matches abc as an a followed by a b followed by a c. This pattern seems simple, but we're giving it a name so we can talk about it later.

Multipliers

We've already seen the asterisk (*) as a grouping pattern. The asterisk indicates zero or more of the immediately previous character (or character class).

Two other grouping patterns that work in the same manner are the plus sign (+), meaning one or more of the immediately previous character, and the question mark (?), meaning zero or one of the immediately previous character. For example, the regular expression /fo+ba?r/ matches an f followed by one or more o's, followed by a b, followed by an optional a, followed by an r.

In all three of these grouping patterns, the patterns are *greedy*. If such a multiplier has a chance to match between five and ten characters, it'll pick the ten-character string every time. For example,

```
$_ = "fred xxxxxxxxx barney";
s/x+/boom/;
```

always replaces all consecutive x's with **boom** (resulting in **fred boom barney**), rather than just one or two x's, even though a shorter set of x's would also match the same regular expression.

If you need to say "five to ten" x's, you could get away with putting five x's followed by five x's each immediately followed by a question mark. But this looks ugly. Instead, an easier way exists: the *general multiplier*. The general multiplier consists of a pair of matching curly braces with one or two numbers inside, as in /x{5,10}/. The immediately preceding character (in this case, the letter x) must be found within the indicated number of repetitions (five through ten here).*

If you leave off the second number, as in /x{5,}/, you indicate "that many or more" (five or more in this case), and if you leave off the comma, as in /x{5}/, you indicate "exactly this many" (five x's). To get five or fewer x's, you must put the zero in, as in /x{0,5}/.

So, the regular expression /a.{5}b/ matches the letter a separated from the letter b by any five non-newline characters at any point in the string. (Recall that a period matches any single non-newline character, and we're matching five here.) The five characters do not need to be the same. (We'll learn how to force them to be the same in the next section.)

We could dispense with *, +, and ? entirely, because they are completely equivalent to {0,}, {1,}, and {0,1}. But it's easier to type the equivalent single punctuation character, and more familiar as well.

If two multipliers occur in a single expression, the greedy rule is augmented with *leftmost is greediest*. For example:

```
$_ = "a xxx c xxxxxxxx c xxx d";
/a.*c.*d/;
```

---

* Of course, /\d{3}/ doesn't only match three-digit numbers. It would also match any number containing more than three digits. To match exactly three, you need to use anchors, described in the next section, titled "Anchoring Patterns."

In this case, the first `.*` in the regular expression matches all characters up to the second c, even though matching only the characters up to the first c would still allow the entire regular expression to match. Right now, this distinction is not important (the pattern would match either way), but later when we can look at parts of the regular expression that matched, the distinction will matter quite a bit.

We can force any multiplier to be nongreedy (or *lazy*) by following it with a question mark:

```
$_ = "a xxx c xxxxxxxx c xxx d";
/a.*?c.*d/;
```

Here, the `a.*?c` matches the fewest characters between the a and c, not the most characters. This means the leftmost c is matched, not the rightmost. You can put such a question-mark modifier after any of the multiplers (`?`, `+`, `*` and `{m,n}`).

What if the string and regular expression were slightly altered, say, to:

```
$_ = "a xxx ce xxxxxxxx ci xxx d";
/a.*ce.*d/;
```

In this case, if the `.*` matches the most characters possible before the next c, the next regular expression character (e) doesn't match the next character of the string (i). In this case, we get automatic *backtracking*. The multiplier is unwound and retried, stopping at someplace earlier (in this case, at the earlier c, next to the e).* A complex regular expression may involve many such levels of backtracking, leading to long execution times. In this case, consider that making that match lazy (with a trailing ?) will actually simplify the work that Perl has to perform.

Parentheses as memory

Another grouping operator is a pair of open and close parentheses around any part pattern. This operator doesn't change whether the pattern matches, but instead causes the part of the string matched by the pattern to be remembered, so that it may be referenced later. So, for example, `(a)` still matches an a, and `([a-z])` still matches any single lowercase letter.

To recall a memorized part of a string, you must include a backslash followed by an integer. This pattern construct represents the same sequence of characters matched earlier in the same-numbered pair of parentheses (counting from one). For example:

```
/fred(.)barney\1/;
```

---

* Well, technically, there was a lot of backtracking of the * operator to find the c's in the first place. But that's a little trickier to describe, and it works on the same principle.

matches a string consisting of `fred`, followed by any single non-newline character, followed by `barney`, followed by that same single character. So, the string matches `fredxbarneyx`, but not `fredxbarneyy`. Compare that string with:

```
/fred.barney./;
```

in which the two unspecified characters can be the same, or different.

Where did the 1 come from? The 1 indicates the first parenthesized part of the regular expression. If there's more than one, the second part (counting the left parentheses from left to right) is referenced as `\2`, the third as `\3`, and so on. For example:

```
/a(.)b(.)c\2d\1/;
```

matches an `a`, a character (call it #1), a `b`, another character (call it #2), a `c`, the character #2, a `d`, and the character #1. So, the string matches `axbycydx`, for example.

The referenced part can be more than a single character. For example,

```
/a(.*)b\1c/;
```

matches an `a`, followed by any number of characters (even zero), followed by `b`, followed by that same sequence of characters, followed by `c`. So, the string would match `aFREDbFREDc`, or even `abc`, but not `aXXbXXXc`.

Alternation

Another grouping construct is alternation, as in `a|b|c`. This construct matches exactly one of the alternatives (`a` or `b` or `c`, in this case). This construct works even if the alternatives have multiple characters, as in `/song|blue/`, which matches either `song` or `blue`. (For single-character alternatives, you're definitely better off with a character class like `/[abc]/`.)

What if we wanted to match `songbird` or `bluebird`? We could write `/songbird|bluebird/`, but that `bird` part shouldn't have to be in there twice. In fact, there's a way out, but we have to talk about the precedence of grouping patterns, which is covered later in the section "Precedence."

Anchoring Patterns

Several special notations anchor a pattern. Normally, when a pattern is matched against the string, the beginning of the pattern is dragged through the string from left to right, matching at the first possible opportunity. Anchors allow you to ensure that parts of the pattern line up with particular parts of the string.

The first pair of anchors requires that a particular part of the match be located either at a word boundary or not at a word boundary. The `\b` anchor requires a word boundary at the indicated point for the pattern to match. A word boundary is the place between characters that match \w and \W, or between characters matching \w and the beginning or ending of the string. Note that this description has little to do with English words and a lot more to do with C symbols, but that's as close as we get. For example:

```
/fred\b/;   # matches fred, but not Frederick
/\bmo/;     # matches moe and mole, but not Elmo
/\bFred\b/; # matches Fred but not Frederick or alFred
/\b\+\b/;   # matches "x+y" but not "++" or " + "
/abc\bdef/; # never matches (impossible for a boundary there)
```

Likewise, \B requires that there not be a word boundary at the indicated point. For example:

```
/\bFred\B/; # matches "Frederick" but not "Fred Flintstone"
```

Two more anchors require that a particular part of the pattern be next to an end of the string. The caret (^) matches the beginning of the string if it is in a place that makes sense to match the beginning of the string. For example, ^a matches an a if, and only if, the a is the first character of the string. However, a^ matches the two characters a and ^ anywhere in the string. In other words, the caret has lost its special meaning. If you need the caret to be a literal caret even at the beginning, put a backslash in front of it.

The $, like the ^, anchors the pattern, but to the end of the string, not the beginning. In other words, c$ matches a c only if it occurs at the end of the string.* A dollar sign anywhere else in the pattern is probably going to be interpreted as a scalar value interpretation, so you'll most likely need to backslash it to match a literal dollar sign in the string.

Other anchors are supported, including \A, \Z, and lookahead anchors created via (?=...) and (?!...). These anchors are described fully in Chapter 2 of *Progamming Perl* and the *perlre* documentation.

Precedence

So what happens when we get a|b* together? Is this a or b any number of times, or is it either a single a or any number of b's?

Well, just as operators have precedence, the grouping and anchoring patterns also have precedence. The precedence of patterns from highest to lowest is given in Table 7-2.

---

* Or just before the newline at the end of the string, for historical simplicity.

Table 7-2. regex Grouping Precedence[a]

Name	Representation
Parentheses	`(  )   (?:  )`
Multipliers	`?  +  *  {m,n}  ??  +?  *?  {m,n}`
Sequence and anchoring	`abc  ^  $  \A \Z  (?=  )   (?!  )`
Alternation	`|`

[a] Some of these symbols are not described in this book. See *Programming Perl* or *perlre* for details.

According to the table, `*` has a higher precedence than `|`. So `/a|b*/` is interpreted as a single **a**, or any number of **b**'s.

What if we want the other meaning, as in "any number of a's or b's"? We simply throw in a pair of parentheses. In this case, we enclose the part of the expression that the `*` operator should apply to inside parentheses, and we are done, as `(a|b)*`. If you want to clarify the first expression, you can redundantly parenthesize it with `a|(b*)`.

When you use parentheses to affect precedence they also trigger the memory, as shown earlier in this chapter. That is, this set of parentheses counts when you are figuring out whether something is `\2`, `\3`, or whatever. If you want to use parentheses without triggering memory, use the form `(?:...)` instead of `(...)`. This form still allows for multipliers, but doesn't cause you to throw off your counting by using up another `$4` or whatever. For example, `/(?:Fred|Wilma) Flintstone/` does not store anything into `$1`; it's just there for grouping.

Here are some other examples of regular expressions, and the effect of parentheses:

```
abc*            # matches ab, abc, abcc, abccc, abcccc, and so on
(abc)*          # matches "", abc, abcabc, abcabcabc, and so on
^x|y            # matches x at the beginning of line, or y anywhere
^(x|y)          # matches either x or y at the beginning of a line
a|bc|d          # a, or bc, or d
(a|b)(c|d)      # ac, ad, bc, or bd
(song|blue)bird # songbird or bluebird
```

More on the Matching Operator

We have already looked at the simplest uses of the matching operator (a regular expression enclosed in slashes). Now let's look at a zillion ways to make this operator do something slightly different.

Selecting a Different Target (the =~ Operator)

Usually the string you'll want to match your pattern against is not within the $_ variable, and it would be a nuisance to put it there (perhaps you already have a value in $_ you're quite fond of). No problem. The =~ operator helps us here. This operator takes a regular expression operator on the right side, and changes the *target* of the operator to something besides the $_ variable—namely, some value named on the left side of the operator. For example:

```
$a = "hello world";
$a =~ /^he/;          # true
$a =~ /(.)\1/;        # also true (matches the double l)
if ($a =~ /(.)\1/) {  # true, so yes...
                      # some stuff
}
```

The target of the =~ operator can be any expression that yields some scalar string value. For example, <STDIN> yields a scalar string value when used in a scalar context, so we can combine this with the =~ operator and a regular expression match operator to get a compact check for particular input, as in:

```
print "any last request? ";
if (<STDIN> =~ /^[yY]/) { # does the input begin with a y?
  print "And just what might that request be? ";
  <STDIN>; # discard a line of standard input
  print "Sorry, I'm unable to do that.\n";
}
```

In this case, <STDIN> yields the next line from standard input, which is then immediately used as the string to match against the pattern ^[yY]. Note that you never stored the input into a variable, so if you wanted to match the input against another pattern, or possibly echo the data out in an error message, you'd be out of luck. But this form frequently comes in handy.

Ignoring Case

In the previous example, we used [yY] to match either a lower- or uppercase y. For very short strings, such as y or fred, this match is easy enough, as in [fF][oO][oO]. But what if the string you wanted to match was the word "procedure" in either lower- or uppercase?

In the Windows NT *findstr* command, a /i flag indicates "ignore case." Perl also has such an option. You indicate the *ignore-case* option by appending a lowercase i to the closing slash, as in /somepattern/i. This says that the letters of the pattern will match letters in the string in either case. For example, to match the word procedure in either case at the beginning of the line, use /^procedure/i.

Now our previous example looks like this:

```
print "any last request? ";
if (<STDIN> =~ /^y/i) { # does the input begin with a y?
  # yes! deal with it
  ...
}
```

Using a Different Delimiter

If you are looking for a string with a regular expression that contains slash characters (/), you must precede each slash with a backslash (\). For example, you can
look for a string that begins with **/wwwroot/docs** like this:

```
$path = <STDIN>; # read a pathname (from "find" perhaps?)
if ($path =~ /^\/wwwroot\/docs/) {
  # begins with /wwwroot/docs...
}
```

As you can see, the backslash-slash combination makes this example look as if
there are little valleys between the text pieces. Using this combination for a lot of
slash characters can get cumbersome, so Perl allows you to specify a different
delimiter character. Simply precede any nonalphanumeric, nonwhitespace character* (your selected delimiter) with an **m**, then list your pattern followed by
another identical delimiter character, and you're done, as in:

```
/^\/wwwroot\/docs/ # using standard slash delimiter
m@^/wwwroot/docs@  # using @ for a delimiter
m#^/wwwroot/docs#  # using # for a delimiter (my favorite)
```

You can even use slashes again if you want, as in **m/fred/**. So the common
regular-expression matching operator is really the **m** operator; however, the **m** is
optional if you choose slash for a delimiter.

Using Variable Interpolation

A regular expression is variable interpolated before it is considered for other
special characters. As a result, you can construct a regular expression from
computed strings rather than just literals. For example:

```
$what = "bird";
$sentence = "Every good bird does fly.";
if ($sentence =~ /\b$what\b/) {
  print "The sentence contains the word $what!\n";
}
```

---

* If the delimiter happens to be the *left* character of a *left-right* pair (parentheses, braces, angle bracket,
or square bracket), the closing delimiter is the corresponding *right* of the same pair. But otherwise, the
characters are the same for begin and end.

In this example we have effectively constructed the regular expression operator /
\bbird\b/ using a variable reference.

Here's a slightly more complicated example:

```
$sentence = "Every good bird does fly.";
print "What should I look for? ";
$what = <STDIN>;
chomp($what);
if ($sentence =~ /$what/) { # found it!
  print "I saw $what in $sentence.\n";
} else {
  print "nope... didn't find it.\n";
}
```

If you enter **bird**, it is found. If you enter **scream**, it isn't. If you enter
[bw]ird, that's also found, showing that the regular expression pattern-matching
characters are indeed still significant.

How would you make them insignificant? You'd have to arrange for the nonalphanumeric characters to be preceded by a backslash, which would then turn
them into literal matches. That process sounds hard, unless you have the \Q
quoting escape at your disposal:

```
$what = "[box]";
foreach (qw(in[box] out[box] white[sox])) {
  if (/\Q$what\E/) {
    print "$_ matched!\n";
  }
}
```

Here, the \Q$what\E contstruct turns into \[box\], making the match look for
a literal pair of enclosing brackets, instead of treating the whole thing as a character class.

Special Read-Only Variables

After a successful pattern match, the variables $1, $2, $3, and so on are set to
the same values as \1, \2, \3, and so on, held inside the pattern. You can use
this feature to look at a piece of the match in later code. For example:

```
$_ = "this is a test";
/(\w+)\W+(\w+)/; # match first two words
              # $1 is now "this" and $2 is now "is"
```

You can also gain access to the same values ($1, $2, $3, and so on) by placing a
match in a list context. The result is a list of values from $1 up to the number of
memorized things, but only if the regular expression matches. (Otherwise, the variables are undefined.) Taking that last example in another way:

```
$_ = "this is a test";
```

```
($first, $second) = /(\w+)\W+(\w+)/; # match first two words
                     # $first is now "this" and $second is now "is"
```

Other predefined read-only variables include `$&`, which is the part of the string that matched the regular expression; `$``, which is the part of the string before the part that matched; and `$'`, which is the part of the string after the part that matched. For example:

```
$_ = "this is a sample string";
/sa.*le/; # matches "sample" within the string
# $` is now "this is a "
# $& is now "sample"
# $' is now " string"
```

Because these variables are set on each successful match, you should save the values elsewhere if you need them later in the program.*

Substitutions

We've already talked about the simplest form of the substitution operator: `s/old-regex/new-string/`. We can now discuss a few variations of this operator.

If you want the replacement to operate on all possible matches instead of just the first match, append a `g` to the substitution, as in:

```
$_ = "foot fool buffoon";
s/foo/bar/g; # $_ is now "bart barl bufbarn"
```

The replacement string is variable interpolated, allowing you to specify the replacement string at runtime:

```
$_ = "hello, world"
$new = "goodbye";
s/hello/$new/; # replaces hello with goodbye
```

Pattern characters in the regular expression allow patterns to be matched, rather than just fixed characters:

```
$_ = "this is a test";
s/(\w+)/<$1>/g; # $_ is now "<this> <is> <a> <test>"
```

Recall that `$1` is set to the data within the first parenthesized pattern match.

An `i` suffix (either before or after the `g`, if present) causes the regular expression in the substitute operator to ignore case, just like the same option on the match operator described earlier.

---

* See O'Reilly's *Mastering Regular Expressions* for the performance ramifications of using these variables.

As with the match operator, an alternate delimiter can be selected if the slash is inconvenient. Just use the same character three times:[*]

```
s#fred#barney#; # replace fred with barney, like s/fred/barney/
```

Also as with the match operator, you can specify an alternate target with the =~ operator. In this case, the selected target must be something you can assign a scalar value to, such as a scalar variable or an element of an array. Here's an example:

```
$which = "this is a test";
$which =~ s/test/quiz/; # $which is now "this is a quiz"
$someplace[$here] =~ s/left/right/; # change an array element
$d{"t"} =~ s/^/x /; # prepend "x " to hash element
```

The split and join Functions

Regular expressions can be used to break a string into fields. The `split` function does this and the `join` function glues the pieces back together.

The split Function

The `split` function takes a regular expression and a string and looks for all occurrences of the regular expression within that string. The parts of the string that don't match the regular expression are returned in sequence as a list of values. For example, here's something to parse semicolon-separated fields, such as the PATH environment variable:

```
$line = "c:\\;;c:\\windows\\;c:\\windows\\system;";
@fields = split(/;/,$line); # split $line, using ; as delimiter
# now @fields is ("c:\", "", "c:\windows","c:\windows\system")
```

Note how the empty second field became an empty string. If you don't want this to happen, match all of the semicolons in one fell swoop:

```
@fields = split(/;+/, $line);
```

This matches one or more adjacent semicolons together, so that there is no empty second field.

One common string to split is the $_ variable, and that turns out to be the default:

```
$_ = "some string";
@words = split(/ /); # same as @words = split(/ /, $_);
```

For this split, consecutive spaces in the string to be split will cause null fields (empty strings) in the result. A better pattern would be / +/, or ideally /\s+/,

---

[*] Or, use two matching pairs if a left-right pair character is used.

which matches one or more whitespace characters together. In fact, this pattern is the default pattern,* so if you're splitting the $_ variable on whitespace, you can use all the defaults and merely say:

```
@words = split; # same as @words = split(/\s+/, $_);
```

Empty trailing fields do not normally become part of the list. This rule is not generally a concern. A solution like this:

```
$line = "c:/;c:/windows;c:/windows/system;";
($first, $second, $third, $fouth) =
    split(/;/,$line); # split $line, using ; as delimiter
```

would simply gives $fourth a null (undef) value if the line isn't long enough, or if it contained empty values in the last field. (Extra fields are silently ignored, because list assignment works that way.)

The join Function

The join function takes a list of values and glues them together with a glue string between each list element. The function looks like this:

```
$bigstring = join($glue,@list);
```

For example, to rebuild the PATH line, try something like:

```
$outline = join(";", @fields);
```

Note that the glue string is not a regular expression—just an ordinary string of zero or more characters.

If you need to get glue ahead of every item instead of just between items, a simple cheat suffices:

```
$result = (join "+", "", @fields;)
```

Here, the extra "" is treated as an empty element, to be glued together with the first data element of @fields. This change results in glue ahead of every element. Similarly, you can get trailing glue with an empty element at the end of the list, like so:

```
$output = join ("\n", @data, "";)
```

---

* Actually, the " " string is the default pattern, and this will cause leading whitespace to be ignored, but that's still close enough for this discussion.

Exercises

See Appendix A for answers.

1. Construct a regular expression that matches:

   (a) At least one **a** followed by any number of **b**'s

   (b) Any number of backslashes followed by any number of asterisks (any number might be zero)

   (c) Three consecutive copies of whatever is contained in `$whatever`

   (d) Any five characters, *including* newline

   (e) The same word written two or more times in a row (with possibly varying intervening whitespace), where "word" is defined as a nonempty sequence of nonwhitespace characters

2. (a) Write a program that accepts a list of words on **STDIN** and looks for a line containing all five vowels (**a**, **e**, **i**, **o**, and **u**). Run this program on some large text file and see what shows up. In other words, enter:

   > `perl myprogram.plx < mytextfile`

   (This presumes you name your program *myprogram.plx*.)

   (b) Modify the program so that the five vowels have to be in order, and intervening letters don't matter.

   (c) Modify the program so that all vowels must be in an increasing order; all five vowels have to be present; and no "e" can occur before an "a", no "i" can occur befor an "e", and so on.

8

Functions

We've already seen and used predetermined, built-in functions, such as `chomp`, `print`, and so on. Now, let's take a look at functions that you define yourself.

Defining a User Function

A user function, more commonly called a *subroutine* or just a *sub*, is defined in your Perl program using a construct like:

```
sub subname {
        statement_1;
        statement_2;
        statement_3;
}
```

The *subname* is the name of the subroutine, which is like the names we've had for scalar variables, arrays, and hashes. Once again, these come from a different namespace, so you can have a scalar variable `$fred`, an array `@fred`, a hash `%fred`, and now a subroutine `fred`.*

The block of statements following the subroutine name becomes the definition of the subroutine. When the subroutine is invoked (described shortly), the block of statements that makes up the subroutine is executed, and any return value (described later) is returned to the caller.

---

* Technically, the subroutine's name is `&fred`, but you seldom need to call it that. See Chapter 2 of *Programming Perl* for all of the gory details.

Here, for example, is a subroutine that displays that famous phrase:

```
sub say_hello {
        print "hello, world!\n";
}
```

Subroutine definitions can be anywhere in your program text (they are skipped on execution), but we like to put them at the end of the file, so that the main part of the program appears at the beginning of the file. (If you like to think in Pascal terms, you can put your subroutines at the beginning and your executable statements at the end, instead. It's up to you.)

Subroutine definitions are global;* there are no local subroutines. If you have two subroutine definitions with the same name, the later one overwrites the earlier one without warning.†

Within the subroutine body, you may access or give values to variables that are shared with the rest of the program (a *global* variable). In fact, by default, any variable reference within a subroutine body refers to a global variable. We'll tell you about the exceptions in the later section entitled "Private Variables in Functions." In the following example:

```
sub say_what {
  print "hello, $what\n";
}
```

`$what` refers to the the global `$what`, which is shared with the rest of the program.

Invoking a User Function

You invoke a subroutine from within any expression by following the subroutine name with parentheses, as in:

```
say_hello(); # a simple expression
$a = 3 + say_hello() # part of a larger expression
for ($x = start_value(); $x < end_value(); $x += increment()) {
    ...
} # invoke three subroutines to define values
```

A subroutine can invoke another subroutine, and *that* subroutine can in turn invoke another subroutine, and so on, until all available memory is filled with return addresses and partially computed expressions. (No mere eight or 32 levels could satisfy a real programmer.)

---

* They are global to the current package, actually, but since this book doesn't really deal with separate packages, you may think of subroutine definitions as global to the whole program.

† This statement is true, unless you are running with the −w switch.

Return Values

A subroutine is always part of some expression. The value of the subroutine invocation is called the *return value*. The return value of a subroutine is the value of the *return* statement or of the last expression evaluated in the subroutine.

For example, let's define this subroutine:

```
sub sum_of_a_and_b {
    return $a + $b;
}
```

The last expression evaluated in the body of this subroutine (in fact, the only expression evaluated) is the sum of $a and $b, so the sum of $a and $b will be the return value. Here's that in action:

```
$a = 3; $b = 4;
$c = sum_of_a_and_b();    # $c gets 7
$d = 3*sum_of_a_and_b(); # $d gets 21
```

A subroutine can also return a list of values when evaluated in a list context. Consider this subroutine and invocation:

```
sub list_of_a_and_b {
return ($a,$b);
}
$a = 5; $b = 6;
@c = list_of_a_and_b(); # @c gets (5,6)
```

The last expression evaluated really means the last expression evaluated, rather than the last expression defined in the body of the subroutine. For example, this subroutine returns $a if $a > 0; otherwise, it returns $b:

```
sub gimme_a_or_b {
        if ($a > 0) {
            print "choosing a ($a)\n";
    return  $a;
        } else {
            print "choosing b ($b)\n";
    return  $b;
        }
}
```

These examples are all rather trivial. It gets better when we can pass values that are different for each invocation into a subroutine, instead of having to rely on global variables. In fact, this discussion is coming right up.

Arguments

Although subroutines that have one specific action are useful, a whole new level of usefulness becomes available when you can pass *arguments* to a subroutine.

In Perl, the subroutine invocation (with the ampersand and the subroutine name) is followed by a list within parentheses, causing the list to be automatically assigned to a special variable named @_ for the duration of the subroutine. The subroutine can access this variable to determine the number of arguments and the value of those arguments. For example:

```
sub say_hello_to {
        print "hello, $_[0]!\n"; # first parameter is target
}
```

Here, we see a reference to $_[0], which is the first element of the @_ array. Special note: although similar in appearance, the $_[0] value (the first element of the @_ array) has nothing whatsoever to do with the $_ variable (a scalar variable of its own). Don't confuse them! The code seems to say hello to whomever we pass as the first parameter. As a result, we can invoke it like this:

```
say_hello_to("world");                   # gives hello, world!
$x = "somebody";
say_hello_to($x);                        # gives hello, somebody!
say_hello_to("me") + say_hello_to("you"); # and me and you
```

Note that in the last line, the return values weren't really used. But in evaluating the sum, Perl has to evaluate all of its parts, so the subroutine was invoked twice.

Here's an example using more than one parameter:

```
sub say {
    print "$_[0], $_[1]!\n";
}

say("hello","world");        # hello world, once again
say("goodbye","cruel world"); # silent movie lament
```

Excess parameters are ignored: if you never look at $_[3], Perl doesn't care. And insufficient parameters are also ignored; you simply get undef if you look beyond the end of the @_ array, as with any other array.

The @_ variable is *private* to the subroutine; if there's a global value for @_, it is saved away before the subroutine is invoked and restored to its previous value upon return from the subroutine. This also means that a subroutine can pass arguments to another subroutine without fear of losing its own @_ variable; the nested subroutine invocation gets its own @_ in the same way.

Let's revisit that "add a and b" routine from the previous section. Here's a subroutine that adds any two values (specifically, the two values passed to the subroutine as parameters):

```
sub add_two {
        $_[0] + $_[1];
}
print add_two(3,4); # prints 7
$c = add_two(5,6);   # $c gets 11
```

Now let's generalize this subroutine. What if we had 3, 4, or 100 values to add together? We could do it with a loop, as shown:

```
sub add {
    $sum = 0;              # initialize the sum
    foreach $_ (@_) {
        $sum += $_;        # add each element
    }
    return $sum;           # the sum of all elements
}
$a = add(4,5,6);           # adds 4+5+6 = 15, and assigns to $a
print add(1,2,3,4,5);      # prints 15
print add(1..5);           # also prints 15, because 1..5 is expanded
```

What if we had a variable named $sum when we called add? We just clobbered it. In the next section, we see how to avoid this situation.

Private Variables in Functions

We've already talked about the @_ variable and how a local copy gets created for each subroutine invoked with parameters. You can create your own scalar, array, and hash variables that work the same way. You do this with the **my** operator, which takes a list of variable names and creates local versions of them (or *instantiations*, if you like bigger words). Here's that **add** function again, this time using **my**:

```
sub add {
        my $sum;           # make $sum a local variable
        $sum = 0;          # initialize the sum
        foreach $_ (@_) {
            $sum += $_;    # add each element
        }
        return $sum;       # last expression evaluated:
                           # the sum of elements
    }
```

When the first body statement is executed, any current value of the global variable $sum is saved away, and a brand new variable named $sum is created (with the value undef). When the subroutine exits, Perl discards the local variable and restores the previous (global) value. This method works even if the $sum variable is currently a local variable from another subroutine (a subroutine that invokes this one, or one that invokes one that invokes this one, and so on). Variables can have many nested local versions, although you can access only one at a time.

Here's a way to create a list of all the elements of an array greater than 100:

```
sub bigger_than_100 {
        my (@result);          # temporary for holding the return value
        foreach $_ (@_) {      # step through the arg list
            if ($_ > 100) {    # is it eligible?
```

```
                    push(@result,$_); # add it
            }
        }
        return @result;            # return the final list
    }
```

What if we wanted all elements greater than 50, rather than all elements greater than 100? We'd have to edit the program, changing each 100 to 50. But what if we need both? Well, we can replace the 50 or 100 with a variable reference instead. This change makes the program look like:

```
sub bigger_than {
        my($n,@values);            # create some local variables
        ($n,@values) = @_;         # split args into limit and values
        my(@result); # temporary for holding the return value
        foreach $_ (@values) {     # step through the arg list
            if ($_ > $n) {         # is it eligible?
                push(@result,$_); # add it
            }
        }
        @result;                   # return the final list
    }
    # some invocations:
    @new = bigger_than(100,@list);    # @new gets all @list > 100
    @this = bigger_than(5,1,5,15,30);  # @this gets (15,30)
```

Notice that this time, we used two additional local variables to give names to arguments. This method is fairly common in practice—you can more easily talk about $n and @values than talk about $_[0] and @_[1..$#_], and $n and @values are safer as well.

The result of **my** is an assignable list, meaning that it can be used on the left side of an array assignment operator. You can give this list initial values for each of the newly created variables. (If you don't give values to the list, the new variables start with a value of **undef**, just like any other new variable.) As a result, we can combine the first two statements of this subroutine, replacing:

```
    my($n,@values);
    ($n,@values) = @_; # split args into limit and values
```

with:

```
    my($n,@values)= @_;
```

This is, in fact, a very common Perl-ish thing to do. Local nonargument variables can be given literal values in the same way, such as:

```
    my($sum) = 0; # initialize local variable
```

Be warned that despite its appearance as a declaration, **my** is really an executable operator. Good Perl hacking strategy suggests that you bunch all of your **my** operators at the beginning of the subroutine definition, before you get into the meat of the routine.

Semiprivate Variables Using local

Perl gives you a second way to create *private* variables, using the local function. You must, however, understand the differences between my and local. For example:

```
$value = "original";

tellme();
spoof();
tellme();

sub spoof {
    local ($value) = "temporary";
    tellme();
}

sub tellme {
    print "Current value is $value\n";
}
```

This prints out:

```
Current value is original
Current value is temporary
Current value is original
```

If my had been used instead of local, the private reading of $value would be available only within the spoof() subroutine. But with local, as the output shows, the private value is not quite so private; it is also available within any subroutines called from spoof(). The general rule is that local variables are visible to functions called from within the block in which those variables are declared.

Whereas my can be used only to declare simple scalar, array, or hash variables with alphanumeric names, local suffers no such restrictions. Also, Perl's built-in variables such as $_, $1, and @ARGV, cannot be declared with my, but work fine with local. Because $_ is so often used throughout most Perl programs, it's probably prudent to place a

```
local $_;
```

at the top of any function that uses $_ for its own purposes. This assures that the previous value will be preserved and automatically restored when the function exits.

In your more advanced programming efforts, you may eventually need to know that local variables are really global variables in disguise. That is, the value of the global variable is saved and temporarily replaced with the locally declared value.

By and large, you should prefer to use my over local because my is faster and safer.

File-Level my() Variables

The **my** operator can also be used at the outermost level of your program, outside of any subroutines or blocks. While **my** isn't really a local variable in the sense defined above, it's actually rather useful, especially when used in conjunction with a Perl pragma:[*]

```
use strict;
```

If you place this pragma at the beginning of your file, you will no longer be able to use variables (scalars, arrays, and hashes) until you have first declared them. And you declare them with **my**, like so:

```
use strict;
my $a;                            # starts as undef
my @b = qw(fred barney betty);    # give initial value
...
push @b, qw(wilma);               # cannot leave her out
@c = sort @b;                     # WILL NOT COMPILE
```

That last statement will be flagged at compile time as an error, because it referred to a variable that had not previously been declared with **my** (that is, @c). In other words, your program won't even start running unless every single variable being used has been declared.

The advantages of forcing variable declarations are twofold:

- Your programs will run slightly faster (variables created with **my** are accessed slightly faster than ordinary variables[†]).

- You'll catch mistakes in typing much faster, because you'll no longer be able to accidentally reference a nonexisting variable named `$freed` when you wanted `$fred`.

Because of these advantages, many Perl programmers automatically begin every new Perl program with **use strict**.

Exercises

See Appendix A for answers.

1. Write a subroutine that takes a numeric value from 1 to 9 as an argument and then returns the English name (such as, **one**, **two**, or **nine**). If the value is

---

[*] A pragma is a compiler directive. Other directives include those used to set up integer arithmetic, overload numeric operators, or request more verbose warnings and error messages. These are documented in *perlmodlib*.

[†] In this case, ordinary variable is really a package variable (so `$x` is really `$main::x`). Variables created with **my** are not found in any package.

out of range, return the original number as the name instead. Test it with some input data; you'll probably have to write some sort of code to call the subroutine. (Hint: the subroutine should *not* perform any I/O.)

2. Taking the subroutine from the previous exercise, write a program that takes two numbers and then adds them together, displaying the result as `Two plus two equals four`. (Don't forget to capitalize the initial word!)

3. Extend the subroutine to return `negative nine` through `negative one` and `zero`. Try it in a program.

9

Miscellaneous Control Structures

The last Statement

In some of the previous exercises, you may have thought, "if I just had a C **break** statement here, I'd be done." Even if you didn't think that, let me tell you about Perl's equivalent for getting out of a loop early: the **last** statement.

The **last** statement breaks out of the innermost enclosing loop block,[*] causing execution to continue with the statement immediately following the block. For example:

```
while (something) {
        something;
        something;
        something;
        if (somecondition) {
            somethingorother;
            somethingorother;
            last; # break out of the while loop
        }
        morethings;
        morethings;
}
# last comes here
```

If *somecondition* is true, the *somethingorother*s are executed, and then the **last** forces the **while** loop to terminate.

The **last** statement counts only looping blocks, not other blocks that are needed to make up some syntactic construct. As a result, the blocks for the **if** and *else*

---

[*] Note that the do {} while/until construct does not count as a loop for purposes of next, last, and redo.

statement, as well as the one for a *do {} while/until*, do not count; only the blocks that make up the `for`, `foreach`, `while`, `until`, and "naked" blocks count. (A naked block is a block that is not otherwise part of a larger construct, such as a loop, subroutine, or `if/then/else` statement.)

Suppose we wanted to see whether a mail message that had been saved in a file was from Erik. Such a message might look like:

```
From: eriko@axtech.com (Erik Olson)
To: rdenn@ora.com
Date: 01-MAY-97 08:16:24 PM MDT -0700
Subject: A sample mail message

Here's the body of the mail message. And
here is some more.
```

We'd have to look through the message for a line that begins with `From:`, and then notice whether the line also contains the login name, `eriko`.

We could do it this way:

```
while (<STDIN>) {           # read the input lines
        if (/^From: /) {    # does it begin with From:? If yes...
                if (/eriko/) { # it's from Erik!
                    print "Email from Erik! It's about time!\n";
                }
                last;       # no need to keep looking for From:, so exit
        }                   # end "if from:"
        if (/^$/) {         # blank line?
                last;       # if so, don't check any more lines
        }
}                           # end while
```

After the line starting with `From:` is found, we exit the main loop because we want to see only the first `From:` line. Also, because a mail message header ends at the first blank line, we can exit the main loop there as well.

The next Statement

Like `last`, `next` alters the ordinary sequential flow of execution. However, `next` causes execution to skip past the rest of the innermost enclosing looping block without terminating the block.* `next` is used like this:

```
while (something) {
        firstpart;
        firstpart;
        firstpart;
        if (somecondition) {
```

---

* If a `continue` block exists for the loop, which we haven't yet discussed, `next` goes to the beginning of the `continue` block rather than to the end of the block. Pretty close.

```
            somepart;
            somepart;
            next;
        }
        otherpart;
        otherpart;
        # next comes here
    }
```

If *somecondition* is true, then *somepart* is executed, and *otherpart* is skipped around.

Once again, the block of an **if** statement doesn't count as a looping block.

The redo Statement

The third way you can jump around in a looping block is with **redo**. This construct causes a jump to the beginning of the current block (without reevaluating the control expression), like so:

```
    while (somecondition) {
        # redo comes here
        something;
        something;
        something;
        if (somecondition) {
            somestuff;
            somestuff;
            redo;
        }
        morething;
        morething;
        morething;
    }
```

Once again, the **if** block doesn't count—just the looping blocks.

With **redo**, **last**, and a naked block, you can make an infinite loop that exits out of the middle, like so:

```
    {
        startstuff;
        startstuff;
        startstuff;
        if (somecondition) {
            last;
        }
        laterstuff;
        laterstuff;
        laterstuff;
        redo;
    }
```

This logic would be appropriate for a `while`-like loop that needed to have some part of the loop executed as initialization before the first test. (In a later section entitled "Expression Modifiers," we'll show you how to write that `if` statement with fewer punctuation characters.)

Labeled Blocks

What if you want to jump out of the block that contains the innermost block—to exit from two nested blocks at once? In C, you'd resort to that much maligned `goto` to get you out. No such kludge is required in Perl. You can use `last`, `next`, and `redo` on any enclosing block by giving the block a name with a *label*.

A label is yet another type of name from yet another namespace following the same rules as scalars, arrays, hashes, and subroutines. As we'll see, however, a label doesn't have a special prefix punctuation character (like `$` for scalars, `&` for subroutines, and so on), so a label named `print` conflicts with the reserved word `print`, and would not be allowed. For this reason, you should choose labels that consist entirely of uppercase letters and digits, which will never be chosen for a reserved word in the future. Besides, using all uppercase makes an item stand out better within the text of a mostly lowercase program.

After you've chosen your label, place it immediately in front of the statement containing the block, and follow it with a colon, like this:

```
SOMELABEL: while (condition) {
        statement;
        statement;
        statement;
        if (nuthercondition) {
            last SOMELABEL;
        }
    }
```

We added **SOMELABEL** as a parameter to `last`. This parameter tells Perl to exit the block named **SOMELABEL**, rather than exiting just the innermost block. In this case, we don't have anything but the innermost block. But suppose we had nested loops:

```
OUTER: for ($i = 1; $i <= 10; $i++) {
        INNER: for ($j = 1; $j <= 10; $j++) {
            if ($i * $j == 63) {
                print "$i times $j is 63!\n";
                last OUTER;
            }
            if ($j >= $i) {
                next OUTER;
            }
        }
    }
```

This set of statements tries all successive values of two small numbers multiplied together until it finds a pair whose product is 63 (7 and 9). After the pair is found, there's no point in testing other numbers, so the first `if` statement exits both `for` loops using `last` with a label. The second `if` ensures that the bigger of the two numbers will always be the first number by skipping to the next iteration of the outer loop as soon as the condition would no longer hold. This means that the numbers will be tested with (`$i`, `$j`) being (1,1), (2,1), (2,2), (3,1), (3,2), (3,3), (4,1), and so on.

Even if the innermost block is labeled, the `last`, `next`, and `redo` statements without the optional parameter (the label) still operate with respect to that innermost block. Also, you can't use labels to jump into a block—just out of a block. The `last`, `next`, or `redo` has to be within the block.

Expression Modifiers

As Yet Another Way to indicate "if this, then that," Perl allows you to tag an *if* modifier onto an expression that is a standalone statement, like this:

```
some_expression if control_expression;
```

In this case, `control_expression` is evaluated first for its truth value (using the same rules as always), and if true, `some_expression` is evaluated next. This method is roughly equivalent to:

```
if (control_expression) {
        some_expression;
}
```

except that you don't need the extra punctuation, the statement reads backwards, and the expression must be a simple expression (not a block of statements). Many times, however, this inverted description turns out to be the most natural way to state the problem. For example, here's how you can exit from a loop when a certain condition arises:

```
LINE: while (<STDIN>) {
        last LINE if /^From: /;
}
```

See how much easier that is to write? And you can even read it in a normal English way: "last line if it begins with From."

Other parallel forms include the following:

```
exp2 unless exp1;# like: unless (exp1) { exp2; }
exp2 while exp1; # like: while (exp1) { exp2; }
exp2 until exp1; # like: until (exp1) { exp2; }
```

All of these forms evaluate *exp1* first, and based on that evaluation, do or don't do something with *exp2*.

For example, here's how to find the first power of two greater than a given number:

```
chomp($n = <STDIN>);
$i = 1;                    # initial guess
$i *= 2 until $i > $n;     # iterate until we find it
```

Once again, we gain some clarity and reduce the clutter.

These forms don't nest: you can't say *exp3* `while` *exp2* `if` *exp1*. This restriction is because the form *exp2* `if` *exp1* is no longer an expression, but a full-blown statement, and you can't tack one of these modifiers on after a statement.

&&, ||, and ?: as Control Structures

These look like punctuation characters, or parts of expressions. Can they really be considered control structures? Well, in Perl-think, almost anything is possible, so let's see what we're talking about here.

Often, you run across "if this, then that." We've previously seen these two forms:

```
if (this) { that; } # one way
that if this;        # another way
```

Here's a third (and believe it or not, there are still others):

```
this && that;
```

Why does this statement work? Isn't that the logical-and operator? Check out what happens when *this* takes on each value of true or false:

- If *this* is true, then the value of the entire expression is still not known, because it depends on the value of *that*. So *that* has to be evaluated.

- If *this* is false, there's no point in looking at *that*, because the value of the whole expression has to be false. Because you don't have to evaluate *that*, we might as well skip it.

And in fact, Perl does just that. Perl evaluates *that* only when *this* is true, making the form equivalent to the previous two examples.

Likewise, the logical `or` works like the `unless` statement (or `unless` modifier). So, you can replace:

```
unless (this) { that; }
```

with

```
this || that;
```

Finally, the C-like ternary operator:

```
exp1 ? exp2 : exp3;
```

evaluates to *exp2* if *exp1* is true, and to *exp3* in all other cases. You might have used:

```
if (exp1) { exp2; } else { exp3; }
```

but you could have eliminated all of that punctuation. For example, you could write:

```
($a < 10) ? ($b = $a) : ($a = $b);
```

Which one should you use? Your choice depends on your mood, sometimes, or on how big each of the expression parts are, or on whether you need to parenthesize the expressions because of precedence conflicts. Look at other people's programs, and see what they do. You'll probably see a little of each. Larry suggests that you put the most important part of the expression first, so that it stands out.

Exercises

See Appendix A for the answers.

1. Extend the problem from the last chapter to repeat the operation until the word **end** is entered for one of the values. (Hint: use an infinite loop, and then do a **last** if either value is **end**.)

2. Rewrite the exercise from Chapter 4, summing numbers up to 999, using a loop that exits from the middle. (Hint: use a naked block with a **redo** at the end to get an infinite loop, and a **last** in the middle based on a condition.)

10

Filehandles and File Tests

What Is a Filehandle?

A *filehandle* in a Perl program is the name for an I/O connection between your Perl process and the outside world. We've already seen and used filehandles implicitly: STDIN is a filehandle, naming the connection between the Perl process and the standard input. Likewise, Perl provides STDOUT (for standard output) and STDERR (for standard error output). These names are the same as those used by the C and C++ standard I/O library package, which Perl uses for most of its I/O.

Filehandle names are like the names for labeled blocks, but they come from yet another namespace (so you can have a scalar $fred, an array @fred, a hash %fred, a subroutine &fred, a label fred, and now a filehandle fred). Like block labels, filehandles are used without a special prefix character, and thus might be confused with present or future reserved words. Once again, the recommendation is that you use ALL UPPERCASE letters in your filehandle; not only will the uppercase stand out better, but it will also guarantee that your program won't fail when a future reserved word is introduced.

Opening and Closing a Filehandle

Perl provides three filehandles—STDIN, STDOUT, and STDERR—which are automatically open to files or devices established by the program's parent process (probably a command console). You use the **open** function to open additional filehandles. The syntax looks like this:

```
open(FILEHANDLE, "somename");
```

where *FILEHANDLE* is the new filehandle and *somename* is the external file-name (such as a file or a device) that will be associated with the new filehandle. This invocation opens the filehandle for reading. To open a file for writing, use the same **open** function, but prefix the filename with a greater-than sign (as with redirection in *cmd.exe* or *command.com*):

```
open(OUT, ">outfile");
```

We'll see in a later section, "Using Filehandles," how to use this filehandle. Also, as at the command prompt, you can open a file for appending by using two greater-than signs for a prefix, as shown:

```
open(LOGFILE, ">>mylogfile");
```

All forms of **open** return true for success and false for failure. (Opening a file for input fails, for example, if the file is not there or cannot be accessed because of permissions; opening a file for output fails if the file is write protected, or if the directory is not writable or accessible.)

When you are finished with a filehandle, you can close it with the **close** operator, like so:

```
close(LOGFILE);
```

Reopening a filehandle also closes the previously opened file automatically, as does exiting the program. Because of this feature, many Perl programs don't bother with **close**. But the function is there if you want to be tidy or make sure that all of the data is flushed out before program termination. A **close** call could also fail if the disk filled up, the remote server that held the file became inaccessible, or any of various other esoteric problems occurred. You should always check the return values of all system calls.

Using Pathnames and Filenames

When working with files and pathnames, you're faced with an interesting choice: what's the best way of specifying pathnames? Perl accepts either a slash or a back-slash as a path delimiter.* The slash is typically used by UNIX systems to delimit paths while the backslash is the traditional MS-DOS path delimiter. The slash is also used as a path delimiter when specifying URLs. The following statements all evaluate to the same thing, as far as Perl is concerned:†

```
"c:\\temp"    # backslash (escaped for double quoted string)
'c:\temp'     # backslash (single quoted string)
"c:/temp"     # slash - no escape needed
```

---

* Acutally, pathnames are just passed to the operating system, which accepts either a slash or a backslash.

† The only portable delimiter is the slash. Of course, if you're using drive letters, your script isn't really portable anyway.

There are a couple of tradeoffs associated with either approach. First we look at the backslash: if you use the backslash to delimit paths, you have compatibilty problems with scripts that need to run on UNIX systems. You also need to remember to escape the backslash inside of double-quoted strings (or use single-quoted strings, because they are not interpolated). Finally, you need to remember to use a slash if you're outputting URL paths.

If you decide to use a slash, you need to consider the following issues: although some Windows NT programs and utilities accept slashes as a delimiter, many do not. Traditionally, the slash is used to specify command-line options to MS-DOS programs, so many programs interpret slashes as command switches. Generally speaking, if your script is self contained, you won't run into any difficulties using slashes. However, if you need to pass pathnames to external programs, you'll probably need to use backslashes (unless you know that the program you're using accepts slashes).

Our practice is to use slashes unless we're passing a path to an external program, in which case we use backslashes. If you're using one style of delimiter, you could easily switch to the other style by doing a simple substitution. You must exercise caution if you're writing code that parses a path to extract components; make sure that your code either regularizes paths to use the same delimiter, or that it handles both delimiters when extracting components.[*]

Another issue to consider is the use of long filenames versus the traditional MS-DOS 8.3 filename (a maximum of eight characters, followed by an optional extension of up to three characters). You'll find that some programs do not handle long filenames gracefully (particularly those with embedded spaces in them). In fact, if you're communicating with 16-bit programs (of either the Windows 3.x or DOS variety), the odds are very high that they won't understand long filenames.

To convert a long filename to an 8.3 filename, use the `Win32::GetShortPath-Name`[†] function:

```
use Win32;
$longname = 'words.secret';
$shortname = Win32::GetShortPathName($longname);
   # $shortname has WORDS~1.SEC
```

Perl can also be used to open files using UNC (Universal Naming Convention) pathnames. A UNC path consists of two backslashes (or slashes) followed by a

---

[*] Or consider using `File::Basename`, which does portable parsing of path components.

[†] For a discussion of the Win32 extensions, see Appendix B, *Libraries and Modules.*

machine name and a share. The following example opens a file using a UNC pathname:

```
open(F, '//someserver/share/somefile') ||
  die "open: $!";
$cnt = 0;
while(<F>) {$cnt++;} # count the number of lines
close(F) || die "close: $!";
print "$cnt lines\n";
```

If you use backslashes, make sure that they're properly escaped:

```
open(F, "\\\\someserver\\share\\somefile") ||
  die "open: $!";
$cnt = 0;
while(<F>) {$cnt++;} # count the number of lines
close(F) || die "close: $!";
print "$cnt lines\n";
```

A Slight Diversion: die

Consider the following a large footnote, but in the middle of the page.

A filehandle that has not been successfully opened can still be used without even so much as a warning throughout the program.* If you read from the filehandle, you'll get end-of-file right away. If you write to the filehandle, the data is silently discarded (like last year's campaign promises).

Typically, you'll want to check the result of the open and report an error if the result is not what you expect. Sure, you can pepper your program with stuff like:

```
unless (open (DATAPLACE,">c:/temp/dataplace")) {
        print "Sorry, I couldn't create c:/temp/dataplace\n";
} else {
        # the rest of your program
}
```

But that sort of change is a lot of work. And it happens often enough for Perl to offer a bit of a shortcut. The **die** function takes a list within optional parentheses, spits out that list (like **print**) on the standard error output, and then ends the Perl program with a nonzero exit status (generally indicating that something unusual happened†). So, rewriting the chunk of code above turns out to look like this:

```
unless (open DATAPLACE,">c:/temp/dataplace") {
        die "Sorry, I couldn't create c:/temp/dataplace\n";
}
# rest of program
```

---

* This statement is true, unless you are running with the –w switch enabled.

† Actually, die () merely raises an exception, but because you aren't being shown how to trap exceptions, it behaves as described. See *Eval {}* in Chapter 3 of *Programming Perl* or *perlfunc* for details.

But we can go even one step further. Remember that we can use the | | (logical or) operator to shorten this up, as in:

```
open(DATAPLACE,">c:/temp/dataplace") ||
        die "Sorry, I couldn't create c:/temp/dataplace\n";
```

So, the **die** gets executed only when the result of the **open** is false. The common way to read this is "open that file or die!" And that's an easy way to remember whether to use the logical **and** or logical **or**.

The message at death (built from the argument to **die**) has the Perl program name and line number automatically attached, so you can easily identify which **die** was responsible for the untimely exit. If you don't like the line number or file revealed, make sure that the death text has a newline on the end. For example:

```
die "you gravy-sucking pigs";
```

prints the file and line number, while

```
die "you gravy-sucking pigs\n";
```

does not.

Another handy thing inside die strings is the $! variable, which contains the text relating to the most recent operating system error value. The variable is used like this:

```
open(LOG, ">>logfile") || die "cannot append: $!";
```

The program might end up saying "**cannot append: Permission denied**" as part of the message.

There's also the *close call* function, which most people know as **warn**. It does everything **die** does, just short of actually dying. Use it to give error messages on standard error without a lot of extra hassle:

```
open(LOG,">>log") || warn "discarding logfile output\n";
```

Using Filehandles

After a filehandle is open for reading, you can read lines from it just as you can read from standard input with **STDIN**. So, for example, to read lines from a text file:

```
open (FIL,"some_file");
while (<FIL>) {
        chomp;
        print "I saw $_ in some_file!\n";
}
```

Note that the newly opened filehandle is used inside the angle brackets, just as we have used **STDIN** previously.

If you have a filehandle open for writing or appending, and if you want to print to it, you must place the filehandle immediately after the print keyword and before the other arguments. No comma should occur between the filehandle and the rest of the arguments:

```
print LOGFILE "Finished item $n of $max\n";
print STDOUT "hi, world!\n";
```

In this case, the message beginning with `Finished` goes to the `LOGFILE` filehandle, which presumably was opened earlier in the program. And `hi, world` still goes to standard output, just as when you didn't specify the filehandle. We say that `STDOUT` is the *default filehandle* for the `print` statement.

Here's a way to copy all of the text from a file specified in `$a` into a file specified in `$b`. It illustrates nearly everything we've learned in the last few pages:[*]

```
open(IN,$a) || die "cannot open $a for reading: $!";
open(OUT,">$b") || die "cannot create $b: $!";
while (<IN>) { # read a line from file $a into $_
        print OUT $_; # print that line to file $b
close(IN);  || die "can't close  $a:$!"
close(OUT);|| die "can't close   $b:$!"
}
```

The -x File Tests

Now you know how to open a filehandle for output, overwriting any existing file with the same name. Suppose you wanted to make sure that there wasn't a file by that name (to keep you from accidentally blowing away your spreadsheet data or that important birthday calendar). Perl uses `-e $filevar` to test for the existence of the file named by the scalar value in `$filevar`. If this file exists, the result is true; otherwise it is false. For example:

```
$name = "index.html";
if (-e $name) {
    print "I see you already have a file named $name\n";
} else {
    print "Perhaps you'd like to make a file called $name\n";
}
```

The operand of the `-e` operator is really just any scalar expression that evaluates to some string, including a string literal. Here's an example that checks to see whether both *index.html* and *index.cgi* exist in the current directory:

```
if (-e "index.html" && -e "index.cgi") {
    print "You have both styles of index files here.\n";
}
```

---

[*] Although this method is entirely redundant when you consider the `File::Copy` module.

Other operators are defined as well. For example, -r $filevar returns true if the file named in $filevar exists and is readable. Similarly, -w $filevar tests whether it is writable. Here's an example that tests a user-specified filename for both readability and writability:

```
print "where? ";
$filename = <STDIN>;
chomp $filename; # toss pesky newline
if (-r $filename && -w $filename) {
        # file exists, and I can read and write it
        ...
}
```

Many more file tests are available, some of which are not applicable to Perl for Win32. Table 10-1 lists some file tests and their meanings; for the whole list, see the *perlfunc* documentation.

Table 10-1. File Tests and Their Meanings

File Test	Meaning
-r	File or directory is readable
-w	File or directory is writable
-e	File or directory exists
-x	File is executable
-z	File exists and has zero size (directories are never empty)
-s	File or directory exists and has nonzero size (the value is the size in bytes)
-f	Entry is a plain file
-d	Entry is a directory
-t	isatty on the filehandle is true (that is, the filehandle is a character device)
-T	File is text
-B	File is binary
-M	Modification age in days (C lang. time_t value)
-A	Access age in days (C lang. time_t value)
-C	Inode-modification age in days (C lang. time_t value)

Most of these tests return a simple true-false condition. A few don't, so let's talk about them.

The -s operator does return true if the file is nonempty, but it's a particular kind of true. It's the length in bytes of the file, which evaluates as true for a nonzero number.

The age operators -M, -A, and -C (yes, they're uppercase) return the number of days since the file was last modified, accessed, or had its information changed.* This age value is fractional with a resolution of one second: 36 hours is returned as 1.5 days. If you compare the age with a whole number (say three), you'll get only the files that were changed exactly that many days ago, not one second more or less. This means that you'll probably want a range comparison rather than an exact comparison to get files that are between three and four days old.†

These operators can operate on filehandles as well as filenames. Giving a file-handle for the operand is all it takes. So to test whether the file opened as SOMEFILE is executable, you can use:

```
if (-x SOMEFILE) {
        # file open on SOMEFILE is executable
}
```

If you leave the filename or filehandle parameter off (that is, if you specify just -r or -s), the default operand is the file named in the $_ variable (there it is again!). So, to test a list of filenames to see which ones are readable, it's as simple as:

```
foreach (@some_list_of_filenames) {
        print "$_ is readable\n" if -r; # same as -r $_
}
```

The stat Function

While these file tests are fine for testing various attributes regarding a particular file or filehandle, they don't tell the whole story. To get at the remaining information about a file, merely call the stat function, which returns pretty much everything that the POSIX system call stat returns (hopefully more than you want to know). Not all of the stat fields are meaningful under Perl for Win32, because they include information not supported by the Windows NT filesystems.

The operand to stat is a filehandle or an expression that evaluates to a file-name. The return value is either undef, indicating that the stat failed, or a 13-element list,‡ most easily described using the following list of scalar variables:

```
($dev,$ino,$mode,$nlink,$uid,$gid,$rdev,
 $size,$atime,$mtime,$ctime,$blksize,$blocks) = stat(...)
```

---

* The age is measured relative to the time the program started, as captured in C-library time into the $^T variable. You can get negative numbers for these ages if the queried value refers to an event that happened after the program began.

† Or, you might want to use the int function.

‡ If you have a hard time remembering the order of stat's return values, you might look at the File::stat module, first introduced in release 5.004 of Perl. It provides access such as:

```
$file_owner = stat($filename)->uid;
```

Table 10-2 lists each field along with a brief description.

Table 10-2. stat Return Values

Field	Description
dev	Device number (drive number)
ino	Inode number: 0 (zero) in Perl for Win32
mode	File permission mode: read/write/execute
nlink	Number of links to file (usually one for Win32 systems—NTFS filesystems may have a value greater than one)
uid	User ID—zero for Win32
gid	Group ID—zero for Win32
rdev	Device Identifier (drive number)
size	File size in bytes
atime	Last access time (C lang. time_t value)
mtime	Last modification time (C lang. time_t value)
ctime	File creation time (C lang. time_t value)
blksize	Disk block size (cluster size): zero for Win32
blocks	Number of blocks for file: zero for Win32

Like the file tests, the operand of **stat** defaults to **$_**, meaning that the stat will be performed on the file named by the scalar variable **$_**.

You can retrieve information about the filesystem of the current active drive using the **Win32::FsType** function:

```
$fstype = Win32::FsType;
if ($fstype =~ /NTFS/) {
    print "NTFS -- good choice!\n";
}
```

Exercises

See Appendix A for answers.

1. Write a program to read in a filename from **STDIN**, and then open that file and display its contents with each line preceded by the filename and a colon. For example, if **fred** was read in, and the file **fred** consisted of the three lines **aaa**, **bbb**, and **ccc**, you would see **fred: aaa**, **fred: bbb**, and **fred: ccc**.

2. Write a program that prompts for an input filename, an output filename, a search pattern, and a replacement string, and then replaces all occurrences of the search pattern with the replacement string while copying the input file to the output file. Try it on some files. Can you overwrite an existing file? (Don't

try it with anything important!) Can you use regular expression characters in the search string? Can you use $1 in the replacement string?

3. Write a program to read in a list of filenames and then display which of the files are readable, writable, and nonexistent. (You can perform each test for each filename as you read them, or you can perform the tests on the entire set of filenames after you've read them all. Don't forget to remove the newline at the end of each filename that you have read.)

4. Write a program to read in a list of filenames and then find the oldest file among them. Print out the name of the file and the age of that file in days.

11

Formats

What Is a Format?

Perl stands, among other things, for "Practical Extraction and Report Language." It's time to learn about that "...report language" business.

Perl provides a simple report-writing template, called a *format.* A format defines a constant part (the column headers, labels, fixed text, or whatever) and a variable part (the current data you're reporting). The shape of the format is very close to the shape of the output, as with formatted output in COBOL or the `print using` clauses of some BASICs.

Using a format consists of doing three things:

1. Defining a format

2. Loading up the data to be printed into the variable portions of the format (fields)

3. Invoking the format

Most often, the first step is done once (in the program text so that it gets defined at compile time[*]), and the other two steps are performed repeatedly.

---

[*] You can also create formats at runtime using the `eval` function, as described in *Programming Perl* and *perlform.*

Defining a Format

A format is defined using a format definition. This format definition can appear anywhere in your program text, like a subroutine. A format definition looks like this:

```
format someformatname =
fieldline
value_one, value_two, value_three
fieldline
value_one, value_two
fieldline
value_one, value_two, value_three
.
```

The first line contains the reserved word `format`, followed by the format name and then an equal sign (=). The format name is chosen from yet another namespace, and follows the same rule as everything else. Because format names are never used within the body of the program (except within string values), you can safely use names that are identical to reserved words. As you'll see in the following section, "Invoking a Format," most of your format names will probably be the same as filehandle names (which then makes them *not* the same as reserved words...oh well).

Following the first line comes the *template* itself, spanning zero or more text lines. The end of the template is indicated by a line consisting of a single dot by itself.* Templates are sensitive to whitespace; this instance is one of the few in which the kind and amount of whitespace (space, newline, or tab) in the text of a Perl program actually matters.

The template definition contains a series of *fieldlines*. Each fieldline may contain fixed text—text that will be printed out literally when the format is invoked. Here's an example of a fieldline with fixed text:

```
Hello, my name is Fred Flintstone.
```

Fieldlines may also contain *fieldholders* for variable text. If a line contains fieldholders, the following line of the template (called the *value* line) dictates a series of scalar values—one per fieldholder—that provide the values that will be plugged into the fields. Here's an example of a fieldline with one fieldholder and the value line that follows:

```
Hello, my name is @<<<<<<<<<
$name
```

---

* In text files, the last line needs to end with a newline to work properly.

The fieldholder is the @<<<<<<<<<, which specifies a left-justified text field with 11 characters. More complete details about fieldholders will be given in the section called "More About the Fieldholders" later in this chapter.

If the fieldline has multiple fieldholders, it needs multiple values, so the values are separated on the value line by commas:

```
Hello, my name is @<<<<<<<<<< and I'm @<< years old.
$name, $age
```

Putting all this together, we can create a simple format for an address label:

```
format ADDRESSLABEL =
=================================
| @<<<<<<<<<<<<<<<<<<<<<<<<< |
$name
| @<<<<<<<<<<<<<<<<<<<<<<<<< |
$address
| @<<<<<<<<<<<<<<<, @< @<<<< |
$city,          $state, $zip
=================================
    .
```

Note that the lines of equal signs at the top and bottom of the format have no fields, and thus have no value lines following. (If you put a value line following such a fieldline, it will be interpreted as another fieldline, and will most likely not do what you want.)

Whitespace within the value line is ignored. Some people choose to use additional whitespace in the value line to line up the variable with the fieldholder on the preceding line (such as putting $zip underneath the third field of the previous line in this example), but that's just for looks. Perl doesn't care, and the change doesn't affect your output.

Text after the first newline in a value is discarded (except in the special case of multiline fieldholders, described later).

A format definition is like a subroutine definition. It doesn't contain immediately executed code, and can therefore be placed anywhere in the file with the rest of the program—we tend to put ours toward the end of the file, ahead of my subroutine definitions.

Invoking a Format

You invoke a format with the **write** function. This operator takes the name of a filehandle and generates text for that filehandle using the current format for that filehandle. By default, the current format for a filehandle is a format with the same name (so for the STDOUT filehandle, the STDOUT format is used), but we'll soon see that you can change it.

Let's take another look at that address label format, and create a file full of address labels. Here's a program segment:

```
format ADDRESSLABEL =
=================================
| @<<<<<<<<<<<<<<<<<<<<<<<<< |
$name
| @<<<<<<<<<<<<<<<<<<<<<<<<< |
$address
| @<<<<<<<<<<<<<<<, @< @<<<< |
$city,            $state, $zip
=================================
.

open(ADDRESSLABEL,">labels-to-print") || die "can't create";
open(ADDRESSES,"addresses") || die "cannot open addresses";
while (<ADDRESSES>) {
        chomp; # remove newline
        ($name,$address,$city,$state,$zip) = split(/:/);
            # load up the global variables
        write (ADDRESSLABEL); # send the output
}
```

Here we see our previous format definition, but now we also have some executable code. First, we open a filehandle onto an output file called **labels-to-print**. Note that the filehandle name (**ADDRESSLABEL**) is the same as the name of the format. This fact is important. Next, we open a filehandle on an address list. The format of the address list is presumed to be something like:

```
Stonehenge:4470 SW Hall Suite 107:Beaverton:OR:97005
Fred Flintstone:3737 Hard Rock Lane:Bedrock:OZ:999bc
```

In other words, the format is five colon-separated fields, which our code parses as described below.

The **while** loop in the program reads each line of the address file, gets rid of the newline, and then splits the remainder into five variables. Note that the variable names are the same names as the ones we used when we defined the format. This fact, too, is important.

After we have all of the variables loaded up (so that the values used by the format are correct), the **write** function invokes the format. Note that the parameter to **write** is the filehandle to be written to, and by default, the format of the same name is also used.

Each field in the format is replaced with the corresponding value from the next line of the format. After the two sample records given above are processed, the file **labels-to-print** contains:

```
=================================
| Stonehenge                    |
| 4470 SW Hall Suite 107        |
| Beaverton        , OR 97005   |
=================================
=================================
| Fred Flintstone               |
| 3737 Hard Rock Lane           |
| Bedrock          , OZ 999bc   |
=================================
```

More About the Fieldholders

So far, by example, you know that the fieldholder @<<<< indicates a 5-character, left-justified field and that @<<<<<<<<<< indicates an 11-character, left-justified field. Here's the whole scoop, as promised earlier.

Text Fields

Most fieldholders start with @. The characters following the @ indicate the type of field, while the number of characters (including the @) indicates the field width.

If the characters following the @ are left-angle brackets (<<<<), you get a left-justified field; that is, the value will be padded on the right with spaces if the value is shorter than the field width. (If a value is too long, it's truncated automatically; the layout of the format is always preserved.)

If the characters following the @ are right-angle brackets (>>>>), you get a right-justified field—that is, if the value is too short, the field gets padded on the left with spaces.

Finally, if the characters following the @ are vertical bars (||||), you get a centered field; if the value is too short, the field gets padded on both sides with spaces, enough on each side to make the value mostly centered within the field.

Numeric Fields

Another kind of fieldholder is a fixed-precision numeric field, useful for those big financial reports. This field also begins with @, and is followed by one or more #'s with an optional dot (indicating a decimal point). Once again, the @ counts as one of the characters of the field. For example:

```
format MONEY =
Assets: @#####.## Liabilities: @#####.## Net: @#####.##
$assets, $liabilities, $assets-$liabilities
.
```

The three numeric fields allow for six places to the left of the decimal place, and two to the right (useful for dollars and cents). Note the use of an expression in the format—perfectly legal and frequently used.

Perl provides nothing fancier than this; you can't get floating currency symbols or brackets around negative values or anything interesting. To do so, you have to write your own spiffy subroutine, like so:

```
format MONEY =
Assets: @<<<<<<<<< Liabilities @<<<<<<<< Net: @<<<<<<<<<
pretty($assets,10), pretty($liab,9), pretty($assets-$liab,10)
.

sub pretty {
        my($n,$width) = @_;
        $width -= 2; # back off for negative stuff
        $n = sprintf("%.2f",$n); # sprintf is in later chapter
        if ($n < 0) {
            return sprintf("[%$width.2f]", -$n);
                # negative numbers get brackets
        } else {
            return sprintf(" %$width.2f ", $n);
                # positive numbers get spaces instead
        }
}

## body of program:
$assets = 32125.12;
$liab = 45212.15;
write (MONEY);
```

Multiline Fields

As mentioned earlier, Perl normally stops at the first newline of a value when placing the result into the output. One kind of fieldholder, the multiline field-holder, allows you to include a value that may have many lines of information. This fieldholder is denoted by @* on a line by itself; as always, the following line defines the value to be substituted into the field, which in this case may be an expression that results in a value containing many newlines.

The substituted value will look just like the original text: four lines of value become four lines of output. For example:

```
format STDOUT =
Text Before.
@*
$long_string
Text After.
.

$long_string = "Fred\nBarney\nBetty\nWilma\n";
write;
```

generates the output:

```
Text Before.
Fred
Barney
Betty
Wilma
Text After.
```

Filled Fields

Another kind of fieldholder is a filled field. This fieldholder allows you to create a filled paragraph, breaking the text into conveniently sized lines at word boundaries, wrapping the lines as needed. There are a few parts that work together here, but let's look at them separately.

First, a filled field is denoted by replacing the @ marker in a text fieldholder with a caret (so you get ^<<<, for example). The corresponding value for a filled field (on the following line of the format) *must* be a scalar variable* containing text, rather than an expression that returns a scalar value. The reason for this is that Perl will alter the variable while filling the filled field, and it's pretty hard to alter an expression.

When Perl is filling the filled field, it takes the value of the variable and grabs as many words (using a reasonable definition of "word")† as will fit into the field. These words are actually ripped out of the variable—the value of the variable after filling this field is whatever is left over after removing the words. You'll see why in a minute.

So far, this isn't much different from how a normal text field works; we're printing only as much as will fit (except that we're respecting a word boundary rather than just cutting it off at the field width). The beauty of this filled field appears when you have multiple references to the same variable in the same format. Take a look at this:

```
format PEOPLE =
Name: @<<<<<<<<<<<< Comment: ^<<<<<<<<<<<<<<<<<<<<<<<<<<<<<
      $name,                  $comment
                            ^<<<<<<<<<<<<<<<<<<<<<<<<<<<<<
                              $comment
                            ^<<<<<<<<<<<<<<<<<<<<<<<<<<<<<
                              $comment
                            ^<<<<<<<<<<<<<<<<<<<<<<<<<<<<<
                              $comment
      .
```

---

* The scalar value can include a single scalar element of an array or hash, like `$a[3]` or `$h{"fred"}`.

† The word-separator characters are defined by the `$:` variable.

Note that the variable $comment appears four times. The first line (the one with the $name field) prints the person's name and the first few words of the value in $comment. But in the process of computing this line, $comment is altered so that the words disappear. The second line once again refers to the same variable ($comment), and will take the next few words from the same variable. This process is also used for the third and fourth lines. Effectively, what we've created is a rectangle in the output that will be filled as best it can with the words from $comment spread over four lines.

What happens if the complete text occupies less than four lines? Well, you'll get a blank line or two. This result is probably OK if you are printing out labels and need exactly the same number of lines for each entry to match them up with the labels. But if you are printing out a report, many blank lines merely use up your printer's paper budget.

To fix this, use the suppression indicator. Any line that contains a tilde (~) character is suppressed (not output) if the line would have otherwise printed blank (just whitespace). The tilde itself always prints as a blank and can be placed anywhere a space could have been placed in the line. We could rewrite that last example as follows:

```
format PEOPLE =
Name: @<<<<<<<<<<<< Comment: ^<<<<<<<<<<<<<<<<<<<<<<<<<<<<
      $name,                  $comment
~                             ^<<<<<<<<<<<<<<<<<<<<<<<<<<<<
                              $comment
~                             ^<<<<<<<<<<<<<<<<<<<<<<<<<<<<
                              $comment
~                             ^<<<<<<<<<<<<<<<<<<<<<<<<<<<<
                              $comment
.
```

Now, if the comment covers only two lines, the third and fourth lines are automatically suppressed.

What if the comment is more than four lines? Well, we could make about 20 copies of the last two lines of that format, hoping that 20 lines will suffice. But that goes against the idea that Perl helps you to be lazy, so there's a lazy way to do it. Any line that contains two consecutive tildes will be repeated automatically until the result is a completely blank line. (The blank line is suppressed.) This changes our format to look like this:

```
format PEOPLE =
Name: @<<<<<<<<<<<< Comment: ^<<<<<<<<<<<<<<<<<<<<<<<<<<<<
      $name,                  $comment
~~                            ^<<<<<<<<<<<<<<<<<<<<<<<<<
                              $comment
.
```

This way, if the comment takes 1 line, 2 lines, or 20 lines, we are still OK.

Note that the criterion for stopping the repeated line requires the line to be blank at some point. That means you probably don't want any constant text (other than blanks or tildes) on the line, or else the line will never become blank.

The Top-of-Page Format

Many reports end up on some hardcopy device, like a laserprinter. Printer paper is generally clipped into page-size chunks, because most of us stopped reading paper in scrolls a long time ago. So the text being fed to a printer typically has to take page boundaries into consideration by putting in blank lines or form-feed characters to skip across the page boundaries. Now, you could take the output of a Perl program and feed it through some utility (maybe even one written in Perl) that does this pagination, but there's an easier way.

Perl allows you to define a top-of-page format that triggers a page-processing mode. Perl counts each line of output generated by any format invocation to a particular filehandle. When the next format output cannot fit on the remainder of the current page, Perl spits out a formfeed followed by an automatic invocation of the top-of-page format, and finally the text from the invoked format. In this manner, the result of one **write** invocation will never be split across page boundaries (unless the result is so large that it won't even fit on a page by itself).

The top-of-page format is defined just like any other format. The default name of a top-of-page format for a particular filehandle is the name of the filehandle followed by _TOP (in uppercase only).

Perl defines the variable **$%** to be the number of times the top-of-page format has been called for a particular filehandle, so you can use this variable in your top-of-page format to number the pages properly. For example, adding the following format definition to the previous program fragment prevents labels from being broken across page boundaries, and also numbers consecutive pages:

```
format ADDRESSLABEL_TOP =
My Addresses -- Page @<
                $%
.
```

The default page length is 60 lines. You can change this default by setting a special variable, described shortly.

Perl doesn't notice whether you also **print** to the same filehandle, so that might throw the number of lines on the current page off a bit. You can either rewrite your code to use formats to send everything or fudge the "number of lines on the current page" variable after you do your **print**. In a moment, we'll see how to change this value.

Changing Defaults for Formats

We have often referred to the default for this or that. Well, Perl provides a way to override the defaults for just about every step. Let's talk about these.

Using select to Change the Filehandle

Back when we talked about `print`, in Chapter 6, *Basic I/O*, we mentioned that `print` and `print STDOUT` were identical, because `STDOUT` was the default for `print`. Not quite. The real default for `print` (and `write`, and a few other operations we'll get to in a moment) is an odd notion called the *currently selected filehandle.*

The currently selected filehandle starts out as `STDOUT`—which makes it easy to print things on the standard output. However, you can change the currently selected filehandle with the `select` function. This function takes a single file-handle (or a scalar variable containing the name of a filehandle) as an argument. After the currently selected filehandle is changed, it affects all future operations that depend on the currently selected filehandle. For example:

```
print "hello world\n";      # like print STDOUT "hello world\n";
select (LOGFILE);           # select a new filehandle
print "howdy, world\n";     # like print LOGFILE "howdy, world\n";
print "more for the log\n"; # more for LOGFILE
select (STDOUT);            # re-select STDOUT
print "back to stdout\n";   # this goes to standard output
```

Note that the `select` operation is sticky—after you've selected a new handle, it stays in effect until the next `select`.

So, a better definition for `STDOUT` with respect to `print` and `write` is that `STDOUT` is the default currently selected handle, or the default default handle.

Subroutines may find a need to change the currently selected filehandle. However, you would be shocked if you called a subroutine and then found out that all of your carefully crafted text lines were going into some bit bucket because the subroutine changed the currently selected filehandle without restoring it. So what's a well-behaved subroutine to do? If the subroutine knows that the current handle is `STDOUT`, the subroutine can restore the selected handle with code similar to that given earlier. However, what if the caller of the subroutine had already changed the selected filehandle?

The return value from `select` is a string containing the name of the previously selected handle. You can capture this value to restore the previously selected file-handle later, using code like this:

```
$oldhandle = select LOGFILE;
print "this goes to LOGFILE\n";
select ($oldhandle); # restore the previous handle
```

Yes, for these examples, putting `LOGFILE` explicitly as the filehandle for the `print` is an easier method, but some operations require the currently selected filehandle to change, as we will soon see.

Changing the Format Name

The default format name for a particular filehandle is the same as the filehandle. However, you can change this name for the currently selected filehandle by setting the new format name into a special variable called `$~`. You can also examine the value of the variable to see what the current format is for the currently selected filehandle.

For example, to use the `ADDRESSLABEL` format on `STDOUT`, simply use the following:

```
$~ = "ADDRESSLABEL";
```

But what if you want to set the format for the `REPORT` filehandle to `SUMMARY`? Just a few steps to do it here:

```
$oldhandle = select REPORT;
$~ = "SUMMARY";
select ($oldhandle);
```

The next time we say:

```
write (REPORT);
```

we get text out on the `REPORT` filehandle in the `SUMMARY` format.

Note that we saved the previous handle into a scalar variable and then restored it later. This maneuver is good programming practice. In fact, in production code, we probably would have handled the previous one-line example similarly and not assumed that `STDOUT` was the default handle.

By setting the current format for a particular filehandle, you can interleave many different formats in a single report.

Changing the Top-of-Page Format Name

Just as we can change the name of the format for a particular filehandle by setting the `$~` variable, we can change the top-of-page format by setting the `$^` variable. This variable holds the name of the top-of-page format for the currently selected filehandle and is read/write, meaning that you can examine its value to see the current format name, and you can change it by assigning to it.

Changing the Page Length

If a top-of-page format is defined, the page length becomes important. By default, the page length is 60 lines; that is, when a `write` won't fit by the end of line 60, the top-of-page format is invoked automatically before printing the text.

Sometimes 60 lines isn't right. You can change this by setting the `$=` variable. This variable holds the current page length for the currently selected filehandle. Once again, to change it for a filehandle other than `STDOUT` (the default currently selected filehandle), you'll need to use the `select()` operator. Here's how to change the `LOGFILE` filehandle to have 30-line pages:

```
$old = select LOGFILE; # select LOGFILE and save old handle
$= = 30;
select $old;
```

Changing the page length won't have any effect until the next time the top-of-page format is invoked. If you set it before any text is output to a filehandle through a format, it'll work just fine because the top-of-page format is invoked immediately at the first `write`.

Changing the Position on the Page

If you `print` your own text to a filehandle, it messes up the page-position line count because Perl isn't counting lines for anything but a `write`. If you want to let Perl know that you've output a few extra lines, you can adjust Perl's internal line count by altering the `$-` variable. This variable contains the number of lines left on the current page on the currently selected filehandle. Each `write` decrements the lines remaining by the lines actually output. When this count reaches zero, the top-of-page format is invoked, and the value of `$-` is then copied from `$=` (the page length).

For example, to tell Perl that you've sent an extra line to `STDOUT`, do something like this:

```
write; # invoke STDOUT format on STDOUT
...;
print "An extra line... oops!\n"; # this goes to STDOUT
$- --; # decrement $- to indicate non-write line went to STDOUT
...;
write; # this will still work, taking extra line into account
```

At the beginning of the program, `$-` is set to zero for each filehandle. This ensures that the top-of-page format will be the first thing invoked for each filehandle upon the first `write`.

The FileHandle Module

Because Perl was designed to be a practical extraction and report language, formats were one of the earliest constructs incorporated into the language. As such, the format interface is starting to show its age, particularly when you have to resort to ugly variable names and esoteric `select` manipulations merely to switch the currently active format.

The FileHandle module provides a more intuitive approach to these matters. For example, here's the easy way to perform the same manipulations we demonstrated earlier in the section "Changing the Format Name."

```
use FileHandle;# load library

format_name REPORT "ADDRESSLABEL";
write REPORT;

format_name REPORT "SUMMARY";
write REPORT;
```

This object-oriented module lets you treat filehandles as though they were objects.* All the filehandle-specific built-in punctuation variables have more mnemonic interfaces. See Chapter 2 of *Programming Perl*, or the *perlform* documentation, for the complete description of these.

Exercises

See Appendix A for answers.

1. Write a program that reads a file containing a list of lines composed of a user name, a company name, and an email address separated by colons. A sample line might look like this:

    ```
    John Doe:Foo Technologies:jdoe@footech.com
    ```

    Print out each field in formatted columns. Use `format` and `write`.

2. Add a top-of-page format to the previous program. (If your file is relatively short, you might need to set the pagelength to something like 10 lines so that you can get multiple instances of the top-of-page.)

3. Add a sequentially increasing page number to the top-of-page, so that you get `page 1`, `page 2`, and so on, in the output.

---

* See Chapter 18, *CGI Programming*, for more explanation about objects.

12

Directory Access

Moving Around the Directory Tree

By now, you're probably familiar with the notion of the current directory and using the *cd* command at the command prompt. If you were programming in C, you'd be invoking the `chdir()` call to change the current directory of a program; this name is also used by Perl.

The `chdir` function in Perl takes a single argument—an expression evaluating to a directory name to which the current directory will be set. As with most other system calls, `chdir` returns true if you've successfully changed to the requested directory and false if you couldn't. Here's an example:

```
chdir("c:/temp") || die "cannot cd to c:/temp ($!)";
```

The parentheses are optional, so you can also get away with stuff like:

```
print "where do you want to go? ";
chomp($where = <STDIN>);
if (chdir $where) {
        # we got there
} else {
        # we didn't get there
}
```

You can't find out where you are without launching a *cc* command (something like *cmd /c cd*, or some moral equivalent*). We'll learn about launching commands in Chapter 14, *Process Management*.

---

* Other solutions are using the `getcwd` function out of the `Cwd` module or the `Win32::GetCwd` function.

Every process* has its own current directory. When a new process is launched, it inherits its parent's current directory, but that's the end of the connection. If your Perl program changes its directory, the change won't affect the parent program that launched the Perl process. Likewise, the processes that the Perl program creates cannot affect that Perl program's current directory. The current directories for these new processes are inherited from the Perl program's current directory.

The chdir function without a parameter defaults to taking you to your home directory, in imitation of a typical UNIX shell's *cd* command. The *cd* command in Windows NT does not normally work this way. In order to guess your home directory, Perl will check to see whether the HOME or LOGDIR environment variables are defined.

Globbing

The command prompt usually takes a solitary asterisk (*) command-line argument and turns it into a list of all of the filenames in the current directory. So, when you say *del* *, you'll remove all of the files from the current directory. (Don't try this unless you like restoring the current directory from your backup device.) Similarly, *.c* as a command-line argument turns into a list of all filenames in the current directory that end in *.c*, and *c:\temp\backup** is a list of all filenames in the directory *c:\temp* that begin with *backup*. (If this information is new to you, you probably want to read some more about using the command line somewhere else before proceeding.)

The expansion of arguments like * or *.c* into the list of matching filenames is called *globbing*. Perl supports globbing through a very simple mechanism—just put the globbing pattern between angle brackets or use the more mnemonically named glob function, like this:

```
@a = <*.plx>;
@a = glob("*.plx");
```

In a list context, as demonstrated here, the glob returns a list of all names that match the pattern or an empty list if none match. In a scalar context, the next name that matches is returned, or undef is returned if there are no more matches; this process is very similar to reading from a filehandle. For example, to look at one name at a time:

```
while (defined($nextname = <c:/scripts/*.plx>)) {
        print "one of the files is $nextname\n";
}
```

---

* A process is the technical jargon for an executing program.

Here the returned filenames begin with *c:\scripts*, so that if you want just the last part of the name, you'll have to whittle it down yourself, like so:

```
while ($nextname = <c:/scripts/*.plx>) {
    $nextname =~ s#.*/##; # remove part before last slash
    print "one of the files is $nextname\n";
}
```

Multiple patterns are permitted inside the file glob argument; the lists are constructed separately and then concatenated as if they were one big list:

```
@fred_barney_files = <fred* barney*>;
```

In other words, the glob returns the same values that an equivalent *dir /B* command with the same parameters would return.

Although file globbing and regular-expression matching function similarly, the meanings of their various special characters are quite different. Don't confuse the two, or you'll be wondering why `<\.c$>` doesn't find all of the files that end in `.c`!

The argument to glob is variable interpolated before expansion. You can use Perl variables to select a wildcard based on a string computed at runtime:

```
if (-d "c:/tmp") {
        $where = "c:/tmp";
} else {
        $where = "c:/temp";
}
@files = <$where/*>;
```

Here we set `$where` to be one of two different directory names, based on whether or not the directory *c:\tmp* exists.* We then get a list of files in the selected directory. Note that the `$where` variable is expanded, which means the wildcard to be globbed is either *c:\tmp* or *c:\temp\\.*

There's one exception to this rule: the pattern `<$var>` (meaning to use the variable `$var` as the entire glob expression) must be written as `<${var}>` for reasons we'd rather not get into at this point.†

Directory Handles

UNIX and POSIX programmers are used to reading directories and their contents using a system library function called *readdir*. As it turns out, this function is what

---

* If we were really trying to find where the temporary directory was, we'd be checking the ENV hash for the TEMP variable:

```
my $tmp = $ENV{'TEMP'} || $ENV{'TMP'};
```

† The construct `<$fred>` reads a line from the filehandle named by the contents of the scalar variable `$fred`. Together with some other features not covered in this book, this construct enables you to use indirect filehandles in which the name of a handle is passed around and manipulated as if it were data.

Perl uses to provide directory access. Perl implements *readdir* (and its companions) using a new type of object called *directory handles*. A directory handle is a name from yet another namespace, and the cautions and recommendations that apply to filehandles also apply to directory handles (you can't use a reserved word, and uppercase is recommended). The filehandle FRED and the directory handle FRED are unrelated.

The directory handle represents a connection to a particular directory. Rather than reading data (as from a filehandle), you use the directory handle to read a list of filenames within the directory. Directory handles are always opened read only; you cannot use a directory handle to change the name of a file or to delete a file.

Opening and Closing a Directory Handle

The opendir function is used to open a directory handle for reading. You give it the name of a new directory handle and a string value denoting the name of the directory to be opened. The return value from opendir is true if the directory can be opened, false otherwise. Here's an example:

```
opendir(NT,"c:/winnt") || die "Cannot opendir c:/winnt: $!";
```

Normally, at this point, we'd go playing with the directory handle NT, but it's probably nice to know how to close the directory handle first. This is done with closedir, in a similar manner to using close, like so:

```
closedir(NT);
```

Like close, closedir is often unnecessary, as all directory handles are automatically closed before they're reopened or at the end of the program.

Reading a Directory Handle

After we have a directory handle open, we can read the list of names with readdir, which takes a single parameter: the directory handle. Each invocation of readdir in a scalar context returns the next filename (just the basename— you'll never get any slashes or backslashes in the return value) in a seemingly random order.* If no more names exist, readdir returns undef. Invoking readdir in a list context returns all of the remaining names as a list with one name per element. Here's an example of listing all of the names from your Windows directory:

```
$windir = $ENV{"WINDIR"};
opendir(NT, $windir) || die "no $windir?: $!";
```

---

* Specifically, this order is the one in which the filenames are kept in the directory—the same unordered order you get back from the *dir* command from the command prompt.

```
while ($name = readdir(NT)) { # scalar context, one per loop
        print "$name\n"; # prints ., .., system.ini, and so on
}
closedir(NT);
```

And here's a way of getting them all in alphabetical order with the assistance of `sort`:

```
$windir = $ENV{"WINDIR"};
opendir(NT, $windir) || die "no $windir?: $!";
foreach $name (sort readdir(NT)) { # list context, sorted
        print "$name\n"; # prints ., .., system.ini, and so on
}
closedir(NT);
```

The names include files that begin with a dot. This method is unlike globbing with `<*>`, which does not return names that begin with a dot. This method is a relic from Perl's UNIX heritage, where the standard filename expansion normally does not include any files that begin with a dot.

In the current version of Perl for Win32, and the current version of the standard distribution, `opendir` fails on UNC paths. You can work around this by mapping a drive to the UNC share before using directory handles, and then using the drive letter as the path instead of the UNC path. You can do this with the `Win32::NetResource` module extension (see the `AddConnection` function) or with the Windows NT *net use* command. For more information on modules and the Win32 extensions, see Appendix B, *Libraries and Modules.*

Exercises

Answers are in Appendix A.

1. Write a program that changes the directory to a location specified as input, and then lists the names of the files found there in alphabetical order. (Don't show a list if the directory change doesn't succeed: merely warn the user.)

2. Modify the program to include all files, not just the ones that don't begin with dot. Try to do so with both a glob and a directory handle.

13

File and Directory Manipulation

This chapter shows you how to manipulate the files themselves, not merely the data contained within. Perl uses UNIX semantics for providing access to files and directories. Some of these names will be familiar to Win32 programmers who have used the C run-time library, while others may not. Perl provides a rich set of file and directory manipulation routines, and not all of these are implemented on Win32 platforms, but we'll cover the most useful ones here.*

Removing a File

Earlier, you learned how to create a file from within Perl by opening it for output with a filehandle. Now, we'll get dangerous and learn how to remove a file (very appropriate for Chapter 13, don't you think?).

The Perl `unlink` function (named for the POSIX system call) deletes a file. This is exactly what the command prompt *del* command does. Here's how to remove a file called *fred* and then remove a file specified during program execution:

```
unlink ("fred"); # say goodbye to fred
print "what file do you want to delete? ";
chomp($name = <STDIN>);
unlink ($name);
```

The `unlink` function can take a list of names to be unlinked as well:

```
unlink ("spottedowl","meadowlark"); # kill two birds
unlink <*.bak>; # just like "del *.bak" in the command prompt
```

---

* In particular, we've omitted discussion of the `link()` and `symlink()` functions, used to create hard and symbolic links under Unix, because these functions are unimplemented in the Windows NT filesystems and thus in Perl for Win32, as well.

The glob is evaluated in a list context, creating a list of filenames that match the pattern. This list is exactly what we need to feed `unlink`.

The return value of `unlink` is the number of files successfully deleted. If only one argument exists, and it is deleted, the result is one; otherwise, the result is zero. If there are three filenames but only two could be deleted, the result is two. You can't tell which two, so if you need to figure out which deletion failed, you must do them one at a time. Here's how to delete all of the backup files (ending in *.bak*) while reporting an error for any file that cannot be deleted:

```
foreach $file (<*.bak>) { # step through a list of .bak files
        unlink($file) || warn "having trouble deleting $file: $!";
}
```

If `unlink` returns one (meaning the one file specified was indeed deleted), the true result skips the `warn` function. If the filename cannot be deleted, the zero result is false, so the `warn` is executed. Once again, this can be read abstractly as "unlink this file or tell me about it."

If the `unlink` function is given no arguments, the `$_` variable is once again used as a default. Thus, we could have written the preceding loop as:

```
foreach (<*.bak>) { # step through a list of .bak files
        unlink || warn "having trouble deleting $_\: $!";
}
```

Renaming a File

In the command shell, you change the name of a file with the *rename* command. And so it is with Perl, too, where this operation is denoted with `rename($old, $new)`. Here's how to change the file named `fred` into `barney`:

```
rename("fred","barney") || die "Can't rename fred to barney: $!";
```

Like most other functions, the `rename` function returns a true value if successful, so test this result to see whether the `rename` has indeed worked.

The `rename` function is perhaps more like the command-prompt *move* command than the command-prompt *rename* command. Perl's `rename` can move a file into a different directory, as can *move*.

The *move* command performs a little behind-the-scenes magic to create a full pathname when you say *move file some-directory*. However, the `rename` function cannot. The equivalent Perl operation is:

```
rename("file","some-directory/file");
```

Note that in Perl we had to say the name of the file within the new directory explicitly. If you try to rename a file to a filename that already exists, `rename` will overwrite the existing file; this result is different than that of the Windows NT *rename* command, which will fail if the file already exists.

Making and Removing Directories

You probably couldn't have made it this far without knowing about the *mkdir* or *md* command, which makes directories that hold other filenames and other directories. Perl's equivalent is the `mkdir` function, which takes a name for a new directory and a mode that will affect the permissions of the created directory. The mode is specified as a number interpreted in internal permissions format. For now, just say `0777` for the mode and everything will work. Here's an example of how to create a directory named `gravelpit`:

```
mkdir("gravelpit",0777) || die "cannot mkdir gravelpit: $!";
```

The command-prompt *rmdir* command removes empty directories—you'll find a Perl equivalent with the same name (*rmdir*). Here's how to make Fred unemployed:

```
rmdir("gravelpit") || die "cannot rmdir gravelpit"; $!
```

Modifying Permissions

The permissions on a file or directory define who (in broad categories) can do what (more or less) to that file or directory. Under UNIX, the typical way to change permissions on a file is with the *chmod* command. As a Windows user, you may be more used to the *attrib* command. Perl changes permissions with the `chmod` function. This operator takes an octal numeric mode and a list of filenames, and attempts to alter the permissions of all the filenames to the indicated mode. To make the files *fred* and *barney* with both read/write attributes, for example, do something like this:

```
chmod(0666,"fred","barney");
```

In short, the UNIX (and Perl) concept of file permissions consists of a bit for read, write, and execute rights for the user, the user's group, and everyone else. These bits are combined to create the mode. Because Win32 systems have a significantly different concept of permissions, you don't need to worry about all of the different possible values for the mode. Table 13-1 presents a couple of key values.

Table 13-1. Key Values for File Permissions

Mode	Meaning
0666	Read/Write
0444	Read only

Win32 systems determine whether or not a file is executable based on the file extension, so we're not going to worry about the execute bits. Furthermore, even though some Windows NT filesystems support advanced user/group rights, the current Perl implementation doesn't support access to these rights via chmod.

The return value of chmod is the number of files successfully adjusted (even if the adjustment does nothing); so chmod works like unlink, and you should treat it as such with regard to error checking. Here's how to change the permissions of *fred* and *barney* while checking the errors for each:

```
foreach $file ("fred","barney") {
        unless chmod (0666,$file) {
            warn "hmm... couldn't chmod $file.\$!";
        }
}
```

The Win32::File[*] extension module provides a way to access and set traditional DOS file attributes like the archive, system, and hidden attributes. This package consists of just two methods: GetFileAttributes and SetFileAttributes. Table 13-2 lists the attributes and their significations.

Table 13-2. DOS File Attributes and Their Significations

Attribute	Explanation
ARCHIVE	The file has been modified since it was last archived.
DIRECTORY	The file is a directory.
HIDDEN	The file is hidden (that is, it won't normally appear in directory listings).
NORMAL	The file is a normal (read/write) file.
READONLY	The file is read-only.
SYSTEM	The file is a system file (among other things, it can't be deleted without first changing the attributes).

To combine attributes, use the bitwise or operator |. Here's an example of how to make a file read-only, without changing its other attributes:

```
use Win32::File;
Win32::File::GetAttributes("foo.txt", $attrib) || die $!;
Win32::File::SetAttributes("foo.txt", $attrib | READONLY) ||
        die $!;
```

Although we won't get to references until Chapter 18, *CGI Programming*, the $attrib is just that. For now, just know that upon returning from GetAttributes, $attrib will contain an attribute mask consisting of some combination of the values outlined above.

---

[*] See Appendix B, *Libraries and Modules*, for an explanation of the Win32 extensions.

To set user permissions on NTFS filesystems, use either the `Win32::FileSecu-rity` extension module, or the Windows NT *cacls.exe* program, which provides a command-line interface to file permissions.

Modifying Timestamps

Associated with each file is a set of three timestamps. These timestamps were discussed briefly when we talked about getting information about a file: the last access time, the last modification time, and the last change time. The first two timestamps can be set to arbitrary values by the `utime` function (which corresponds directly to the same-named C library call). Setting these two values automatically sets the third value to the current time, so there's no point in having a way to set the third value.

The values are measured in internal time, namely an integer number of seconds past midnight GMT, January 1, 1970—a figure that had reached eight-hundred-million-something when this book was being written. (Internally, it's represented as a 32-bit unsigned number, and if we haven't all upgraded to 64-bit machines (or beyond), will overflow sometime well into the next century. We have much more to worry about in the year 2000*).

The `utime` function works like `chmod` and `unlink`. It takes a list of filenames and returns the number of files affected. Here's how to make the *fred* and *barney* files look as though they were modified sometime in the recent past:

```
$atime = $mtime = 700_000_000; # a while ago
utime($atime,$mtime,"fred","barney")
```

No "reasonableness" value exists for the timestamps; you can make a file look arbitrarily old or as though it were modified at some time in the distant future (useful if you are writing science fiction stories). For example, using the `time` function (which returns the current time as a timestamp), here's how to make the file *max_headroom* look like it was updated 20 minutes into the future:

```
$when = time()+ 20*60; # 20 minutes from now
utime($when,$when,"max_headroom");
```

---

* Perl's `localtime` and `gmtime` functions work just like C's do: they return the year with 1,900 subtracted. In 2003, `localtime` will give the year as 103.

Exercises

See Appendix A for answers.

1. Write a program that works like *del*, deleting the files given as command-line arguments when the program is invoked. (You don't need to handle any options of *del*.)

   Be careful to test this program in a mostly empty directory so that you don't accidentally delete useful stuff! Remember that the command-line arguments are available in the @ARGV array when the program starts.

2. Write a program that works like *rename*, renaming the first command-line argument to the second command-line argument. (You don't need to handle any options of *rename*, or more than two arguments.) You may wish to consider how to handle the rename when the destination is a directory.

14

Process Management

Using system and exec

Like the command shell, a Perl program can launch new processes, and like most other operations, has more than one way to do so.

The simplest way to launch a new process is to use the `system` function. In its simplest form, this function hands a single string to a brand new command shell to be executed as a command. When the command is finished, the `system` function returns the exit value of the command (typically `0` if everything went OK). Here's an example of a Perl program executing a *dir* command using a shell:

```
system("dir");
```

We're ignoring the return value here, but the *dir* command is not likely to fail anyway.

Where does the command's output go? In fact, where does the input come from, if it was a command that wanted input? These are good questions, and the answers to these questions are most of what distinguishes the various forms of process creation.

For the `system` function, the three standard files (standard input, standard output, and standard error) are inherited from the Perl process. So, for the *dir* command in the previous example, the output goes wherever the `print STDOUT` output goes—probably to the invoker's command prompt. Because you are firing off another command shell, you can change the location of the standard output using the normal I/O redirections. For example, to put the output of the *directory* command into a file named *this_dir*, something like this will work just fine:

```
system("dir >this_dir") && die "cannot create this_dir";
```

This time, we not only send the output of the *dir* command into a file with a redirection to the new command shell, but also check the return status. If the return status is true (nonzero), something went wrong with the shell command, and the `die` function will do its deed. This is backwards from normal Perl operator convention—a nonzero return value from the `system` operator generally indicates that something went wrong. You can feed anything to the `system` function that you can feed to your command shell.

Here's an example of generating a *dir* command and sending the output to a filename specified by a Perl variable:

```
$where = "dir_out.".++$i; # get a new filename
system "dir >$where";
```

The double-quoted string is variable interpolated, so Perl replaces `$where` with its value.

In addition to the standard filehandles, the current directory and the environment variables are inherited by the child. These variables are typically created by the command shell *set* command and accessed or altered using the *%KEYNAME%* construct. Environment variables are used by many utilities, including the command shell itself, to alter or control the way that utility operates.

Perl gives you a way to examine and alter current environment variables through a special hash called `%ENV` (uppercase). Each key of this hash corresponds to the name of an environment variable, with the corresponding value being, well, the corresponding value. Examining this hash shows you the environment handed to Perl by the parent process—altering the array affects the environment used by Perl and by its children processes, but not that of its parents.

For example, here's a simple program that prints out all of your environment variables:

```
foreach $key (sort keys %ENV) {
        print "$key=$ENV{$key}\n";
}
```

Note that the equal sign here is not an assigment, but simply a text character that the `print` function is using to say stuff like `USERNAME=eriko` or `COMSPEC=c:\nt\system32\cmd.exe`.

Here's a program snippet that alters the value of `PATH` to make sure that the *nmake* command run by `system` is looked for only in the correct places:

```
$oldPATH = $ENV{"PATH"};               # save previous path
$ENV{"PATH"} = "c:\\msdev\\bin;c:\\winnt;c:\\winnt\\system32";
                                       # force known path
system("nmake myproj.mak >output"); # run command
$ENV{"PATH"} = $oldPATH;               # restore previous path
```

That's a lot of typing. It'd be faster just to set a local value for this hash element.

Despite its other shortcomings, the `local` operator can do one thing that `my` cannot: it can give just one element of an array or a hash a temporary value. For example:

```
{
    local $ENV{"PATH"} =
    "c:\\msdev\\bin;c:\\winnt;c:\\winnt\\system32";
    system("nmake fred bedrock >output");
}
```

The `system` function can also take a list of arguments rather than a single argument. In this case, rather than handing the list of arguments off to a command shell, Perl treats the first argument as the command to run (located according to the `PATH` if necessary) and the remaining arguments as arguments to the command *without* normal shell interpretation. In other words, you don't need to quote whitespace or worry about arguments that contain angle brackets because those are all merely characters to hand to the program. So, the following two commands are equivalent:

```
system "nmake 'fred flintstone.mak' buffaloes";   # using command shell
system "nmake","fred flintstone.mak","buffaloes"; # using list
```

Giving `system` a list rather than giving it a simple string saves one command shell process as well, so do this when you can. (In fact, when the one-argument form of `system` is simple enough, Perl itself optimizes away the shell invocation entirely, calling the resulting program directly as if you had used the multiple-argument invocation.)

Here's another example of equivalent forms:

```
@cfiles = ("fred.c","barney.c");           # what to compile
@options = ("-DHARD","-DGRANITE");         # options
system "cc -o slate @options @cfiles";     # using shell
system "cc","-o","slate",@options,@cfiles; # avoiding shell
```

Using Backquotes

Another way to launch a process is to put a shell command line between backquotes. This fires off a command and waits for its completion, capturing the standard output as it goes along:

```
@files = `dir`; # gets dir output
```

The value of `@files` is the text from the *dir* command, so it might look something like:

```
Volume in drive D has no label.
Volume Serial Number is 9C5D-713A
```

```
 Directory of D:\ora\eg
05/19/97  11:54p        <DIR>          .
05/19/97  11:54p        <DIR>          ..
04/12/97  11:12a                    23 bell.pl
04/12/97  10:56a                    73 console.pl
```

The standard input and standard error of the command within backquotes are inherited from the Perl process.* In other words, the value of the backquoted string is normally just the standard output of the commands within the backquotes.

Using Processes as Filehandles

Yet another way to launch a process is to create a process that looks like a file-handle (similar to the **popen** C library routine, if you're familiar with that). We can create a process filehandle that either captures the output from or provides input to the process.† Here's an example of creating a filehandle out of a *netstat* process. Because the process is generating output that we want to read, we make a filehandle that is open for reading, like so:

```
open(NETPROC, "netstat|"); # open netstat for reading
```

Note the vertical bar on the right side of **netstat**. That bar tells Perl that this **open** is not about a filename, but rather, is about a command to be started. Because the bar is on the right of the command, the filehandle is opened for reading, and the standard output of *netstat* is going to be captured. (The standard input and standard error remain shared with the Perl process.) To the rest of the program, the **NETPROC** handle is merely a filehandle that is open for reading, and all normal file I/O operators apply. Here's a way to read data from the *netstat* command into an array:

```
@netstat = <NETPROC>;
```

Similarly, to open a command that expects input, we can open a process file-handle for writing by putting the vertical bar on the left of the command, like so:

```
open(FIND,"|find $pattern");
print FIND @filedata;
close(FIND);
```

In this case, after opening **FIND**, we wrote some data to it and then closed it. Opening a process with a process filehandle allows the command to execute in parallel with the Perl program. Saying **close** on the filehandle forces the Perl program to wait until the process exits. If you don't close the filehandle, the process can continue to run even beyond the execution of the Perl program.

---

* Actually, the situation is a bit more complicated. See the question in Section 8 of the Perl FAQ on "How can I capture STDERR from an external command?"

† But not both at once. See Chapter 6 of *Programming Perl* for examples of bidirectional communication.

You don't have to open just one command at a time. You can open an entire pipeline. For example, the following line starts up a *dir* process, which pipes its output into a *sort* process, which finally sends its output along to the DIRPR filehandle:

```
open(DIRPR, "dir | sort |");
```

The **exit** function causes an immediate exit from the current Perl process. You'd use this to abort a Perl program from somewhere in the middle. The **exit** function takes an optional parameter, which serves as the numeric exit value that can be noticed by the parent process. The default is to exit with a zero value, indicating that everything went OK.

Summary of Process Operations

Table 14-1 summarizes the operations that you have for launching a process.

Table 14-1. Summary of Subprocess Operations

Operation	Standard Input	Standard Output	Standard Error	Waited for?
system()	Inherited from program	Inherited from program	Inherited from program	Yes
Backquoted string	Inherited from program	Captured as string value	Inherited from program	Yes
open() command as filehandle for output	Connected to filehandle	Inherited from program	Inherited from program	Only at time of close()
open() command as filehandle for input	Inherited from program	Connected to filehandle	Inherited from program	Only at time of close()
fork, exec, wait, waitpid	Not implemented	Not implemented	Not implemented	Not implemented

The simplest way to create a process is with the **system** function. Standard input, output, and error are unaffected (they're inherited from the Perl process). A backquoted string creates a process, capturing the standard output of the process as a string value for the Perl program. Standard input and standard error are unaffected. Both methods require that the process finish before any more code is executed.

A simple way to get an asynchronous process (one that allows the Perl program to continue before the process is complete) is to open a command as a filehandle, creating a pipe for the command's standard input or standard output. A command opened as a filehandle for reading inherits the standard input and standard error from the Perl program; a command opened as a filehandle for writing inherits the standard output and standard error from the Perl program.

Win32::Process

The most flexible way of starting a process on Windows NT is to use the `Win32::Process` module.* Using this module, you can select whether or not you want to wait for the child process to run to completion, configure priorities, and suspend or resume processes.

Even though we haven't covered all of the relevant concepts, we are going to run through a `Win32::Process` example.

As shown, the `Win32::Process` module contains a method (subroutine) called `Create` that does all the work of creating a process:

```
use Win32::Process;
Win32::Process::Create($Process,
        "c:\\nt\\system32\\notepad.exe",
        "notepad",
        0,
        DETACHED_PROCESS,
        ".") || die "Create: $!";
```

This code creates an asynchronous instance of *Notepad*. Let's take a look at the parameters. The first parameter `$Process` is a scalar reference that receives the process object if the call succeeds. We'll discuss references in Chapter 18, *CGI Programming*, but for now, you can just think of it as a parameter that receives output.

The second argument is a fully qualified (system-dependent) path to the executable. The third argument is the command line passed to the program. In this case, we're just invoking *Notepad* without any documents or options. The next argument specifies whether or not the new process inherits handles from the parent process (the Perl program). A value of one indicates that the process inherits any inheritable open handle in the parent process. Inheritable handles include I/O handles, socket handles, synchronization handles, and so on. Unless you really know what you're doing here, you're better off specifying this value as zero.

The next argument specifies various create options for the new process. The flag that we've passed is `DETACHED_PROCESS`, which indicates that the new process does not have access to the console of the calling process (our Perl program).

---

* Of course, this method won't work at all on non-Windows platforms.

Other flags that you may be interested in include CREATE_SUSPENDED, which creates a process that is initially suspended, and CREATE_SEPARATE_WOW_VDM, which runs a 16-bit process in its own Virtual DOS Machine (VDM). For more information on the various options, see the *win32mod* documentation for Win32::Process.

Exercises

1. Write a program that takes two directory arguments and then uses the *xcopy* command to copy the first directory (and all related subdirectories) to the second directory.

2. Write a program that uses the Windows NT *net view* command to list all hosts in your domain or workgroup, in sorted order.

In this chapter:
- *Finding a Substring*
- *Extracting and Replacing a Substring*
- *Formatting Data with sprintf( )*
- *Advanced Sorting*
- *Transliteration*
- *Exercises*

15

Other Data Transformation

Finding a Substring

Finding a substring depends on where you have lost it. If you happen to have lost it within a bigger string, you're in luck, because **index** can help you out. Here's how **index** looks:

```
$x = index($string,$substring);
```

Perl locates the first occurrence of *substring* within *string*, returning an integer location of the first character. The index value returned is zero-based; if the *substring* is found at the beginning of the *string*, you get a zero. If it's one character later, you get a one, and so on. If the *substring* can't be found in *string*, you get negative one.

Take a look at these:

```
$where   = index("hello","e");                      # $where gets 1
$person  = "barney";
$where   = index("fred barney",$person);            # $where gets 5
@rockers = ("fred","barney");
$where   = index(join(" ",@rockers),$person);       # same thing
```

Notice that both the string being searched and the string being searched for can each be a literal string, a scalar variable containing a string, or even an expression that has a string value. Here are some more examples:

```
$which = index("a very long string","long"); # $which gets 7
$which = index("a very long string","lame"); # $which gets -1
```

If the string contains the substring at more than one location, the **index** function returns the leftmost location. To find later locations, you can give **index** a third parameter. This parameter is the minimum value that will be returned by **index**, allowing you to look for the next occurrence of the substring that follows a selected position. This `index` looks like this:

```
$x = index($bigstring,$littlestring,$skip);
```

Here are some examples of how this third parameter works:

```
$where = index("hello world","l");   # returns 2 (first l)
$where = index("hello world","l",0); # same thing
$where = index("hello world","l",1); # still same
$where = index("hello world","l",3); # now returns 3
# (3 is the first place greater than or equal to 3)
$where = index("hello world","o",5); # returns 7 (second o)
$where = index("hello world","o",8); # returns -1 (none after 8)
```

Going the other way, you can scan from the right to get the rightmost occurrence using `rindex`. The return value is still the number of characters between the left end of the string and the start of the substring, as before, but you'll get the rightmost occurrence instead of the leftmost occurrence if there are more than one. The `rindex` function also takes a third parameter like `index` does, so that you can get an occurrence that is less than or equal to a selected position. Here are some examples of what you get:

```
$w = rindex("hello world","he");  # $w gets 0
$w = rindex("hello world","l");   # $w gets 9 (rightmost l)
$w = rindex("hello world","o");   # $w gets 7
$w = rindex("hello world","o ");  # now $w gets 4
$w = rindex("hello world","xx");  # $w gets -1 (not found)
$w = rindex("hello world","o",6); # $w gets 4 (first before 6)
$w = rindex("hello world","o",3); # $w gets -1 (not found before 3)
```

Extracting and Replacing a Substring

Pulling out a piece of a string can be done with careful application of regular expressions, but if the piece is always at a known character position, this method is inefficient. Instead, you should use `substr`. This function takes three arguments: a string value, a start position (measured as with `index`), and a length, like so:

```
$s = substr($string,$start,$length);
```

The start position works like `index`: the first character is zero, the second character is one, and so on. The length is the number of characters to grab at that point: a length of zero means no characters, one means get the first character, two means two characters, and so on. (`substr` stops at the end of the string, so if you ask for too many characters, don't worry.) `substr` looks like this:

```
$hello = "hello, world!";
$grab  = substr($hello, 3, 2);   # $grab gets "lo"
$grab  = substr($hello, 7, 100); # 7 to end, or "world!"
```

You could even create a "10 to the power of" operator for small integer powers, as in:

```
$big = substr("10000000000",0,$power+1); # 10**$power
```

If the count of characters is zero, an empty string is returned. If either the starting position or ending position is less than zero, the position is counted that many characters from the end of the string. So −1 for a start position and 1 (or more) for the length gives you the last character. Similarly, −2 for a start position starts with the second-to-last character. The following example illustrates the point:

```
$stuff = substr("a very long string",-3,3); # last three chars
$stuff = substr("a very long string",-3,1); # the letter "i"
```

If the starting position is before the beginning of the string (like a huge negative number bigger than the length of the string), the beginning of the string is the start position (as if you had used zero for a starting position). If the start position is a huge positive number, the empty string is always returned. In other words, `substr` probably does what you expect it to do, as long as you expect it to always return something other than an error.

Omitting the length argument provides the same result as including a huge number for that argument—grabbing everything from the selected position to the end of the string.*

If the first argument to `substr` is a scalar variable (in other words, it could appear on the left side of an assignment operator), then the `substr` itself could appear on the left side of an assignment operator. This case may look strange if you come from a C background, but if you've ever played with some dialects of BASIC, it's quite normal.

What gets changed as the result of such an assignment is the part of the string that would have been returned had the `substr` been used on the right-hand side of the expression instead. In other words, `substr($var,3,2)` returns the fourth and fifth characters (starting at 3, for a count of 2), so assigning a value to `substr($var,3,2)` changes those two characters as shown:

```
$hw = "hello world!";
substr($hw, 0, 5) = "howdy"; # $hw is now "howdy world!"
```

The length of the replacement text (what gets assigned into the `substr`) doesn't have to be the same as the text it is replacing, as shown in this example. The

---

* Very old Perl versions did not allow the third argument to be omitted, leading to the use of a huge number for that argument by pioneer Perl programmers. You may come across such cases in your Perl archeological expeditions.

string will automatically grow or shrink as necessary to accommodate the text. Here's an example in which the string gets shorter:

```
substr($hw, 0, 5) = "hi"; # $hw is now "hi world!"
```

and here's an example that makes the string longer:

```
substr($hw, -6, 5) = "nationwide news"; # replaces "world"
```

The shrinking and growing are fairly efficient, so don't worry about using them arbitrarily, although replacing a string with a string of equal length is a faster solution.

Formatting Data with sprintf( )

The `printf` function is sometimes handy when used to take a list of values and produce an output line that displays the values in controllable ways. The `sprintf` function is identical to `printf` for its arguments, but returns whatever would have been output by `printf` as a single string. (Think of it as "string `printf`.") For example, to create a string consisting of the letter X followed by a five-digit zero-padded value of $y, simply use this:

```
$result = sprintf("X%05d",$y);
```

See Chapter 6, *Basic I/O*, or Chapter 3 of *Programming Perl* for a description of the format strings understood by `printf` and `sprintf`.

Advanced Sorting

Earlier, you learned that you could take a list and sort it in ascending ASCII order (as you do with strings) using the built-in `sort` function. What if you don't want an ascending ASCII sort, but something else instead, like a numeric sort? Well, Perl gives you the tools you need to do the job. In fact, you'll see that the Perl `sort` is completely general and able to perform any well-defined sort order.

To define a sort of a different color, you need to define a comparison routine that describes how two elements compare. Why is this necessary? Well, if you think about it, sorting is putting a bunch of things in order by comparing them all. Because you can't compare them all at once, you need to compare two at a time, eventually using what you find out about each pair's order to put the whole kit'n'caboodle in line.

The comparison routine is defined as an ordinary subroutine. This routine will be called repeatedly, each time passing two elements of the list to be sorted. The routine must determine whether the first value is less-than, equal-to, or greater-than the second value, and return a coded value (described in a moment). This process is repeated until the list is sorted.

To save a little execution speed, the two values are not passed in an array, but rather are handed to the subroutine as the values of the global variables $a and $b. (Don't worry: the original values of $a and $b are safely protected.) The routine should return any negative number if $a is less than $b, 0 if $a is equal to $b, and any positive number if $a is greater than $b. Now remember, the less-than sign is defined by you; it could be a numeric comparison, according to the third character of the string, or even according to the values of a hash using the passed-in values as keys. It's really pretty flexible.

Here's an example of a sort subroutine that sorts in numeric order:

```
sub by_number {
        if ($a < $b) {
            return -1;
        } elsif ($a == $b) {
            return 0;
        } elsif ($a > $b) {
            return 1;
        }
    }
```

Notice the name **by_number**. There's nothing special about the name of this subroutine, but you'll see why we like names that start with **by_** in a minute.

Let's look through this routine. If the value of $a is less than (numerically in this case) the value of $b, we return a -1 value. If the values are numerically equal, we get back a 0, and otherwise a 1. So, according to our specification for a sort comparison routine, this method should work.

How do we use it? Let's try sorting the following list:

```
@somelist = (1,2,4,8,16,32,64,128,256);
```

If we use the ordinary **sort** without any adornment on the list, we get the numbers sorted as if they were strings, and in their ASCII order, like so:

```
@wronglist = sort @somelist;
# @wronglist is now (1,128,16,2,256,32,4,64,8)
```

This **sort** is certainly not very numeric. Well, let's give **sort** our newly defined sort routine. The name of the sort routine immediately follows the **sort** keyword, like so:

```
@rightlist = sort by_number @wronglist;
# @rightlist is now (1,2,4,8,16,32,64,128,256)
```

This **sort** does the trick. Note that you can read the **sort** with its companion sort routine in a human-like fashion: "sort by number." This feature is why we named the subroutine with a **by_** prefix.

This kind of three-way value of -1, 0, and +1 on the basis of a numeric comparison occurs often enough in sort routines that Perl has a special operator to do this in one fell swoop. The operation is often called the *spaceship* operator, and looks like <=>. Using the spaceship operator, the preceding sort subroutine can be replaced with this:

```
sub by_number {
        $a <=> $b;
}
```

Note the spaceship between the two variables. Yes, it is indeed a three-character-long operator. The spaceship returns the same values as the if/elsif chain from the previous definition of this routine. Now this is pretty short, but you can reduce the sort invocation even further, by replacing the name of the sort routine with the entire sort routine in line, like so:

```
@rightlist = sort { $a <=> $b } @wronglist;
```

There are some who argue that this shortcut decreases readability. They are wrong. Others argue that it removes the need to go somewhere else for the definition. Perl doesn't care. Our personal rule is that if it doesn't fit on one line or we have to use it more than once, it goes into a subroutine.

The spaceship operator for numeric comparison has a comparable string operator called cmp. The cmp operator returns one of three values depending on the relative string comparisons of the two arguments. So, another way to write the default sort order* is:

```
@result = sort { $a cmp $b } @somelist;
```

You probably won't ever write this exact subroutine (mimicking the built-in default sort), unless you're writing a book about Perl. However, the cmp operator does have its uses in the construction of cascaded ordering schemes. For example, you might need to put the elements in numeric order unless they're numerically equal, in which case they should go in ASCII string order. (By default, the by_number routine above just sticks nonnumeric strings in some random order because there's no numeric ordering when comparing two values of zero.) Here's a way to say "numeric, unless they're numerically equal, then string":

```
sub by_mostly_numeric {
        ($a <=> $b) || ($a cmp $b);
}
```

How does this work? Well, if the result of the spaceship is -1 or 1, the rest of the expression is skipped, and the -1 or 1 is returned. If the spaceship evaluates to zero, however, the cmp operator gets its turn at bat, returning an appropriate ordering value considering the values as strings.

---

* This statement is not exactly true. The built-in sort discards undef elements, but this one doesn't.

The values being compared are not necessarily the values being passed in. For example, say you have a hash where the keys are the login names and the values are the real names of each user. Suppose you want to print a chart where the login names and real names are sorted in the order of the real names. How would you do that?

Actually, the solution is fairly easy. Let's assume the values are in the array %names. The login names are thus the list of keys(%names). What we want to end up with is a list of the login names sorted by the corresponding value, so for any particular key $a, we need to look at $names{$a} and sort based on that. If you think of the sort that way, it almost writes itself, as in:

```
@sortedkeys = sort by_names keys(%names);

sub by_names {
        return $names{$a} cmp $names{$b};
}

foreach (@sortedkeys) {
        print "$_ has a real name of $names{$_}\n";
}
```

To this we should also add a fallback comparison. Suppose the real names of two users are identical. Because of the whimsical nature of the sort routine, we might get one value ahead of another the first time through and the values in the reversed order the next time. This difference is bad if the report might be fed into a comparison program for reporting, so try very hard to avoid such things. With the cmp operator, you can avoid this case like this:

```
sub by_names {
        ($names{$a} cmp $names{$b}) || ($a cmp $b);
}
```

Here, if the real names are the same, we sort based on the login name instead. Because the login name is guaranteed to be unique (after all, login names are the keys of this hash, and no two keys are the same), then we can ensure a unique and repeatable order. Good defensive programming during the day is better than a late-night call from a system administrator wondering why the security alarms are going off.

Transliteration

When you want to take a string and replace every instance of some character with some new character, or delete every instance of some character, you can do so with carefully selected s/// commands. But suppose you had to change all of the a's into b's, and all of the b's into a's? You can't do that with two s///

commands because the second one would undo all of the changes that the first one made.

Perl provides a `tr` operator that does the trick:

```
tr/ab/ba/;
```

The `tr` operator takes two arguments: an *old string* and a *new string*. These arguments work like the two arguments to `s///`; in other words, there's some delimiter that appears immediately after the `tr` keyword that separates and terminates the two arguments (in this case, a slash, but nearly any character will do).

The `tr` operator modifies the contents of the `$_` variable (just like `s///`), looking for characters of the old string within the `$_` variable. All such characters found are replaced with the corresponding characters in the new string. Here are some examples:

```
$_ = "fred and barney";
tr/fb/bf/;         # $_ is now "bred and farney"
tr/abcde/ABCDE/;   # $_ is now "BrED AnD fArnEy"
tr/a-z/A-Z/;       # $_ is now "BRED AND FARNEY"
```

Notice how a range of characters can be indicated by two characters separated by a dash. If you need a literal dash in either string, precede it with a backslash.

If the new string is shorter than the old string, the last character of the new string is repeated enough times to make the strings equal length, like so:

```
$_ = "fred and barney";
tr/a-z/x/; # $_ is now "xxxx xxx xxxxxx"
```

To prevent this behavior, append a `d` to the end of the `tr///` operator, which means *delete*. In this case, the last character is not replicated. Any character that matches in the old string without a corresponding character in the new string is simply removed from the string. For example:

```
$_ = "fred and barney";
tr/a-z/ABCDE/d; # $_ is now "ED AD BAE"
```

Notice how any letter after `e` disappears because there's no corresponding letter in the new list, and that spaces are unaffected because they don't appear in the old list. This processing is similar in operation to the `-d` option of the *tr* command.

If the new list is empty and there's no d option, the new list is the same as the old list. This default may seem silly. Why replace an I for an I and a 2 for a 2? But the command actually does something useful. The return value of the `tr///` operator is the number of characters matched by the old string, and by changing characters into themselves, you can get the count of that kind of character within the string.* For example:

```
$_ = "fred and barney";
$count = tr/a-z//;       # $_ unchanged, but $count is 13
$count2 = tr/a-z/A-Z/;   # $_ is uppercased, and $count2 is 13
```

If you append a c (like appending the d), you complement the old string with respect to all 256 characters. Any character you list in the old string is removed from the set of all possible characters; the remaining characters, taken in sequence from lowest to highest, form the resulting old string. So, a way to count or change the nonletters in our string could be:

```
$_ = "fred and barney";
$count = tr/a-z//c; # $_ unchanged, but $count is 2
tr/a-z/_/c;         # $_ is now "fred_and_barney" (non-letters => _)
tr/a-z//cd;         # $_ is now "fredandbarney" (delete non-letters)
```

Notice that the options can be combined, as shown in that last example, where we first complement the set (the list of letters become the list of all nonletters) and then use the d option to delete any character in that set.

The final option for tr/// is s, which squeezes multiple consecutive copies of the same resulting translated letter into one copy. As an example, look at this:

```
$_ = "aaabbbcccdefghi";
tr/defghi/abcddd/s; # $_ is now "aaabbbcccabcd"
```

Note that the def became abc, and ghi (which would have become ddd without the s option) becomes a single d. Also note that the consecutive letters at the first part of the string are not squeezed because they didn't result from a translation. Here are some more examples:

```
$_ = "fred and barney, wilma and betty";
tr/a-z/X/s;  # $_ is now "X X X, X X X"
$_ = "fred and barney, wilma and betty";
tr/a-z/_/cs; # $_ is now "fred_and_barney_wilma_and_betty"
```

In the first example, each word (consecutive letters) was squeezed down to a single letter X. In the second example, all chunks of consecutive nonletters became a single underscore.

Like s///, the tr operator can be targeted at another string besides $_ using the =~ operator:

```
$names = "fred and barney";
$names =~ tr/aeiou/X/; # $names now "frXd Xnd bXrnXy"
```

---

* This method works only for single characters. To count strings, use the /g flag to a pattern match:

```
while (/pattern/g) {
    $count++;
}
```

Exercises

See Appendix A for answers.

1. Write a program to read a list of filenames, breaking each name into its head and tail components. (Everything up to the last backslash is the head, and everything after the last slash is the tail. If there's no backslash, everything is in the tail.) Try this exercise with things like *fred*, *barney*, and *fred**barney*. Do the results make sense?

2. Write a program to read in a list of numbers on separate lines, and then sort them numerically, printing out the resulting list in a right-justified column. (Hint: the format to print a right-justified column is something like "%20g".)

3. Create a file that consists of sentences, one per line. Write a program that makes the first character of each sentence uppercase, and the rest of the sentence lowercase. (Does the program work even when the first character is not a letter? How would you alter the program if the sentences were not already one per line?)

In this chapter:
- *Getting User and Machine Information*
- *Packing and Unpacking Binary Data*
- *Getting Network Information*
- *The Registry*
- *Opening and Reading Registry Values*
- *Setting Registry Values*
- *Exercises*

16

System Information

Getting User and Machine Information

Perl provides several facilities for finding out information about the user and machine that you are running on. These functions are provided via Win32 extensions (see Appendix B, *Libraries and Modules*, for more information).

To retrieve the name of the user executing the script, use the `Win32::Login-Name` function:

```
use Win32;
$name = Win32::LoginName;
```

To retrieve the name of the machine executing the script, use the `Win32::Node-Name` function:

```
use Win32;
$machine = Win32::NodeName;
```

The `Win32::NetAdmin` module provides extensive functionality for administering users and groups. Here's an simple example of how you might use it to retrieve the current user's home directory:

```
use Win32::NetAdmin;
$user = Win32::LoginName; # grab the name of the current user
Win32::NetAdmin::UserGetAttributes("",
     $username, $password, $passwordage,
     $privilege, $homedir, $comment,
     $flags, $scriptpath);
print "The homedir for $username is $homedir\n";
```

For more information on using `Win32::NetAdmin`, explore the *win32mod* documentation.

As you explore Perl scripts on the Net, you'll no doubt find scripts that refer to any of a myriad of Perl functions that access UNIX password and group files. At the time of this writing, these functions are not implemented in Perl on Win32 platforms, but you can usually duplicate the functionality (if it's applicable) using one of the Win32 extension modules.

Packing and Unpacking Binary Data

While most of the user information is nicely represented in textual form, other system information is more naturally represented in other forms. For example, the IP address of an interface is internally managed as a four-byte number. While it is frequently decoded into a textual representation consisting of four small integers separated by periods, this encoding and decoding is wasted effort if a human is not interpreting the data in the meantime.

As a result, the network routines in Perl that expect or return an IP address use a four-byte string that contains one character for each sequential byte in memory. While constructing and interpreting such a byte-string is fairly straightforward using `chr` and `ord` (not presented here), Perl provides a short cut that is equally applicable to more difficult structures.

The `pack` function works a bit like `sprintf`, taking a format control string and a list of values, and creating a single string from those values. The `pack` format string is geared towards creating a binary data structure, however. For example, to take four small integers and pack them as successive unsigned bytes in a composite string, use the following format:

```
$buf = pack("CCCC", 140, 186, 65, 25);
```

Here, the `pack` format string is four C's. Each C represents a separate value taken from the following list (similar to what a `%` field does in `sprintf`). The C format (according to the Perl manpages, the reference card, *Programming Perl*, the HTML files, or even *Perl: The Motion Picture*) refers to a single byte computed from an unsigned character value (a small integer). The resulting string in `$buf` is a four-character string—each character being one byte from the four values 140, 186, 65, and 25.

Similarly, the format 1 generates a signed long value. On many machines, this is a four-byte number, although this format is machine-dependent. On a four-byte *long* machine, the statement:

```
$buf = pack("l",0x41424344);
```

generates a four-character string that looks like either **ABCD** or **DCBA**, depending on whether the machine is little-endian or big-endian. These results occur because we are packing one value into four characters (the length of a long integer), and the one value just happens to be composed of the bytes representing the ASCII values for the first four letters of the alphabet. Similarly:

```
$buf = pack("ll", 0x41424344, 0x45464748);
```

creates an eight-byte string consisting of **ABCDEFGH** or **DCBAHGFE**, once again depending on whether the machine is little- or big-endian.

The exact list of the various pack formats is given in the reference documentation (*perlfunc*, or *Programming Perl*). You'll see a few here as examples, but we're not going to list them all.

What if you were given the eight-byte string **ABCDEFGH** and were told that it was really the memory image (one character is one byte) of two long (four-byte) signed values? How would you interpret it? Well, you'd need to do the inverse of **pack**, called **unpack**. This function takes a format control string (usually identical to the one you'd give **pack**) and a data string, and returns a list of values that make up the memory image defined in the data string. For example, let's take that string apart:

```
($val1,$val2) = unpack("ll","ABCDEFGH");
```

This statement gives us back something like `0x41424344` for `$val1`, or possibly `0x44434241` instead (depending on big-endian-ness). In fact, by the values that come back, we can determine if we are on a little- or big-endian machine.

Whitespace in the format control string is ignored, and can be used for readability. A number in the format control string generally repeats the previous specification that many times. For example, **CCCC** can also be written **C4** or **C2C2** with no change in meaning. (A few of the specifications use a trailing number as a part of the specification, and thus cannot be multiplied in this manner.)

A format character can also be followed by a *****, which repeats the format character enough times to swallow up the rest of the list or the rest of the binary image string (depending on whether you are packing or unpacking). So, another way to pack four unsigned characters into a string is:

```
$buf = pack("C*", 140, 186, 65, 25);
```

The four values here are swallowed up by the one format specification. If you had wanted two short integers followed by "as many unsigned chars as possible," you could say something like:

```
$buf = pack("s2 C*", 3141, 5926, 5, 3, 5, 8, 9, 7, 9, 3, 2);
```

Here, we take the first two values as shorts (generating four or eight characters, probably) and the remaining nine values as unsigned characters (generating nine characters, almost certainly).

Going in the other direction, **unpack** with an asterisk specification can generate a list of elements of unpredetermined length. For example, unpacking with **C*** creates one list element (a number) for each string character. Therefore, this statement:

```
@values = unpack("C*", "hello, world!\n");
```

yields a list of 14 elements, one for each of the characters of the string.

Getting Network Information

Perl supports network programming in a way that is very familiar to those who have written network code in C programs. In fact, most of the Perl functions that provide network access have the same names and similar parameters as their C counterparts. We can't teach a complete course on network programming in this chapter, but let's take a look at one of the task fragments to see how it's done in Perl.

One of the things you need to find out is the network address that goes with a network name, or vice versa. In C, you use the **gethostbyname** routine to convert a network name to a network address. You then use this address to create a connection from your program to another program somewhere else.

The Perl function to translate a host name to an address has the same name and similar parameters as the C routine, and looks like this:

```
($name, $aliases, $addrtype, $length, @addrs) =
    gethostbyname($name); # generic form of gethostbyname
```

The parameter to this function is a hostname—for example, *slate.bedrock.com*. The return value is a list of four or more parameters, depending on how many addresses are associated with the name. If the hostname is not valid, the function returns an empty list.

If **gethostbyname** is called in a scalar context, only the (first) address is returned.

When **gethostbyname()** completes successfully, **$name** is the *canonical name*, which differs from the input name if the input name is an alias. **$aliases** is a list of space-separated names by which the host is also known. **$addrtype** gives a coded value to indicate the form of the addresses. In this case, for *slate.bedrock.com*, we can presume that the value indicates an IP address, usually represented as four numbers under 256, separated by dots. **$length** gives the number of addresses, which is actually redundant information because you can look at the length of **@addrs** anyway.

But the useful part of the return value is **@addrs**. Each element of the list is a separate IP address, stored in an internal format, handled in Perl as a four-character string.* While this four-character string is exactly what other Perl networking functions are looking for, suppose we wanted to print out the result for the user to see. In this case, we need to convert the return value into a human-readable format with the assistance of the **unpack** function and a little additional massaging. Here's some code that prints one of *slate.bedrock.com*'s IP addresses:

```
($addr) = (gethostbyname("slate.bedrock.com"))[4];
print "Slate's address is ",
      join(".",unpack("C4", $addr)), "\n";
```

The **unpack** takes the four-byte string and returns four numbers. This just happens to be in the right order for the **join** to glue in a dot between each pair of numbers to make the human-readable form. See Appendix C, *Networking Clients*, for information about building simple networking clients.

The Registry

The Windows NT Registry is a database that stores all sorts of information about your system. It includes operating system and hardware information, file extension associations, environment information, application information, and much more. In addition to being used heavily by the operating system, most Win32 applications keep registration and state information in the Registry. If you've never taken a look at it before, you really ought to run the *regedit.exe* (or *regedt32.exe*) utility included with your system and take a look at what the Registry contains. For a detailed programmer's reference to the Windows 95 Registry, you might try Ron Petrusha's *Inside the Windows 95 Registry*, published by O'Reilly & Associates.

Many operating system and application behaviors are controlled by Registry data; therefore, one of the most valuable tools an administrator can have at his disposal is an efficient way to update Registry data. Enter Perl's **Win32::Registry** package, which provides a powerful interface to the Registry. This package lets you retrieve information from the Registry, as well as add new information and modify or delete existing information.

A strong word of caution is in order before we begin. The Registry contains vital system data and you could render your system inoperable by deleting or changing Registry information. Before modifying the Registry, make certain that

---

* Well, at least until IPv6.

you have a good backup of your entire Registry. The exercises in this chapter will only read data or write to harmless areas of the Registry, but taking precautions is still a good idea. To make a backup, use the *regedit* utility included with your system.

The Registry Structure

The Registry is organized into four main subtrees of keys that contain machine and user data. Each subtree is organized into clusters of keys called hives (by analogy to the cellular structure of beehives). A hive is a collection of keys, subkeys, and values that is rooted at the subtree. For example, one of the Registry subtrees, as shown in Figure 16-1, is `HKEY_LOCAL_MACHINE`, which contains information about the local machine and the software installed on it. The hives under `HKEY_LOCAL_MACHINE` are `HARDWARE`, `SAM`, `SECURITY`, `SOFTWARE`, and `SYSTEM`.

Each registry key can have data items called *values*, or additional child keys called *subkeys*. Some users like to think of this in terms of a filesystem: keys are similar to directories and values are similar to files.

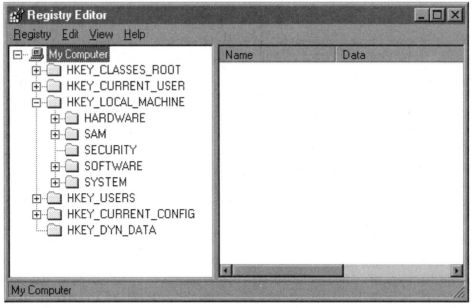

Figure 16-1. Sample Registry

Table 16-1 details the four main subtrees of the Registry, and a general description of what each one is used for.

Table 16-1. Sample Registry Subtrees

Registry Subtree	Description
HKEY_LOCAL_MACHINE	Contains information about the local computer, including information about the hardware and operating system
HKEY_CLASSES_ROOT	Contains OLE and file association information
HKEY_CURRENT_USER	Contains user profile information for the currently logged-on user including environment, desktop, and preference settings
HKEY_USERS	Contains all actively loaded user profiles (including HKEY_ CURRENT_USER) and default user profile information

The `Win32:Registry` package creates an instantiated registry key object[*] for each of these subtrees, so you can open keys relative to these trees.

The Registry can contain several different data types including strings, dwords (unsigned four-byte integers), unicode strings, expanding strings (e.g., environment variables that rely on the value of another environment variable), binary data, and more. `Win32::Registry` defines constants (in the form of subroutines) for these values. Table 16-2 gives some of the most useful constants.

Table 16-2. Win32::Registry Constants

Win32::Registry Constant	Data Type
REG_SZ	String Data
REG_DWORD	Unsigned four-byte integer
REG_MULTI_SZ	Multiple strings, delimited with NULL
REG_EXPAND_SZ	Strings that expand (e.g., based on environment variables)
REG_BINARY	Binary data (no particular format is assumed)

Opening and Reading Registry Values

Let's start our exploration of the Registry by finding out how to get information out of it. As an example, let's see what we can find out about the current build version of Windows NT on our system. If you're using this book on a Windows 95 system, you'll need to change the *Windows NT* key to *Windows*:

```
use Win32::Registry;
$p = "SOFTWARE\\Microsoft\\Windows NT\\CurrentVersion";
$main::HKEY_LOCAL_MACHINE->Open($p, $CurrVer) ||
        die "Open: $!";
$CurrVer->GetValues(\%vals); # get sub keys and value -hash ref
foreach $k (keys %vals) {
    $key = $vals{$k};
    print "$$key[0] = $$key[2]\n"; # see below for explanation
}
```

---

[*] See Chapter 18, *CGI Programming*, for a discussion of Perl objects.

Running this script on one of our systems produces the following output:

```
CurrentBuildNumber: 1381
CSDVersion = Service Pack 3
CurrentBuild = 1.511.1 () (Obsolete data - do not use)
RegisteredOrganization = Axiom Technologies
CurrentType = Uniprocessor Free
InstallDate = Ö?L3
RegisteredOwner = Erik Olson
CurrentVersion = 4.0
SystemRoot = D:\NT
CurrentBuildNumber = 1381
SoftwareType = SYSTEM
ProductId = 50036419013877247607
SourcePath = E:\I386
PathName = D:\NT
```

Let's see what's going on here. The first line of the script employs the **use** operator to include the **Win32::Registry** package. We then have a variable **$p** containing a Registry path relative to **HKEY_LOCAL_MACHINE**. The third line uses **$main::HKEY_LOCAL_MACHINE** (one of the Registry keys declared in *registry.pm* that we mentioned) to open the **CurrentVersion** key. If the **Open** method succeeds, **$CurrVer** will contain the Registry object corresponding to the **CurrentVersion** key.

Line four uses the **$CurrVer** key to call the **GetValues** method. **GetValues** takes a reference to a hash as a parameter and populates that hash with all of the values under **$CurrVer**. Each hash element consists of a key with the name of the Registry value and a value containing a reference to a three-element list. The list contains the value name, the data type of the value, and the value data. The remaining lines of the example iterate over each value using the **foreach** operator and print its value name and data value. For example:

```
foreach $k (keys %vals) {        # iterate over keys
    $key = $vals{$k};            # get ref to list
    print "$$key[0] = $$key[2]\n"; # dereference as list
}
```

We've seen how the **Open** method will open a Registry key relative to one of the main subtrees (or another key). We can also use the **Create** method to open a key, creating it if it doesn't exist. **Create** won't create more than one level deep, so we need to have a handle to the parent key before calling create. Here's an example that creates a new key under the HKEY_CURRENT_USER\SOFTWARE hive:

```
use Win32::Registry;
$main::HKEY_CURRENT_USER->Open("SOFTWARE", $Software) ||
        die "Open: $!";
$Software->Create("ERIKO", $eriko) ||
        die "Create: $!"; # new key is in $eriko
```

In order to create a key under SOFTWARE, we first need to obtain the key to SOFTWARE. We do so by using Open again, this time with the HKEY_CURRENT_ USER subtree. After we have the SOFTWARE key open, we can create keys directly beneath it.

Setting Registry Values

In addition to creating keys, we can also set Registry values. To do so, we once again need an open key and the SetValue or SetValueEx function. SetValue sets the default (unnamed) value for a key, while SetValueEx allows you to create a new named value and set its information. The following example assumes that we already have the $eriko key open:

```
$eriko->SetValue("blah", REG_SZ, "some_string");
$eriko->SetValueEx("foo", 0, REG_SZ, "bar");
```

Even though these two functions look similar, they do quite different things. The first line (SetValue) creates a new key called blah and sets its default (unnamed) value to some_string. The second line (SetValueEx) creates a new value under $eriko with a name of foo and a value of bar. In both cases, we're using the REG_SZ data type, which indicates string data.

More Registry Operations

You can do more with the Registry than just read and modify key values. You can also delete keys and export/import hives from the Registry. As we mentioned above, be extremely prudent when deleting or importing things into your registry.

Here's an example of deleting a key:

```
use Win32::Registry;
$main::HKEY_CURRENT_USER->Open("SOFTWARE", $Software) ||
    die "Open: $!";
$Software->Create("ERIKO", $eriko) ||
    die "Create: $!";    # open parent key
$eriko->DeleteKey("blah"); # delete blah
```

DeleteKey will delete a key and all of its values—it will *not* delete a key with subkeys. To do that, you need to remove all of the subkeys first. Here's how you do that:

```
use Win32::Registry;
$main::HKEY_CURRENT_USER->Open("SOFTWARE", $Software) ||
    die "Open: $!";
$Software->Create("ERIKO", $eriko) ||
    die "Create: $!";
$eriko->Open("blah", $blah); # open blah
$blah->GetKeys(\@kids);      # get all child keys
```

```
foreach $k (@kids) {          # kill all of them
    $blah->DeleteKey($k);
}
$eriko->DeleteKey("blah");    # now, remove blah
```

This code assumes that none of the child keys of **blah** have child keys themselves. If they do, you'll need to do something recursive to iterate over each subkey and all of its subkeys.

The following example saves a Registry hive to an external file using the **Save** method:

```
use Win32::Registry;
$main::HKEY_LOCAL_MACHINE->Open("SOFTWARE", $Software) ||
        die "Open: $!";
$Software->Open("ActiveState", $ActiveState) ||
        die "Open: $!";
# write ActiveState hive to perlkeys.reg
$ActiveState->Save("perlkeys.reg") ||
        die "Save: $!";
```

You can connect to the Registry of a remote machine (but only to the HKEY_LOCAL_MACHINE or HKEY_USERS hives) using the **RegConnectRegistry** function:

```
use Win32::Registry;
Win32::Registry::RegConnectRegistry("\\\\somemachine",
        HKEY_LOCAL_MACHINE, $key) || die "connect: $!";
```

Exercises

See Appendix A for the answers.

1. Write a program that takes a machine name as input and then prints a list of all of the IP addresses for that machine (skip this example if you don't have TCP/IP installed). Try your program on something like *www.microsoft.com* that has lots of IP addresses to make sure you get it right.

2. Write a program that takes as an argument a single Registry key relative to HKEY_LOCAL_MACHINE and prints all of the values under it (don't worry about recursing into child keys or about binary data for now, just print whatever you get).

3. Write a subroutine that creates all of the keys in a path if they don't exist. To make things easier, pass in the subtree to which the path is relative.

4. Using what you know about **unpack**, write a routine that will print a hexidecimal representation of a REG_DWORD value (that is, a four-byte integer value).

17

Database Manipulation

DBM Databases and DBM Hashes

Most UNIX systems have a standard library called DBM that many Win32 programmers have never heard about. This library provides a simple database management facility that allows programs to store a collection of key-value pairs into a pair of disk files. These files retain the values in the database between invocations of the programs using the database, and these programs can add new values, update existing values, or delete old values.

The DBM library is fairly simple, but being readily available, it has been used for many programs with modest database needs. For example, the famous UNIX mail program, *sendmail* (and its variants and derivatives), stores its user alias database (the mapping of mail addresses to recipients) as a DBM database. The most popular Usenet news software uses a DBM database to track current and recently seen articles. In spite of this, it is unlikely that you will have DBM files laying around on your Windows system (unless you've already created them using Perl).

Perl provides access to this same DBM mechanism through a rather clever means: a hash can be associated with a DBM database through a process similar to opening a file. This hash (called a *DBM array*) is then used to access and modify the DBM database. Creating a new element in the array modifies the DBM database immediately. Deleting an element deletes the value from the DBM database, and so on.*

---

* This case is actually just a special use of the general `tie` mechanism. If you want something more flexible, check out the *SDBM_File* and *perltie* documentation.

The size, number, and kind of keys and values in a DBM database are restricted, and depending on which version of DBM library you're using, a DBM array may share these same restrictions. Perl for Win32 includes the SDBM database routines. In general, if you keep both the keys and the values down to 1000 arbitrary binary characters or less, you'll probably be OK.

Opening and Closing DBM Hashes

To associate a DBM database with a DBM array, use the **dbmopen** function, which looks like this:

```
dbmopen(%ARRAYNAME, "dbmfilename", $mode);
```

The **%ARRAYNAME** parameter is a Perl hash. (If this hash already has values, the values are discarded.) This hash becomes connected to the DBM database called *dbmfilename*, usually stored on disk as a pair of files called *dbmfilename.dir* and *dbmfilename.pag*.

The **$mode** parameter is a number that controls the permission bits of the pair of files if the files need to be created. The number is typically specified in octal format; the frequently used value of **0666** provides read-write access to the database. If the files already exist, this parameter has no effect. For example:

```
dbmopen(%FRED, "mydatabase", 0666); # open %FRED onto mydatabase
```

This invocation associates the hash **%FRED** with the disk files *mydatabase.dir* and *mydatabase.pag* in the current directory. If the files don't already exist, they are created with read/write attributes.

The return value from **dbmopen** is true if the database could be opened or created, and false otherwise, just like an **open** invocation. If you don't want the files created, use a **$mode** value of **undef**. For example:

```
dbmopen(%A,"c:/temp/xx",undef) || die "cannot open DBM c:/temp/xx";
```

In this case, if the files *c:\temp\xx.dir* and *c:\temp\xx.pag* cannot be opened, the **dbmopen** call returns false, rather than attempting to create the files.

The DBM array stays open throughout the program. When the program terminates, the association is terminated. You can also break the association in a manner similar to closing a filehandle, by using the **dbmclose** function:

```
dbmclose(%A);
```

Like **close**, **dbmclose** returns false if something goes wrong.

Using a DBM Hash

After the database is opened, accesses to the DBM hash are mapped into references to the database. Changing or adding a value in the hash causes the corresponding entries to be immediately written into the disk files. For example, once %FRED is opened from the earlier example, we can add, delete, or access elements of the database, like this:

```
$FRED{"fred"} = "bedrock";  # create (or update) an element
delete $FRED{"barney"};     # remove an element of the database
foreach $key (keys %FRED) { # step through all values
        print "$key has value of $FRED{$key}\n";
}
```

That last loop has to scan through the entire disk file twice: once to access the keys, and a second time to look up the values from the keys. If you are scanning through a DBM hash, it's generally more disk-efficient to use the **each** operator, which makes only one pass:

```
while (($key, $value) = each(%FRED)) {
        print "$key has value of $value\n";
}
```

Fixed-Length Random-Access Databases

Another form of persistent data is the fixed-length, record-oriented disk file. In this scheme, the data consists of a number of records of identical length. The numbering of the records is either not important or determined by some indexing scheme.

For example, we might have a series of records in which the data has 40 characters of first name, a one-character middle initial, 40 characters of last name, and then a two-byte integer for the age. Each record is then 83 bytes long. If we were reading all of the data in the database, we'd read chunks of 83 bytes until we got to the end. If we wanted to go to the fifth record, we'd skip ahead four times 83 bytes (332 bytes) and read the fifth record directly.

Perl supports programs that use such a disk file. A few things are necessary in addition to what you already know:

- Opening a disk file for both reading and writing, and setting the filehandle to binary mode
- Moving around in this file to an arbitrary position
- Fetching data by a length rather than up to the next newline
- Writing data down in fixed-length blocks

The **open** function takes an additional plus sign before its I/O direction specification to indicate that the file is really being opened for both reading and writing. For example:

```
open(A,"+<b");  # open file b read/write (error if file absent)
open(C,"+>d");  # create file d, with read/write access
open(E,"+>>f"); # open or create file f with read/write access
```

Notice that all we've done was to prepend a plus sign to the I/O direction.

Next, we need to set the filehandle to binary mode using the **binmode** function:

```
binmode(A);  # set the filehandle to binary mode
```

Some operating systems don't need to use **binmode**, so you may find scripts that don't do this. Windows NT (and Windows 95) systems *do* need to use **binmode**, so if you find yourself getting strange results while using a random-access database file, this is the first place you should check.

After we've got the file open, we need to move around in it. You do this with the **seek** function, which takes the same three parameters as the C **fseek** library routine. The first parameter is a filehandle; the second parameter gives an offset, which is interpreted in conjunction with the third parameter. Usually, you'll want the third parameter to be zero so that the second parameter selects a new absolute position for the next read from or write to the file. For example, to go to the fifth record on the filehandle **NAMES** (as described above), you can do this:

```
seek(NAMES,4*83,0);
```

After the file pointer has been repositioned, the next input or output will start there. For output, use the **print** operator, but be sure that the data you are writing is the right length. To obtain the right length, we can call upon the **pack()** operator:

```
print NAMES pack("A40 A A40 s", $first, $middle, $last, $age);
```

That **pack()** specifier gives 40 characters for **$first**, a single character for **$middle**, 40 more characters for **$last**, and a short (two bytes) for the **$age**. This should be 83 bytes long, and will be written at the current file position.

Last, we need to fetch a particular record. Although the **<NAMES>** operator returns all of the data from the current position to the next newline, that's not correct; the data is supposed to go for 83 bytes, and there probably isn't a newline right there. Instead, we use the **read** function, which looks and works a lot like its C language counterpart:

```
$count = read(NAMES, $buf, 83);
```

The first parameter for **read** is the filehandle. The second parameter is a scalar variable that holds the data that will be read. The third parameter gives the number of bytes to read. The return value from **read** is the number of bytes actually read; typically, this number is the same number as the number of bytes asked for unless the filehandle is not opened or you are too close to the end of the file.

After you have the 83-character data, break the data into its component parts with the **unpack** operator:

```
($first, $middle, $last, $age) = unpack("A40 A A40 s", $buf);
```

Note that the **pack** and **unpack** format strings are the same. Most programs store this string in a variable early in the program, and even compute the length of the records using **pack** instead of sprinkling the constant 83 everywhere:

```
$names = "A40 A A40 s";
$names_length = length(pack($names)); # probably 83
```

Variable-Length (Text) Databases

Some system databases (and quite a few user-created databases) are a series of human-readable text lines, with one record per line. For example, the TCP/IP hosts file contains one line per hostname.

Most often, these databases are updated with simple text editors. Updating such a database consists of reading it all into a temporary area (either memory or another disk file), making the necessary changes, and then either writing the result back to the original file or creating a new file with the same name (after deleting or renaming the old version). You can think of this process as a *copy pass*: the data is copied from the original database to a new version of the database, and changes are made during the copy.

Perl supports a copy-pass-style edit on line-oriented databases using *inplace editing*. Inplace editing is a modification of the way the diamond operator (<>) reads data from the list of files specified on the command line. Most often, this editing mode is accessed by setting the **-i** command-line argument, but we can also trigger inplace editing mode from within a program, as shown in the examples that follow.

To trigger the inplace editing mode, set a value into the **$^I** scalar variable. The value of this variable is important and will be discussed in a moment.

When the **<>** construct is used and **$^I** has a value other than **undef**, the steps marked **##INPLACE##** in the following code are added to the list of implicit actions the diamond operator takes:

```
$ARGV = shift @ARGV;
open(ARGV,"<$ARGV");
rename($ARGV,"$ARGV$^I");  ## INPLACE ##
unlink($ARGV);             ## INPLACE ##
```

```
open(ARGVOUT,">$ARGV");    ## INPLACE ##
select(ARGVOUT);           ## INPLACE ##
```

The effect is that reads from the diamond operator come from the old file, and writes to the default filehandle go to a new copy of the file. The old file remains in a backup file, which is the filename with a suffix equal to the value of the $^I variable. (A bit of magic is also used to copy the attributes from the old file to the new file.) These steps are repeated each time a new file is taken from the @ARGV array.

Typical values for $^I are things like .bak or ~, to create backup files much like the editor creates. A strange and useful value for $^I is the empty string, `""`, which causes the old file to be neatly eliminated after the edit is complete. Unfortunately, if the system or program crashes during the execution of your program, you lose all of your old data, so this method is recommended only for brave, foolish, or trusting souls.

Here's a way to change everyone's login name to lowercase in some file that contains a list of user logins, one per line:

```
@ARGV = ("userlist.txt");  # prime the diamond operator
$^I = ".bak";              # write userlist.bak for safety
while (<>) {               # main loop, once for each line
        tr/A-Z/a-z/;       # change everything to lower case
        print;             # send output to ARGVOUT: the new
userlist.txt
}
```

As you can see, this program is pretty simple. In fact, the same program can be generated entirely with a few command-line arguments:

```
perl -p -i.bak -e 'tr/A-Z/a-z/' userlist.txt
```

The -p switch brackets your program with a **while** loop that includes a **print** statement. The -i switch sets a value into the $^I variable. The -e switch defines the following argument as a piece of Perl code for the loop body. The final argument gives an initial value to @ARGV.

Command-line arguments are discussed in greater detail in *Programming Perl* or the *perlrun* documentation.

Win32 Database Interfaces

We have seen how Perl can be used to create and maintain databases. What we haven't talked about is how Perl can also be used to access data stored in many popular database formats.

One of the handiest extension modules for Perl for Win32 is `Win32::ODBC`. Written by Dave Roth, `Win32::ODBC` provides an interface to any ODBC data source for which you have a driver.

A detailed discussion of `Win32::ODBC` is beyond the scope of this book, but you can find `Win32::ODBC` at any CPAN site (try *www.perl.com/CPAN/authors/Dave_Roth/*).

Another popular way to access data from Perl for Win32 is to use the OLE Automation interface to Microsoft's *ActiveX Data Objects* (ADO). ADO is an OLE interface that provides uniform data access to any compliant data source (including ODBC). See Chapter 19, *OLE Automation*, for a couple of examples of how to use ADO. For more information on ADO, see *www.microsoft.com/ado*.

Exercises

See Appendix A for answers.

1. Create two programs: one program that reads the data from <>, splits the data into words, and then updates a DBM file noting the number of occurrences of each word; and another program to open the DBM file and display the results sorted by descending count. Run the first program on a few files and see if the second program picks up the proper counts.

18

CGI Programming

Unless you've been holed up in a log cabin without electricity for the last few years, you've heard of the World Wide Web. Web addresses (better known as URLs) pop up everywhere from billboards to movie credits, from magazines and newspapers to government reports.

Many of the more interesting web pages include some sort of entry form. You supply input to this form and click on a button or picture. This step fires up a program at the web server that examines your input and generates new output. Sometimes this program (commonly known as a *Common Gateway Interface (CGI) program*) is just an interface to an existing database, massaging your input into something the database understands and massaging the database's output into something a web browser can understand (usually HTML).

CGI programs do more than process form input. They are also invoked when you click on a graphic image and may in fact be used to provide whatever output that your browser sees. Instead of being dull and boring, CGI-enabled web pages can be marvelously alive with dynamic content. Dynamic information is what makes the Web an interesting and interactive place, and not just a way to read a book from your terminal.

Despite what all those bouncing balls and jumping adverts might lead you to believe, the web contains a lot of text. Because we're dealing with text, files, network communications, and a little bit of binary data now and then, Perl is perfect for web programming.

In this chapter, we'll not only explore the basics of CGI programming, but we'll also steal a little introductory knowledge about references, library modules, and object-oriented programming with Perl as we go along. Then, at the end, we'll make a quick survey of Perl's usefulness for other sorts of web programming.

As a standalone tutorial, this chapter (and most any other document shorter than a couple of hundred pages) will not be adequate to teach the more complex topics touched on here, such as object programming and the use of references. But as a means to gain a preliminary taste of what's ahead of you, the examples presented here, together with their explanations, may whet your appetite and give you some practical orientation as you slog through the appropriate textbooks. And if you're the learn-by-doing type, you'll actually start writing useful programs based on the models you find here.

We assume you already possess a basic familiarity with HTML.

The CGI.pm Module

Starting with the 5.004 release, the standard Perl distribution includes the all-singing, all-dancing CGI.pm module.*

Written by Lincoln Stein, author of the acclaimed book *How to Setup and Maintain Your Web Site* (Addison-Wesley), this module makes writing CGI programs in Perl a breeze. Like Perl itself, *CGI.pm* is platform independent, so you can use it on systems running everything from Windows NT to UNIX and VMS.

Assuming *CGI.pm* is already installed on your system, you can read its complete documentation in the included HTML documentation. If all else fails, just read the source file for *CGI.pm*: the documentation for the module is embedded in the module itself, written in simple *pod* format.†

While developing CGI programs, keep a copy of the *CGI.pm* documentation handy. Not only does it describe the module's functions, it's also loaded with examples and tips.

---

* If you have the ActiveState distribution or an earlier release of Perl (but at least version 5.001), and haven't gotten around to upgrading yet, just grab *CGI.pm* from CPAN. To install it, follow the directions in the *README* file.

† Pod stands for "plain old documentation," the simplistic markup used for all Perl documentation. See the *perlpod* documentation for how it works.

Your CGI Program in Context

Figure 18-1 shows the relationships between a web browser, web server, and CGI program. When you click on a link while using your browser, there is a URL associated with the link. This URL specifies a web server and a resource accessible through that server. So the browser communicates with the server, requesting the given resource. If, say, the resource is an HTML fill-out form, the web server responds by downloading the form to the browser, which then displays the form for you to fill out.

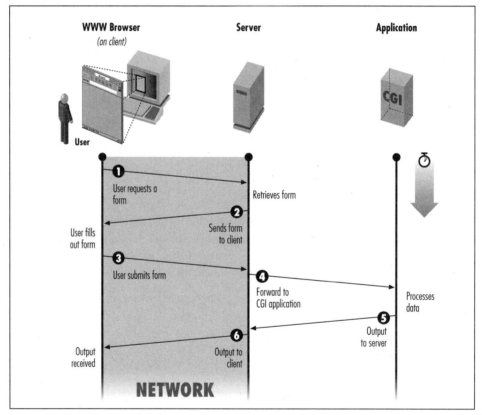

Figure 18-1. CGI application flow

Each text-input field on the form has a name (given in the form's HTML code), and an associated value, which is whatever you type into the field. The form itself is associated (via the HTML <FORM> tag) with a CGI program that processes the form input. When you fill out the form and click on *Submit*, the browser accesses the URL of the CGI program. But first it tacks onto the end of the URL a *query string* consisting of one or more `name=value` pairs; each name is the name of a text input field, and each value is the corresponding input you provided. So the URL to which the browser submits your form input looks something like this (where the query string is everything after the question mark):

```
http://www.SOMEWHERE.org/cgi-bin/some_cgi_prog?flavor=vanilla&size=double
```

In this case, there are two `name=value` pairs. Such pairs are separated by an ampersand (&): a detail you won't have to worry about when you use the *CGI.pm* module. The part of the URL that reads */cgi-bin/some_cgi_prog/* will receive further explanation later; at the moment, you need only note that this part provides a path to the CGI program that will process the HTML form input.

When the web server (*www.SOMEWHERE.org* in this case) receives the URL from your browser, it invokes the CGI program, passing the `name=value` pairs to the program as arguments. The program then does whatever it does, and (usually) returns HTML code to the server, which in turn downloads the code to the browser for display to you.

The conversation between the browser and the server, and also between the server and the CGI program, follows the protocol known as HTTP. You needn't worry much about this when writing your CGI program, because *CGI.pm* takes care of the protocol requirements for you.

The way in which the CGI program expects to receive its arguments (and other information) from the browser via the server is governed by the CGI specification. Again, you don't need to worry too much about this; as you will see, *CGI.pm* automatically unpacks the arguments for you.

Finally, you should know that CGI programs can work with any HTML document, not just forms. For example, you could write the HTML code:

```
Click <a href="http://www.SOMEWHERE.org/cgi-bin/fortune.cgi">here</a>
to receive your fortune.
```

In this case, there wouldn't be any argument supplied to the CGI program with the URL. Or the HTML document could give two links for the user to click on— one to receive a fortune, and one to receive the current date. Both links could point to the same program, in one case with the argument `fortune` following the question mark in the URL, and in the other case with the argument `date`. The HTML links would look like this:

```
<a href="http://www.SOMEWHERE.org/cgi-bin/fortune_or_date?fortune>
<a href="http://www.SOMEWHERE.org/cgi-bin/fortune_or_date?date>
```

The CGI program (*fortune_or_date* in this case) would then see which of the two possible arguments it received and execute either the *fortune* or *date* program accordingly.

So you see that arguments do not have to be of the **name=date** variety character-
istic of fill-out forms. You can write a CGI program to do most anything you
please, and you can pass it most any arguments you please.

In this chapter, we will primarily illustrate HTML fill-out forms. And we will
assume that you understand basic HTML code already.*

Simplest CGI Program

Here's the source code for your first CGI program. It's so simple it doesn't even
need to use the *CGI.pm* module.

```
# howdy--the easiest of CGI programs
print <<END_of_Multiline_Text;
Content-type: text/html

<HTML>
 <HEAD>
 <TITLE>Hello World</TITLE>
 </HEAD>
 <BODY>
 <H1>Greetings, Terrans!</H1>
 </BODY>
</HTML>

END_of_Multiline_Text
```

Each and every time this program is called, it displays exactly the same thing. It's
not particularly dynamic, or interesting. But we'll spice it up later.

This little program contains just one statement: a call to the **print** function. That
somewhat funny looking argument is a *here document*. It starts with two less-than
signs and a word that we'll call the *end token*. Although this may look like I/O
redirection, it's really just a convenient way to quote a multiline string. The string
begins on the next line and continues up to a line containing the end token,
which must stand by itself at the start of the line. Here documents are especially
handy for generating HTML.

The first part in that long string is arguably the most important: the **Content-
Type** line identifies the type of output you're generating. It's immediately
followed by a blank line, which must not contain any spaces or tabs. Most begin-
ners' first CGI programs fail because they forget that blank line, which separates
the header (somewhat like a mail header) from an optional body following it.†

---

* For the full story about HTML, see *HTML: The Definitive Guide, Second Edition*, O'Reilly & Associates.

† This header is required by the HTTP protocol we mentioned above.

After the blank line comes the HTML, which is sent on to be formatted and displayed on the user's browser.

First make sure your program runs correctly from the command line. This is a necessary but not a sufficient step to making sure your program will run as a server script. A lot of other things can go wrong; see the section on "Troubleshooting CGI Programs" later in this chapter.

After it runs properly from the command line, you need to get the program installed on the server machine. Acceptable locations are server- and machine-dependent, although the *scripts* or *cgi-bin* directory of your server installation is a good place to start looking. Consult your server documentation or options to be sure.

After your program is installed in a CGI directory, you can execute it by giving its pathname to your browser as part of a URL. For example, if your program is called *howdy.plx*, the pathname would be:

```
http://www.SOMEWHERE.org/cgi-bin/howdy.plx
```

Servers typically define aliases for long pathnames. The server at *www.SOMEWHERE.org* might well translate *cgi-bin/howdy.plx* in this URL to something like *c:\inetpub\scripts\howdy.plx*.

Passing Parameters via CGI

You don't need a form to pass a parameter to (most) CGI programs. This feature is convenient because it lets programs be called via simple links, not just by full-blown forms. To test this out, take the original URL and add a question mark followed by the parameter name, an equal sign, and the value desired. For example, the following URL would call the *ice_cream* script with the `flavor` parameter set to the value `mint`:

```
http://www.SOMEWHERE.org/cgi-bin/ice_cream.plx?flavor=mint
```

When you point your browser at this URL, the browser not only requests the web server to invoke the *ice_cream.plx* program, but it also passes the string `flavor=mint` to the program. Now it's up to the program to read the argument string and pick it apart. Doing this properly is not as easy as you might think. Many programs try to wing it and parse the request on their own, but most hand-rolled algorithms only work some of the time. Given how hard it is to get it right in all cases, you probably shouldn't try to write your own code, especially when perfectly fine modules already handle the tricky parsing business for you.

Enter the *CGI.pm* module, which always parses the incoming CGI request correctly. To pull this module into your program, merely say:

```
use CGI;
```

somewhere near the top of your program.*

The **use** statement is somewhat like a **#include** statement in C programming in that it pulls in code from another file at compile time. But it also allows optional arguments specifying which functions and variables you'd like to access from that module. Put those in a list following the module name in the **use** statement. You can then access the named functions and variables as if they were your own.

In this case, all we need to use from *CGI.pm* is the **param()** function.†

If given no arguments, **param()** returns a list of all the fields that were in the HTML form that this CGI script is responding to. (In the current example, this list contains the **flavor** field. In general, the list contains all the names in **name=value** strings received from the submitted form.) If given an argument naming a field, **param()** returns the value (or values) associated with that field. Therefore, **param("flavor")** returns **"mint"**, because we passed in **?flavor=mint** at the end of the URL.

Even though we have only one item in our import list for **use**, we'll employ the **qw()** notation; this way it will be easier to expand the list later:

```
# ice_cream.plx: program to answer ice cream
# favorite flavor form (version 1)
use CGI qw(param);

print <<END_of_Start;
Content-type: text/html

<HTML>
 <HEAD>
 <TITLE>Hello World</TITLE>
 </HEAD>
 <BODY>
 <H1>Greetings, Terrans!</H1>
END_of_Start

my $favorite = param("flavor");
print "<P>Your favorite flavor is $favorite.";
print <<All_Done;
 </BODY>
</HTML>
All_Done
```

---

* All Perl modules end in the suffix *.pm*; in fact, the **use** statement assumes this suffix. You can learn how to build your own modules in Chapter 5 of *Programming Perl* or the *perlmod* documentation.

† Some modules automatically export all their functions, but because *CGI.pm* is really an object module masquerading as a traditional module, we have to ask for its functions explicitly.

Less Typing

That's still a lot of typing. Luckily, *CGI.pm* includes a whole slew of convenience functions for simplifying this. Each of these routines returns a string for you to output. For example, `header()` returns a string containing the `Content-type` line with a following blank line, `start_html(`*string*`)` returns *string* as an HTML title, `h1(`*string*`)` returns `string` as a first-level HTML heading, and `p(`*string*`)` returns *string* as a new HTML paragraph.

We could list all these functions in the import list given with `use`, but that would eventually grow too unwieldy. However, *CGI.pm*, like many modules, provides you with *import tags*—labels that stand for groups of functions to import. You simply place the desired tags (each of which begins with a colon) at the beginning of your import list. The tags available with *CGI.pm* include these:

`:cgi`
> Import all argument-handling methods, such as `param()`.

`:form`
> Import all fill-out form generating methods, such as `textfield()`.

`:html2`
> Import all methods that generate HTML 2.0 standard elements.

`:html3`
> Import all methods that generate HTML 3.0 proposed elements (such as `<table>`, `<super>`, and `<sub>`).

`:netscape`
> Import all methods that generate Netscape-specific HTML extensions.

`:shortcuts`
> Import all HTML-generating shortcuts (that is, "html2" + "html3" + "netscape").

`:standard`
> Import "standard" features: "html2," "form," and "cgi."

`:all`
> Import all the available methods. For the full list, see the *CGI.pm* module, where the variable `%TAGS` is defined.

We'll just use `:standard`. (For more information about importing functions and variables from modules, see the Exporter module in Chapter 7 of *Programming Perl*.)

Here's our program using all the shortcuts CGI.pm provides:

```
# cgi-bin/ice_cream.plx: program to answer ice cream
# favorite flavor form (version 2)
use CGI qw(:standard);
```

```
print header(), start_html("Hello World"), h1("Hello World");
my $favorite = param("flavor");
print p("Your favorite flavor is $favorite.");
print end_html();
```

See how much easier that is? You don't have to worry about form decoding, headers, or HTML if you don't want to.

Form Generation

Perhaps you're tired of typing your program's parameter to your browser. Just make a fill-out form instead, which is what most folks are used to. The parts of the form that accept user input are typically called *widgets*, a much handier term than graphical input devices. Form widgets include single- and multiline text-fields, pop-up menus, scrolling lists, and various kinds of buttons and checkboxes.

Create the following HTML page, which includes a form with one textfield widget and a submit button. When the user clicks on the submit button,* the *ice_cream* script specified in the ACTION tag will be called:

```
<!-- ice_cream.html -->
<HTML>
 <HEAD>
 <TITLE>Hello Ice Cream</TITLE>
 </HEAD>
 <BODY>
 <H1>Hello Ice Cream</H1>
 <FORM ACTION="http://www.SOMEWHERE.org/cgi-bin/ice_cream.plx">
 What's your flavor? <INPUT NAME="favorite" VALUE="mint">
 <P>
 <INPUT TYPE="submit">
 </FORM>
 </BODY>
</HTML>
```

Remember that a CGI program can generate any HTML output that you want, which will then be passed to any browser that fetches the program's URL. A CGI program can, therefore, produce the HTML page with the form on it, just as a CGI program can respond to the user's form input. Moreover, the same program can perform both tasks, one after the other. All you need to do is divide the program into two parts, which do different things depending on whether or not the program was invoked with arguments. If no arguments were received, then the program sends the empty form to the browser; otherwise, the arguments contain a user's input to the previously sent form, and the program returns a response to the browser based on that input.

---

* Some browsers allow you to leave out the submit button when the form has only a single input text field. When the user types a return in this field, it is treated as a submit request. But you should use proper HTML here.

Keeping everything in a single CGI file this way eases maintenance. The cost is a little more processing time when loading the original page. Here's how it works:

```
# ice_cream.plx: program to answer *and generate* ice cream
# favorite flavor form (version 3)
use CGI qw(:standard);
my $favorite = param("flavor");
print header, start_html("Hello Ice Cream"),
        h1("Hello Ice Cream");
if ($favorite) {
    print p("Your favorite flavor is $favorite.");
} else {
    # hr() emits horizontal rule: <HR>
    print hr(), start_form();
    print p("Please select a flavor: ",
            textfield("flavor","mint"));
    print end_form(), hr();
}
```

If, while using your browser, you click on a link that points to this program (and if the link does not specify `?whatever` at the end of the URL), you'll see a screen like Figure 18-2.

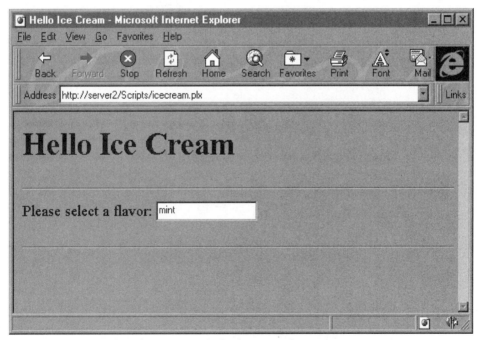

Figure 18-2. Screen shot of ice_cream.plx (without input)

Now, fill in the `flavor` field and press Return. Figure 18-3 will appear.

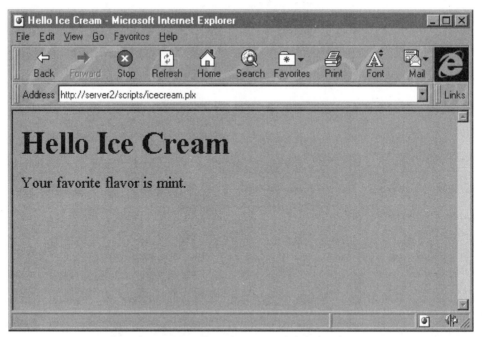

Figure 18-3. Screen shot of ice_cream.plx with params (after input)

Other Form Elements

Now that you know how to create simple text fields in your form and respond to them, you're probably wondering how to make the other kinds of widgets you've seen, like buttons, checkboxes, and menus.

Here's a more elaborate version of our program. We've thrown in some new widgets: pop-up menus, a submit button (named "order"), and a button to reset the entire form and erase all user input. Pop-up menus are pretty much just what they say they are, but the arguments given to `popup_menu` may perplex you until you've read the following section on "References." The `textfield()` function creates a text-input field with the indicated name. We'll give more details about this function when describing the guestbook program later in this chapter. Here's an example:

```
# ice_cream.plx: program to answer and generate ice cream
# order form (version 4)
use strict; # enforce variable declarations and quoting
use CGI qw(:standard);

print header, start_html("Ice Cream Stand"),
    h1("Ice Cream Stand");
if (param()) { # the form has already been filled out
    my $who = param("name");
```

```
        my $flavor = param("flavor");
        my $scoops = param("scoops");
        my $taxrate = 1.0743;
        my $cost = sprintf("%.2f", $taxrate *
            (1.00 + $scoops * 0.25));
        print p("Ok, $who, have $scoops scoops of $flavor
            for \$$cost.");
    } else { # first time through, so present clean form
        print hr(); # draw a horizontal rule before the form
        print start_form();
        print p("What's your name? ", textfield("name"));
        # FOR EXPLANATION OF FOLLOWING TWO LINES, SEE NEXT SECTION
        print p("What flavor: ", popup_menu("flavor",
            ['mint','cherry','mocha']));
        print p("How many scoops? ",
            popup_menu("scoops", [ 1..3 ]));
        print p(submit("order"), reset("clear"));
        print end_form(), hr();
    }
    print end_html;
```

Figure 18-4 shows the initial screen the `textfield` function generates.

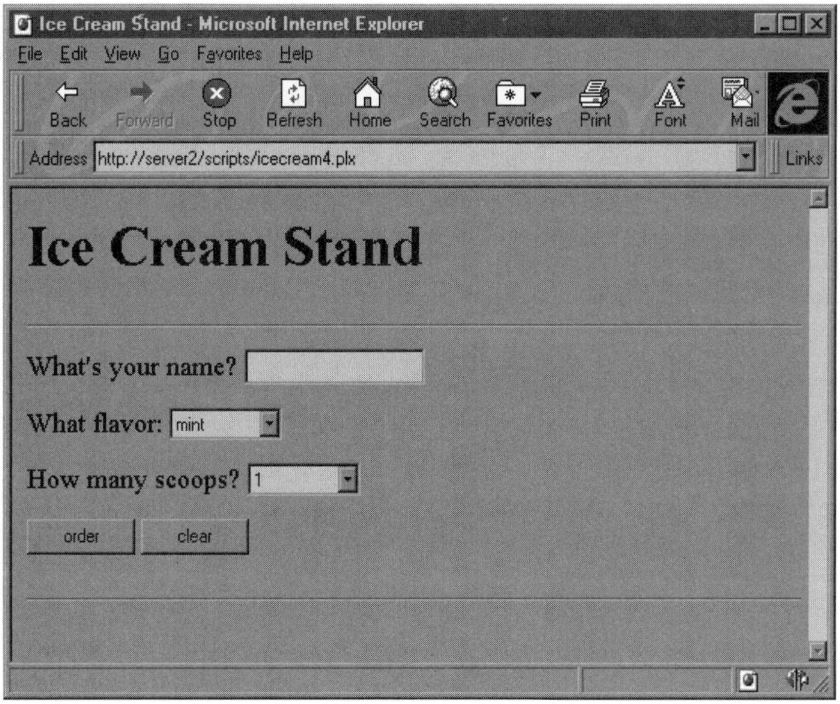

Figure 18-4. Screen shot of ice_cream.plx (final version)

As you'll recall, the `param()` function, when called without arguments, returns the names of all form-input fields that were filled out. As a result, you can tell whether or not the URL was called from a filled-out form. If you have parameters, then the user filled in some of the fields of an existing form, so respond to them. Otherwise, generate a new form, expecting to have this very same program called a second time.

References

You may have noticed that the `popup_menu()` functions in the previous example both have a strange kind of argument. Just what are `[',' cherry','mocha']` and `[ 1..3 ]` doing there? The brackets create something you haven't seen before: a reference to an anonymous array. The `popup_menu()` function expects an array reference for an argument. Another way to create an array reference is to use a backslash in front of a named array, as in `\@choices`. So this:

```
@choices = ('mint','cherry','mocha');
print p("What flavor: ", popup_menu("flavor", \@choices));
```

works just as well as this:

```
print p("What flavor: ", popup_menu("flavor", [
```

References behave somewhat as pointers do in other languages, but with less danger of error. They're values that refer to other values (or variables). Perl references are very strongly typed (and uncastable), and they can never cause general protection faults. Even better, the memory storage pointed to by references is automatically reclaimed when it's no longer used. References play a central role in object-oriented programming. They're also used in traditional programming, forming the basis for data structures more complex than simple one-dimensional arrays and hashes. Perl supports references to both named and anonymous scalars, arrays, hashes, and functions.

Just as you can create references to named arrays with `\@array` and to anonymous arrays with `[ list ]`, you can also create references to named hashes using `\%hash` and to anonymous hashes using:[*]

```
{ key1, value1, key2, value2, ... }
```

You can learn more about references in Chapter 4 of *Programming Perl*, or the *perlref* documentation.

---

[*] Yes, braces now have quite a few meanings in Perl. The context in which you use them determines what they're doing.

Fancier Calling Sequences

We'll round out the discussion of form widgets by creating a really fancy widget—one that allows the user to select any number of its items. The `scrolling_list()` function of *CGI.pm* can take an arbitrary number of argument pairs, each of which consists of a named parameter (beginning with -) and a value for the parameter.

To add a scrolling list to a form, here's all you need to do:

```
print scrolling_list(
    -NAME => "flavors",
    -VALUES => [ qw(mint chocolate cherry vanilla peach) ],
    -LABELS => {
        mint => "Mighty Mint",
        chocolate => "Cherished Chocolate",
        cherry => "Cheery Cherry",
        vanilla => "Very Vanilla",
        peach => "Perfectly Peachy",
    },
    -SIZE => 3,
    -MULTIPLE => 1, # 1 for true, 0 for false
);
```

The parameter values have meanings as follows:

-NAME

The name of the widget. You can use the value of this later to retrieve user data from the form with **param()**.

-VALUES

A reference to an anonymous array. The array consists of the keys of the hash referenced by -LABELS.

-LABELS

A reference to an anonymous hash. The values of the hash provide the labels (list items) seen by the form user. When a particular label is selected by the user, the corresponding hash key is what gets returned to the CGI program. That is, if the user selects the item given as **Perfectly Peachy**, the CGI program will receive the argument **peach**.

-SIZE

A number determining how many list items will be visible to the user at one time.

-MULTIPLE

A true or false value (in Perl's sense of true and false) indicating whether the form user will be allowed to choose more than one list item.

When you've set −MULTIPLE to true, you'll want to assign param()'s return list to an array:

```
@choices = param("flavors");
```

Here's another way to create the same scrolling list, passing a reference to an existing hash instead of creating one on the fly:

```
%flavors = (
    mint => "Mighty Mint",
    chocolate => "Cherished Chocolate",
    cherry => "Cheery Cherry",
    vanilla => "Very Vanilla",
    peach => "Perfectly Peachy",
);
print scrolling_list(
    -NAME => "flavors",
    -LABELS => \%flavors,
    -VALUES => [ keys %flavors ],
    -SIZE => 3,
    -MULTIPLE => 1, # 1 for true, 0 for false
);
```

This time we send in values computed from the keys of the %flavors hash, which is itself passed in by reference using the backslash operator. Notice how the −VALUES parameter is still wrapped in square brackets? Passing in the result of keys as a list wouldn't work because the calling convention for the scrolling_list() function requires an array reference there, which the brackets happily provide. Think of the brackets as a convenient way to treat multiple values as a single value.

Creating a Guestbook Program

If you have followed the examples above, you can now get some simple CGI programs going. But what about harder ones? A common request is to create a CGI program to manage a guestbook, so that visitors to your web site can record their own messages.*

Actually, the form for this kind of thing is quite easy—easier in fact than some of our ice cream forms. Other matters get trickier. But don't worry, we'll explain everything as we go.

You probably want guestbook messages to survive a user's visit to your site, so you need a file to store them in. The CGI program (probably) runs under a different user, not as you; therefore, it won't normally have permission to update a file of yours. So, first, create a file (make sure it has read-write permissions for

---

* As we will note later on, this application might also be called a *webchat* program.

whatever user your program runs as). You can either use a text editor to create an empty file, or do something like:

```
> echo. > c:\temp\chatfile
```

Okay, but how will you accommodate several folks using the guestbook program simultaneously? The operating system doesn't block simultaneous access to files, so if you're not careful, you could get a jumbled file as everyone writes to it at the same time. To avoid this, we'll use Perl's `flock` function to request exclusive access to the file we're going to update. It will look something like this:

```
# Perl 5.004
use Fcntl qw(:flock); # imports LOCK_EX, LOCK_SH, LOCK_NB
....
flock(CHANDLE, LOCK_EX) || bail("cannot flock $CHATNAME: $!");

# ActiveState distribution
$LOCK_EX = 2; # hard coded value of standard LOCK_EX
....
flock(CHANDLE, $LOCK_EX) || bail("cannot flock $CHATNAME: $!");
```

The LOCK_EX argument to `flock` is what buys us exclusive file access.* `bail` is a subroutine that prints an error message back to the browser and then calls die.

`flock` presents a simple but uniform locking mechanism even though its underlying implementation varies wildly between systems. It reliably blocks, not returning until it gets the lock. Note that file locks are purely advisory; they only work when all processes accessing a file honor the locks in the same way. If three processes honor them, but another doesn't, all bets are off.

Object-Oriented Programming in Perl

Finally, and most importantly, you must learn how to use objects and classes. Although building your own object module is beyond the scope of this book, you don't have to know about that in order to use existing, object-oriented library modules. For in-depth information about using and creating object modules, see Chapter 5 of *Programming Perl* and the *perltoot* documentation (Perl 5.004 distribution and beyond).

We won't go into the theory behind objects here, but you can just treat them as packages (which they are!) of wonderful and marvelous things that you invoke indirectly. Objects provide subroutines that do anything you need to do with the object.

---

* With Perl versions prior to the 5.004 release, you must comment out the use Fcntl and just use 2 as the argument to *flock*.

For instance, suppose the *CGI.pm* module returns an object called `$query` that represents the user's input. If you want to get a parameter from the query, invoke the `param()` subroutine like this:

```
$query->param("answer");
```

This says, "Run the `param()` subroutine on the `$query` object, with **answer** as an argument." It's just like invoking any other subroutine, except that you employ the name of the object followed by the `->` syntax. Subroutines associated with objects, by the way, are called *methods*.

If you want to retrieve the return value of the `param()` subroutine, just use the usual assignment statement and store the value in a regular old variable named `$he_said`:

```
$he_said = $query->param("answer");
```

Objects look like scalars; you store them in scalar variables (like `$query` in our example), and you can make arrays or hashes of objects. But you don't treat them as you would strings or numbers. They're actually a particular kind of reference,[*] but you don't even treat them as you would ordinary references. Instead, you treat them like a special, user-defined type of data.

The type of a particular object is known as its *class*. The class name is normally just the module name—without the *.pm* suffix—and often the words *class* and *module* are used interchangeably. So we can speak of the CGI module and also the CGI class. Objects of a particular class are created and managed by the module implementing that class.

You access classes by loading in a module, which looks just like any other module except that object-oriented ones don't usually export anything. You can think of the class as a factory that cranks out brand-new objects. To get the class to produce one of these new objects, you invoke special methods called *constructors*. Here's an example:

```
$query = CGI->new(); # call method new() in class "CGI"
```

What you have there is the invocation of a *class method*. A class method looks just like an `object method` (which is what we were talking about a moment ago), except that instead of using an object to call the method, you use the name of the class as though it were itself an object. An object method is saying "call the function by this name that is related to this object"; a class method is saying "call the function by this name that is related to this class."

Sometimes you'll see that same thing written this way:

```
$query = new CGI; # same thing
```

---

[*] A blessed reference, to be precise.

The second form is identical in behavior to the first. It's got less punctuation, so is sometimes preferred. But it's less convenient to use as part of a larger expression, so we'll use the first form exclusively in this book.

From the standpoint of the designer of object modules, an object is a reference to a user-defined data structure, often an anonymous hash. Inside this structure is stored all manner of interesting information. But the well-behaved user of an object is expected to get at this information (to inspect or change it), not by treating the object as a reference and going straight for the data it points to, but by employing only the available object and class methods. Changing the object's data by other means amounts to hanky-panky that is bound to get you talked about. To learn what those methods are and how they work, just read the object module's documentation, usually included as embedded pods.

Objects in CGI.pm

The CGI module is unusual in that it can be treated either as a traditional module with exported functions or as an object module. Some kinds of programs are more easily written using the object interface to *CGI.pm* rather than the procedural one. A guestbook program is one of these. We access the input that the user supplied to the form via a CGI object, and we can, if we want, use this same object to generate new HTML code for sending back to the user.

First, however, we need to create the object explicitly. *For CGI.pm*, as for so many other classes, the method that generates objects is the class method named **new()**.[*]

This method constructs and returns a new CGI object corresponding to a filled-out form. The object contains all the user's form input. Without arguments, **new()** builds the object by reading the data passed by the remote browser. With a filehandle as an argument, it reads the handle instead, expecting to find form input saved from previous communication with a browser.

We'll show you the program and explain its details in a moment. Let's assume that the program is named *guestbook.plx* and is in the *cgi-bin* directory. While this program does not look like one of the two-part scripts shown earlier (where one part outputs an HTML form, and the other part reads and responds to form input from a user), you will see that it nevertheless does handle both functions. So you do not need a separate HTML document containing a guestbook form. The user might first trigger our program simply by clicking on a link like this:

```
Please sign our
<A HREF="http://www.SOMEWHERE.com/cgi-bin/guestbook.plx">guestbook</A>.
```

---

[*] Unlike C++, Perl doesn't consider new a keyword; you're perfectly free to have constructor methods called gimme_another() or fred(). But most classes end up naming their constructors new() anyway.

The program then downloads an HTML form to the browser, and for good measure also downloads any previous guest messages (up to a stated limit) for the user to review. The user then fills out the form, submits it, and the program reads what is submitted. This information is added to the list of previous messages (saved in a file), which is then output to the browser again, along with a fresh form. The user can continue reading the current set of messages and submitting new messages via the supplied forms as long as he wishes.

Here's the program. You might want to scan it quickly before we step you through it.

```perl
use strict; # enforce declarations and quoting
use CGI qw(:standard); # import shortcuts

sub bail { # function to handle errors gracefully
    my $error = "@_";
    print h1("Unexpected Error"), p($error), end_html;
    die $error;
}

my (
    $CHATNAME,     # name of guestbook file
    $MAXSAVE,      # how many to keep
    $TITLE,        # page title and header
    $cur,          # new entry in the guestbook
    @entries,      # all cur entries
    $entry,        # one particular entry
    $LOCK_EX,      # hardcoded value for flock
);

$LOCK_EX = 2;    # hardcoded value for flock

$TITLE = "Simple Guestbook";
$CHATNAME = "c:/temp/chatfile"; # wherever makes sense on your system
$MAXSAVE = 10;
print header, start_html($TITLE), h1($TITLE);
$cur = CGI->new(); # current request
if ($cur->param("message")) { # good, we got a message
    $cur->param("date", scalar localtime); # current time
    @entries = ($cur); # save message to array
}

# open the file for read-write (preserving old contents)
open(CHANDLE, "+< $CHATNAME") ||
    bail("cannot open $CHATNAME: $!");
# get exclusive lock on the guestbook
# ($LOCK_EX == exclusive lock)
flock(CHANDLE, $LOCK_EX) || bail("cannot flock $CHATNAME: $!");

# grab up to $MAXSAVE old entries, newest first
while (!eof(CHANDLE) && @entries < $MAXSAVE) {
    # pass the filehandle by reference
```

```
        $entry = CGI->new(\*CHANDLE);
        push @entries, $entry;
    }
    seek(CHANDLE, 0, 0) || bail("cannot rewind $CHATNAME: $!");
    foreach $entry (@entries) {
        $entry->save(\*CHANDLE); # pass the filehandle by reference
    }
    truncate(CHANDLE, tell(CHANDLE)) ||
        bail("cannot truncate $CHATNAME: $!");
    close(CHANDLE) || bail("cannot close $CHATNAME: $!");

    print hr, start_form; # hr() emits html horizontal rule: <HR>
    print p("Name:", $cur->textfield(
        -NAME => "name"));
    print p("Message:", $cur->textfield(
        -NAME => "message",
        -OVERRIDE => 1, # clears previous message
        -SIZE => 50));
    print p(submit("send"), reset("clear"));
    print end_form, hr;
    print h2("Prior Messages");
    foreach $entry (@entries) {
        printf("%s [%s]: %s",
        $entry->param("date"),
        $entry->param("name"),
        $entry->param("message"));
        print br();
    }
    print end_html;
```

Figure 18-5 shows a sample screen dump after running the program a few times.

Because every execution of the program results in the return of an HTML form to the particular browser that sought us out, the program begins by getting a start on the HTML code:

```
    print header, start_html($TITLE), h1($TITLE);
```

The program then creates a new CGI object:

```
    $cur = CGI->new(); # current request
    if ($cur->param("message")) { # good, we got a message
        # set to the current time
        $cur->param("date", scalar localtime);
        @entries = ($cur); # save message to array
    }
```

If we are being called via submission of a form, then the $cur object now contains information about the input text given to the form. The form we supply (as shown later) has two input fields: a *name field* for the name of the user, and a *message field* for the message. In addition, the code shown above puts a date stamp on the form data after it is received. Feeding the param() method two arguments is a way to set the parameter named in the first argument to the value given in the second argument.

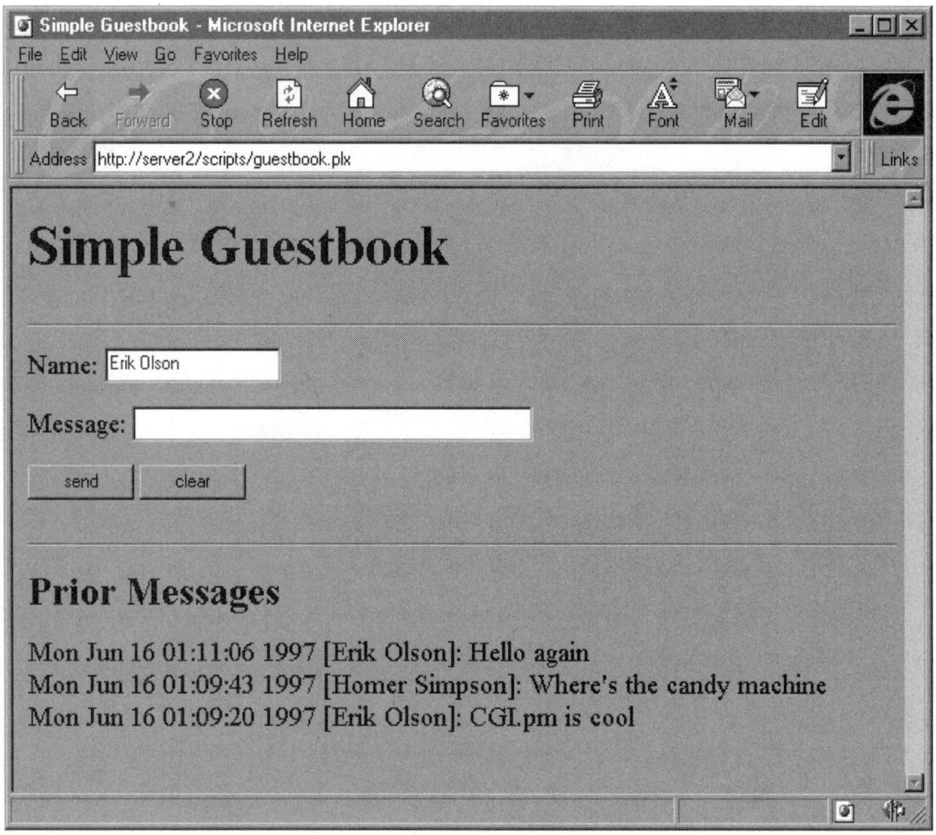

Figure 18-5. Sample screen dump

If we are not being called via submission of a form, but rather because the user has clicked on "Please sign our guestbook," then the query object we create here will be empty. The `if` test will yield a false value, and no entry will be added to the `@entries` array.

In either case, we proceed to check for any entries previously saved in our save-file. We will read those into the `@entries` array. (Recall that we have just now made the current form input, if any, the first member of this array.) But, first, we have to open the savefile:

```
open(CHANDLE, "+< $CHATNAME") || bail("cannot open $CHATNAME: $!");
```

This opens the file in nondestructive read-write mode. Alternatively, we could have used `sysopen()`.* This way a single call opens an old file (if it exists)

---

* For you C programmers, `sysopen()` is implemented in terms of `open()` rather than `fopen()`.

without clobbering it, or else creates a new one (note the use of the permission bits again):

```
# need to import two "constants" from Fcntl module for sysopen
use Fcntl qw( O_RDWR O_CREAT );
sysopen(CHANDLE, $CHATFILE, O_RDWR|O_CREAT, 0666)
    || bail "can't open $CHATFILE: $!";
```

Then we lock the file, as described earlier, and proceed to read up to a total of $MAXSAVE entries into @entries:

```
flock(CHANDLE, $LOCK_EX) || bail("cannot flock $CHATNAME: $!");
while (!eof(CHANDLE) && @entries < $MAXSAVE) {
    # pass the filehandle by reference
    $entry = CGI->new(\*CHANDLE);
    push @entries, $entry;
}
```

eof is a Perl built-in function that tells whether we have hit the end-of-file. By repeatedly passing the new() method a reference to the savefile's filehandle,* we retrieve the old entries—one entry per call. Then, we update the file so that it now includes the new entry we (may) have just received:

```
seek(CHANDLE, 0, 0) || bail("cannot rewind $CHATNAME: $!");
foreach $entry (@entries) {
    $entry->save(\*CHANDLE); # pass the filehandle by reference
}
truncate(CHANDLE, tell(CHANDLE)) ||
    bail("cannot truncate $CHATNAME: $!");
close(CHANDLE) || bail("cannot close $CHATNAME: $!");
```

seek, truncate, and tell are all built-in Perl functions whose descriptions you will find in any Perl reference work. Here seek repositions the file pointer to the beginning of the file, truncate truncates the indicated file to the specified length, and tell returns the current offset of the file pointer from the beginning of the file. The effect of these lines is to save only the most recent $MAXSAVE entries, beginning with the one just now received, in the savefile.

The save() method handles the actual writing of the entries. The method can be invoked here as $entry->save because $entry is a CGI object, created with CGI->new() as discussed above.

The format of a savefile entry looks like this, where the entry is terminated by = standing alone on a line:

```
NAME1=VALUE1
NAME2=VALUE2
NAME3=VALUE3
=
```

---

* Actually, this reference is a glob reference, not a filehandle reference, but it's close enough.

Now it's time to return a fresh form to the browser and its user. (This form will be, of course, the first form he is seeing if he has just clicked on "Please sign our guestbook.") First, consider some preliminaries:

```
print hr, start_form; # hr() emits html horizontal rule: <HR>
```

As already mentioned, *CGI.pm* allows us to use either straight function calls or method calls via a CGI object. Here, for basic HTML code, we've reverted to the simple function calls. But for generation of form input fields, we continue to employ object methods:

```
print p("Name:", $cur->textfield(
    -NAME => "name"));
print p("Message:", $cur->textfield(
    -NAME => "message",
    -OVERRIDE => 1, # clears previous message
    -SIZE => 50));
print p(submit("send"), reset("clear"));
print end_form, hr;
```

The `textfield()` method returns a text input field for a form. The first of the two invocations here generates HTML code for a text input field with the HTML attribute `NAME="name"`, while the second one creates a field with the attribute `NAME="message"`.

Widgets created by *CGI.pm* are by default sticky—they retain their values between calls. (This statement is true only during a single session with a form, beginning when the user clicks on "Please sign our guestbook.") Consequently, the `NAME="name"` field generated by the first `textfield()` above will have the value of the user's name if he already filled out and submitted the form at least once during this session. So the input field we are now creating will actually have these HTML attributes:

```
NAME="name" VALUE="Sam Smith"
```

The second invocation of `textfield()` is a different matter. We don't want the message field to contain the value of the old message. So the `-OVERRIDE => 1` argument pair says, in effect, "throw out the previous value of this text field and restore the default value." The `-SIZE => 50` argument pair of `textfield()` gives the size of the displayed input field in characters. Other optional argument pairs besides those shown include: `-DEFAULT => 'initial value'` and `-MAXLENGTH => n`, where n is the maximum number of input characters the field will accept.

Finally, we output for the user's delectation the current set of saved messages, including, of course, any he has just submitted:

```
print h2("Prior Messages");
foreach $entry (@entries) {
```

```
            printf("%s [%s]: %s",
            $entry->param("date"),
            $entry->param("name"),
            $entry->param("message"));
            print br();
    }
    print end_html;
```

As you will doubtless realize, the h2 function outputs a second-level HTML heading. For the rest, we simply iterate through the current list of saved entries (the same list we earlier wrote to the savefile), printing out date, name, and message from each one.

Users can sit with the guestbook form, continually typing messages and pressing the submit button. This method simulates an electronic bulletin-board system, letting users see each other's new messages each time they send off their own. When they do this, they call the same CGI program repeatedly, which means that the previous widget values are automatically retained between invocations. This result is particularly convenient when creating multistage forms, such as those used in so-called "shopping cart" applications.

Troubleshooting CGI Programs

CGI programs launched from a web server run under a fundamentally different environment than they do when invoked from the command line. While you should always verify that your CGI program runs properly from the command line,* this isn't enough to guarantee that your program will work when called from the web server.

You should get the CGI programming FAQ and a good book on CGI programming to help you in this. Some of these references are listed at the end of this chapter. Here's a brief list of the frequent problems that arise in CGI programming. Almost all of them trigger those annoyingly unhelpful 500 **Server Error** messages that you will soon come to know and hate.

- If, when sending HTML to a browser, you forget the blank line between the HTTP header (that is, the Content-Type line) and the body, your program won't work. Remember to output a proper Content-Type line (and possibly other HTTP headers) plus a totally blank line before you do anything else.

- The server needs to be able to read and execute the script, so you need to make sure that whatever user your script runs as (e.g., IUSR_MYSERVER under IIS) has read and execute rights to the script.

---

* See the *CGI.pm* documentation for tips on command-line debugging.

- The directory where the script resides must have read and execute rights for the script user.

- The script must be installed in the proper directory for your server configuration. For example, on some systems, the directory may be *c:\inetpub\scripts.**

- You need to have your script's filename end in a particular suffix, like *.cgi* or *.plx*, so that your web server knows that it needs to invoke the Perl interpreter on your script. Make sure that your script directory is not writable by FTP clients. We suggest using a suffix of *.plx*, and associating *.plx* with your Perl interpreter.

- Your server configuration requires CGI execution specially enabled for the directory you put your CGI script in. Make sure both **GET** and **POST** are allowed.

- Normally, the web server doesn't execute your script using your account. Make sure the files and directories accessed by the script are open to whatever user the script will run as; this might be the IUSR_INTERNET or *anoynmous* account, or whatever account you use on your system. You may need to pre-create such files and directories and give them appropriate permissions. Always be alert to the risks when you grant such access to files.

- Always run your script under Perl's **-w** flag to get warnings. These warnings go to the web server error log, which contains any errors and warnings generated by your script. Learn the path to that logfile from your webmaster and check it for problems. See also the standard **CGI::Carp** module for how to handle errors better.

- Make sure that the versions and paths to Perl and any libraries you use (like *CGI.pm*) are what you're expecting them to be over on the machine the web server is running on.

- Enable **autoflush** on the STDOUT filehandle at the top of your script by setting the **$|** variable to a true value, like one. If you've used the **FileHandle** module or any of the IO modules (like **IO::File**, **IO::Socket**, and so on), then you can use the more mnemonically named **autoflush()** method on the filehandle instead:

  ```
  use FileHandle;
  STDOUT->autoflush(1);
  ```

- Check the return value of every system call your program makes, and take appropriate action if the call fails.

---

* This directory is the default for IIS, Microsoft's Internet Information Server.

Perl and the Web: Beyond CGI Programming

Perl is used for much more than CGI programming. Other uses include logfile analysis, cookie and password management, clickable images, and image manipulation. And this list is still just the tip of the iceberg.

Custom Publishing Systems

Commercial web publishing systems may make things easy, especially for nonprogrammers, but they just aren't infinitely flexible the way a real programming language is. Without source code, you're locked into someone else's design decisions: if something doesn't work quite the way you want it to, you can't fix it. No matter how many whiz-bang programs become available for the consumer to purchase, a programmer will always be needed for those special jobs that don't quite fit the mold. And, of course, someone has to write the publishing software in the first place.

Perl is great for creating custom publishing systems tailored to your unique needs. You can easily convert raw data into zillions of HTML pages *en masse*. Sites all over the web use Perl to generate and maintain their entire web site. *The Perl Journal* (*www.tpj.com*) uses Perl to generate its pages. The Perl Language Home Page (*www.perl.com*) has nearly ten thousand web pages automatically maintained and updated by various Perl programs.

PerlIS and PerlScript

Each time a user invokes a CGI program or script, the web server needs to create a new instance of that program. While this is a reliable, proven way of doing things, there are more efficient ways to generate dynamic content. ActiveState provides for their distribution of Perl for Win32 two excellent alternatives. One is PerlIS, which enables Perl to be run as an ISAPI extension under an ISAPI compliant webserver (more on this shortly). Another is PerlScript, which is an ActiveX scripting version of Perl that can be used to generate Active Server Pages with a compatible web server (such as Microsoft's *IIS* or O'Reilly's *Website Professional 2.0*).

We said that PerlIS runs as an ISAPI extension. Accordingly, the web server loads Perl as part of its process when the web server starts. Each CGI request destined for the Perl interpreter is then run in-process with the web server as a separate thread. Consequently, the web server doesn't need to start a new instance of the Perl interpreter for each request; it merely creates a new thread and tells its copy of the Perl interpreter to handle the request from the new thread. This can provide significant performance benefits in situations where the server receives a high number of hits.

The current version of PerlIS (Build 306) has some instability when launching external processes and when creating socket connections. If you can't get something to work that you need, we suggest running your script as a CGI program using the standalone interpreter. Look for improved stability in future releases of PerlIS.

PerlScript can not only be used to generate Active Server Pages, but also as a client-side scripting language in the same manner as VBScript or JavaScript. For more information on PerlScript, see *www.activestate.com*. For more information on Active Server Pages, see the Microsoft ASP roadmap at *www.microsoft.com/iis/usingiis/resources/ASPdocs/roadmap.asp*, which provides a detailed overview of Active Server Pages and the automation objects that a server provides to PerlScript.

Further Reading

There's quite a bit more to modules, references, objects, and web programming than we can possibly hope to cover in this one small chapter. A whole book could be written on CGI programming. In fact, dozens have been. For your continued research into these matters, check out the following reference list:

- *CGI.pm* documentation
- The LWP library from CPAN (runs under Windows NT with a few modifications—see the documentation for more information)
- *CGI Programming on the World Wide Web* (Shishir Gundavaram, O'Reilly & Associates, 1996)
- *Web Client Programming with Perl* (Clinton Wong, O'Reilly & Associates, 1997)
- *HTML: The Definitive Guide*, Second Edition (Chuck Musciano & Bill Kennedy, O'Reilly & Associates, 1997)
- *How to Set Up and Maintain a Web Site,* Second Edition (Lincoln D. Stein, Addison-Wesley, 1996)
- Nick Kew's CGI FAQ
- Perl documentation: *perltoot, perlref, perlmod, perlobj*

Exercises

See Appendix A for answers.

1. Write a form that provides two input fields that are added together when the user submits it.

2. Write a CGI script that detects the browser type making the request, and then prints something appropriate (hint: look at the HTTP_USER_AGENT environment variable).

19

OLE Automation

Introduction to OLE Automation

OLE Automation is a method for a client program to control an OLE server. Microsoft designed automation to be a solution for the problem of cross-application macro programming. Because there seemed to be little chance of convincing users to use a single language, the best solution was to make a way for any language to access the capabilities that an application chose to offer.

Automation objects provide two types of interactivity: *properties* and *methods*. Properties are values that you can get and set.* Methods are functions that can be called with (optional) parameters and (optionally) provide a return value, possibly even another automation object. PerlScript also provides support for OLE events, which are a type of handler that get invoked when certain things happen, such as when the user clicks on a button in a browser. However, we will limit our discussion to automation and to properties and methods.

Perl implements support for automation objects in the same way as for any other Perl object. Object methods can be called using the pointer arrow:

```
$obj->some_func();  # call some_func() method of $obj
```

Properties are stored in a hash, and can also be accessed through the pointer arrow:

```
$obj->{foo} = "Some String";   # set foo to Some String
$val = $obj->{foo};            # get the value of foo
```

---

* Although, it is possible to have read only properties.

Notice that we normally don't need to enclose the property name in quotes. If you're getting a property value, you can also use a short form:

```
$val = $obj->foo;          # get the value of foo
$obj->foo = $val;          # WRONG, set requires {foo}
```

Now, we know that we can control our favorite automation servers from Perl. But how do we know what methods, properties, and objects a server exposes? The answer, unfortunately, it that these things are completely server dependent. No standards for object names, methods, or properties exist. The best solution is to turn to your server's documentation for answers. If the server doesn't provide documentation, your situation is still not completely hopeless. If the automation server provides typelib information (an OLE mechanism to describe the interfaces that an OLE server provides), you can use an OLE object viewer (such as Microsoft's *OLE2VW32.EXE*) that can read OLE typelib information and try to figure out what methods and properties the object exposes on your own.

Automation servers come in a couple of different flavors. There are local servers that live in an application (*.exe file*) and run as their own processes. There are in-proc servers that live in DLLs (dynamic-link libraries) and run in the process of the automation controller. There are also remote servers that may run on a different machine using Distributed COM (DCOM).

Perl for Win32 cannot currently use OCX controls, which require additional OLE support.

Creating Automation Objects

Unfortunately, automation is one of the areas in which the ActiveState distribution differs slightly from the *libwin32* OLE module for use with the standard Perl distribution. Both distributions use the `CreateObject` function to create an automation object, but the syntax (and module name) is slightly different:

```
# ActiveState distribution
use OLE;
$obj = CreateObject OLE "Excel.Application" ||
        die "CreateObject: $!";

# libwin32 Win32::OLE
use Win32::OLE;
Win32::OLE::CreateObject("Excel.Application", $obj) ||
        die "CreateObject: $!";
```

The ActiveState CreateObject takes two arguments: a class type (currently, always OLE), and a ProgID (program ID) string of the object to create. When an automation server is registered on the system, it stores a CLSID (class ID), which is a token that uniquely identifies an OLE object, and a ProgID that provides a human readable way to access the CLSID. Perl does the conversion internally, so you just need to provide the ProgID. A server generally has two types of ProgIDs: one is a version-independent ProgID that typically identifies the most current version of the server, the other is a version-specific ProgID that denotes a specific application version.

Here are some examples of ProgIDs that you might use:

```
Excel.Application (Microsoft Excel Application Object)
Excel.WorkSheet   (Microsoft Excel Worksheet Object)
Word.Document.8   (Microsoft Word Document Object, Ver 8)
Word.Basic.8      (Microsoft WordBasic Object, Ver 8)
```

You'll need to check the documentation for the automation server that you want to use in order to discover what its ProgID is.

CreateObject returns a reference to the automation object if it succeeds, and `undef` if it fails.

The *libwin32* version of `CreateObject` uses `Win32::OLE` as the module name (this was done for conformity with the other Win32 extensions). `CreateObject` takes the same ProgID, and a scalar that will contain the automation object if the function returns successfully.

Throughout this chapter, we'll be using the ActiveState syntax for our automation examples.

Using Automation Objects

In this section, we're going to explore automation objects by building a simple progam that sends a message using Microsoft's *Active Messaging Library*. If you don't have Active Messaging (if you have MAPI, you probably have it) on your system, you can still follow the concepts, which are generally applicable to using automation. Remember, though, that the specific methods, properties, and objects that a server exposes are specific to that server. To learn more about Active Messaging, try the Microsoft MSDN* web site at *www.microsoft.com/msdn/sdk/* and look for the for Active Messaging Library documentation. The Active Message Library is a complex API that provides complete services for messaging, message stores, providers, transports, and more; but we're just going to touch on the basics of sending a message here.

---

* Microsort Developer Network—you might also have it on CD, if you're a Win32 programmer and subscribe to MSDN.

The first thing we need to do is to create a Active Messaging session. This happens to be the top-level automation object for our purposes, so we'll start here with `CreateObject`:

```
use OLE;
$ActiveSession = CreateObject OLE "MAPI.Session" ||
        die "CreateObject: $!";
```

The ProgID for the Active Messaging Session object is MAPI.Session, so that's the argument that we give to `CreateObject`. After we have an Active Messaging session, we need to logon. Active Messaging provides a couple of options for doing this. If you don't supply a valid username/password combination, you'll get a logon dialog that lets you supply a user and password:

```
$LogonName = "Erik Olson";
$LogonPasswd = undef; # use stored one, or prompt
die "Logon: $!" if $ActiveSession->Logon($LogonName,
        $LogonPasswd); # Logon returns 0 on success
```

Here, we're calling the `Logon` method of the Active Messaging Session object. Because `Logon` returns 0 on success, we are only dying if we get a return value (indicating an error code). If we successfully logon to the Active Messsaging session, we're ready to create a Message object. A message object is another automation object that (appropriately enough) encapsulates a message. For example:

```
$Message = $ActiveSession->Outbox->Messages->Add();
```

Now, things are starting to get interesting. We're using the $ActiveSession object to call a method named `Outbox` that returns an automation object (the Outbox object). We're then calling a method of the Outbox object called `Messages` that returns another automation object (the Message object). We're then calling a method of the Message object named `Add` that returns yet another automation object, which we're assiging to our `$Message` variable. Perl lets you merrily create as many nested automation objects as you need.

Now that we have a Message object, we can start doing things with the message. First, we need to add a recipient. This involves another nested automation-object call:

```
$Recipient = $Message->Recipients->Add();
```

Here we're calling the Recipients method of the message object that returns a recipients object. We then call the Add method of the recipients object to get a Recipient object that we can use. Let's set some properties of the recipient object:

```
$Recipient->{Name} = "Erik Olson"; # to address
$Recipient->{Type} = 1; # ugly constant, means this is a To address
```

We've set the **Name** property of the Recipient object by setting the property using the object's hash. As for that assignment to the **Type** property, we've set it to 1, which is the Active Messaging value for a TO recipient (as opposed to a CC or BCC recipient). Table 19-1 displays the values for the recipient types.

Table 19-1. Recipient Type Values

Recipient Type	Value
MAPI_ORIG (recipient is message originator)	0
MAPI_TO (recipient is a primary recipient)	1
MAPI_CC (recipient is a copy recipient)	2
MAPI_BCC (recipient is a blind copy recipient)	3

After setting the recipient information, we need to resolve it to a name in the Active Messaging address book. We do this by calling the Resolve member of the Recipient object:

```
$Recipient->Resolve();
```

Now that we know where our message is going, let's add some data to it. We need at least a subject and a body, both of which are properties of the Message object.

```
$Message->{Subject} = "A Message From Perl";
$Message->{text} = "Perl does automation!";
```

All that remains is to save the message, send it, and terminate our session:

```
$Message->Update();
$Message->Send(1, 0, 0);
$Message->Logoff();
```

We call the **Update** method of the message object to save it, then the **Send** method to actually send the message. The parameters to **Send** are shown in Table 19-2.

Table 19-2. Send Parameters

Parameter	Meaning
saveCopy	Save a copy of the message in the Sent-Items folder (one or zero)
showDialog	Display a send-message dialog where the user can change the message contents or recipients (1 or 0)
parentWindow	Parent-window handle for the dialog, if **showDialog** is true; in Perl, you'll normally be passing this as 0

Let's put everything together:

```
use OLE;
$LogonName = "Erik Olson";          # send message to me
$LogonPasswd = undef;               # use stored passwd
$ActiveSession = CreateObject OLE "MAPI.Session" ||
      die "CreateObject: $!";       # create session
```

```
die "Logon: $!" if $ActiveSession->Logon($LogonName,
        $LogonPasswd);            # logon (returns 0 on success)
$Message = $ActiveSession->Outbox->Messages->Add();
$Recipient = $Message->Recipients->Add();
$Recipient->{Name} = "Erik Olson"; # to address
                                # ugly constant, means this is a To address
$Recipient->{Type} = 1;
$Recipient->Resolve();            # resolve name - hope it's there
$Message->{Subject} = "A Message From Perl";
$Message->{text} = "Perl does automation!";
$Message->Update();               # save it
$Message->Send(1, 0, 0);          # send it - don't show UI
$ActiveSession->Logoff();         # end session
```

Data-Access Objects

If you are a Perl programmer looking for a database solution, you owe it to your-self to check out Microsoft's *ActiveX Data Objects* (ADO), which provide an automation interface to database access. ADO is a powerful data-access layer that you can use from Perl, PerlIS, or PerlScript. This layer is particularly interesting in conjunction with Active Server pages and PerlScript. See *www.microsoft.com/ADO/* for more information on ADO. The ActiveState site (*www.activestate.com*) has several samples using PerlScript and ADO for database access.

Just to tempt you, here's a quick example that uses the sample database shipped with the OLEDB SDK (OLE Database Software Development Kit), with which ADO is included. For more information on the OLEDB SDK, see *www.microsoft.com/oledb*. The sample database contains a table called *Employees*, which includes the fields *LastName*, *FirstName*, and *EmployeeID*. The following program just opens the data source (you have to have an ODBC driver installed for Microsoft Access database files) and lists all the rows in the *Employees* table. Regardless of which data source you choose to use ADO with, you'll find the procedure to be similiar.

```
use OLE;
$conn = CreateObject OLE "ADODB.Connection" ||
        die "CreateObject: $!";   # create ADO auto object
$conn->Open('OLE_DB_NWind_Jet');  # connect to data source
$sql = "SELECT * FROM Employees ORDER BY LastName, FirstName";
$rs = $conn->Execute($sql);       # grab all records in table
while(!$rs->EOF()) {
    $lastname = $rs->Fields('LastName')->Value;
    $firstname = $rs->Fields('FirstName')->Value;
    $empid = $rs->Fields('EmployeeId')->Value;
    write;                        # print them out
    $rs->MoveNext();
}

$rs->Close();                     # shut down the recordset
$conn->Close();                   # close the data source
# some formats for a quick printout
```

```
format STDOUT =
@<<<<<        @<<<<<<<<<<<<<<<<<<<    @<<<<<<<<<<<<<<<<<<<<<<<<<
$empid,       $firstname,            $lastname
.
format STDOUT_TOP =
Page @<<
$%
ID            First                  Last
=====         ===================    =========================
.
```

Our first task is to create the automation object using the now familiar
`CreateObject` function. We then use the ADO Connection object to execute a
SQL statement. The Execute function returns a Recordset object, which we then
use to iterate through all the rows, printing out the data.

Here's another quick program that inserts an employee into the *Employees* table:

```
use OLE;
$firstname = "Homer";              # hardcode some values to insert
$lastname = "Simpson";
$empid = "3001";
$conn = CreateObject OLE "ADODB.Connection" ||
        die "CreateObject: $!";    # create the ADO object
$conn->Open('OLE_DB_NWind_Jet');   # connect to the data source
# build a simple SQL INSERT
$sql = "INSERT into Employees (LastName, FirstName, EmployeeID)";
$sql .= "VALUES ('$lastname', '$firstname', '$empid')";
$conn->Execute($sql);              # run it
$conn->Close();
```

Variants

In order for automation controllers and servers to cooperate, they have to have
some way to agree on the type of data that they're passing. Automation accom-
plishes this through a data type called a **VARIANT**. The **VARIANT** data type is
built on a C-language union. It contains a type field that identifies that type of
data in the union (things such as strings, numbers, automation objects, etc.) and a
field that contains the data.

Usually, Perl handles data-type conversion for you. If you need more control,
though, you can create a **Variant** object and specify the type yourself. Perl
provides access to the types listed in Table 19-3.

Table 19-3. Variant Types

Variant Type	Description
VT_UI1	Unsigned character (1 byte)
VT_I2	Signed integer (2 bytes)
VT_I4	Signed integer (4 bytes)

Table 19-3. Variant Types (continued)

Variant Type	Description
VT_R4	Floating point (4 bytes)
VT_R8	Floating point (8 bytes)
VT_DATE	OLE Date (floating-point value measuring days since midnight, Dec. 30, 1899)
VT_BSTR	OLE String
VT_CY	OLE Currency
VT_BOOL	OLE Boolean

By default, Perl converts integer data to the VT_I4 type, string data to the VT_BSTR type, and floating-point data to the VT_R8 type. Usually, these conversions are what you'd expect, but let's look at how you might specify your own type:

```
$vt = new OLE::Variant(OLE::VT_DATE, "May 31, 1997" );
$Message->{TimeSent} = $vt;
```

This example first creates a Variant object, setting the type to **VT_DATE** and the date to "May 31, 1997." It then assigns the date to the **Message** object TimeSent property (something you might do if you were posting a message to a folder, for example).

Tips and Techniques

Here are a couple of tips for using OLE automation from Perl.

Translating Samples from Visual Basic

Finding documentation and examples that show you how to use an automation server from Perl can be difficult. You'll more likely find examples for Visual Basic. Converting automation examples from Visual Basic to Perl is quite easy.

Visual Basic also uses a **CreateObject** call to create automation objects. Visual Basic uses a **set** statement to assign an object, whereas Perl just needs a normal assignment. Visual Basic references properties and methods using the dot operator, while Perl uses the pointer arrow for methods, and the pointer arrow and a hash for properties. Here's a brief snippet from Visual Basic:

```
set Message = ActiveSession.Outbox.Messages.Add
Message.Subject = "Subject"
Message.Text = "Text"
```

And here's the translation into Perl:

```
$Message = $ActiveSession->Outbox->Messages->Add();
$Message->{Subject} = "Subject";
$Message->{Text} = "Text";
```

Exercises

1. Write a program that will invoke your favorite automation-enabled web browser and take it to the O'Reilly & Associates Perl home page (*http:// www.ora.com/publishing/perl*).

2. Write a program that reads a list of numbers and uses automation to put them in sequential rows in your favorite spreadsheet.

A

Exercise Answers

This appendix gives the answers for the exercises found at the end of each chapter.

Chapter 2, Scalar Data

1. Here's one way to do it:

```
$pi = 3.141592654;
$result = 2 * $pi * 12.5;
print "radius 12.5 is circumference $result\n";
```

First, we give a constant value (π) to the scalar variable $pi. Next, we compute the circumference using this value of $pi in an expression. Finally, we print the result using a string containing a reference to the result.

2. Here's one way to do it:

```
print "What is the radius: ";
chomp($radius = <STDIN>);
$pi = 3.141592654;
$result = 2 * $pi * $radius;
print "radius $radius is circumference $result\n";
```

This is similar to the previous exercise, but in this case, we've asked the person running the program for a value, using a **print** statement for a prompt, and then the **<STDIN>** operator to read a line from the terminal.

If we had left off the **chomp**, we'd get a newline in the middle of the displayed string at the end. You must get that newline off the string as soon as you can.

3. Here's one way to do it:

```
print "First number: "; chomp($a = <STDIN>);
print "Second number: "; chomp($b = <STDIN>);
$c = $a * $b; print "Answer is $c\n";
```

The first line does three things: prompts you with a message, reads a line from standard input, and then gets rid of the inevitable newline at the end of the string. Note that because we are using the value of $a strictly as a number, we can omit the chomp here, because 45\n is 45 when used numerically. However, such careless programming would likely come back to haunt us later on (for example, if we were to include $a in a message).

The second line does the same thing for the second number and places it into the scalar variable $b.

The third line multiplies the two numbers together and prints the result. Note the newline at the end of the string here, contrasted with its absence in the first two lines. The first two messages are prompts, for which user input was desired on the same line. This last message is a complete statement; if we had left the newline out of the string, the shell prompt would appear immediately after the message. Not very cool.

4. Here's one way to do it:

```
print "String: "; $a = <STDIN>;
print "Number of times: "; chomp($b = <STDIN>);
$c = $a x $b; print "The result is:\n$c";
```

As with the previous exercise, the first two lines ask for, and accept, values for the two variables. Unlike the previous exercise, we don't chomp the newline from the end of the string, because we need it! The third line takes the two entered values and performs a string repetition on them, and then displays the answer. Note that the interpolation of $c is not followed by a newline, because we believe that $c will always end in a newline anyway.

Chapter 3, Arrays and List Data

1. Here's one way to do it:

```
print "Enter the list of strings:\n";
@list = <STDIN>;
@reverselist = reverse @list;
print @reverselist;
```

The first line prompts for the strings. The second reads the strings into an array variable. The third line computes the list in the reverse order, storing it into another variable. The final line displays the result.

We can actually combine the last three lines, resulting in:

```
print "Enter the list of strings:\n";
print reverse <STDIN>;
```

This method works because the print operator is expecting a list, and reverse returns a list—so they're happy. And reverse wants a list of values to reverse, and <STDIN> in a list context returns a list of the lines, so they're happy, too!

2. One way to do this is:

```
print "Enter the line number: "; chomp($a = <STDIN>);
print "Enter the lines, end with ^Z:\n"; @b = <STDIN>;
print "Answer: $b[$a-1]";
```

The first line prompts for a number, reads it from standard input, and removes that pesky newline. The second line asks for a list of strings, then uses the <STDIN> operator in a list context to read all of the lines until end-of-file into an array variable. The final statement prints the answer, using an array reference to select the proper line. Note that we don't have to add a newline to the end of this string, because the line selected from the @b array still has its newline ending. You'll need to type CTRL-Z at the console to indicate an end-of-file.

3. One way to do this is:

```
srand;
print "List of strings: "; @b = <STDIN>;
print "Answer: $b[rand(@b)]";
```

The first line initializes the random number generator. The second line reads a bunch of strings. The third line selects a random element from that bunch of strings and prints it.

Chapter 4, Control Structures

1. Here's one way to do it:

```
print "What temperature is it? ";
chomp($temperature = <STDIN>);
if ($temperature > 72) {
  print "Too hot!\n";
} else {
  print "Too cold!\n";
}
```

The first line prompts you for the temperature. The second line accepts the temperature for input. The if statement on the final five lines selects one of two messages to print, depending on the value of $temperature.

2. Here's one way to do it:

```
print "What temperature is it? ";
chomp($temperature = <STDIN>);
if ($temperature > 75) {
  print "Too hot!\n";
} elsif ($temperature < 68) {
  print "Too cold!\n";
} else {
  print "Just right!\n";
}
```

Here, we've modified the program to include a three-way choice. First, the temperature is compared to 75, then to 68. Note that only one of the three choices will be executed each time through the program.

3. Here's one way to do it:

```
print "Enter a number (999 to quit): ";
chomp($n = <STDIN>);
while ($n != 999) {
  $sum += $n;
  print "Enter another number (999 to quit): ";
  chomp($n = <STDIN>);
}
print "the sum is $sum\n";
```

The first line prompts for the first number. The second line reads the number from the terminal. The **while** loop continues to execute as long as the number is not 999.

The **+=** operator accumulates the numbers into the **$sum** variable. Note that the initial value of **$sum** is **undef**, which makes a nice value for an accumulator, because the first value added in will be effectively added to 0 (remember that **undef** used as a number is 0).

Within the loop, we must prompt for and receive another number, so that the test at the top of the loop is against a newly entered number.

When the loop is exited, the program prints the accumulated results.

Note that if you enter **999** right away, the value of **$sum** is not 0, but an empty string—the value of **undef** when used as a string. If you want to ensure that the program prints 0 in this case, you should initialize the value of **$sum** at the beginning of the program with **$sum = 0**.

4. Here's one way to do it:

```
print "Enter some strings, end with ^Z:\n";
@strings = <STDIN>;
while (@strings) {
  print pop @strings;
}
```

First, this program asks for the strings. These strings are saved in the array variable **@strings**, one per element.

The control expression of the **while** loop is **@strings**. The control expression is looking for a single value (*true* or *false*), and is therefore computing the expression in a scalar context. The name of an array (such as **@strings**) when used in a scalar context is the number of elements currently in the array. As long as the array is not empty, this number is non-zero, and therefore true. This is a very common Perl idiom for "do this while the array is non-empty."

The body of the loop prints a value, obtained by **pop**'ing off the rightmost element of the array. Thus, each time through the loop, the array is one element shorter, because that element has been printed.

You may have considered using subscripts for this problem. As we say, there's more than one way to do it. However, you'll rarely see subscripts in a true Perl Hacker's programs because a better way almost always exists.

5. Here's a way to do it *without* a list:

```
for ($number = 0; $number <= 32; $number++) {
  $square = $number * $number;
  printf "%5g %8g\n", $number, $square;
}
```

And here's how to do it *with* a list:

```
foreach $number (0..32) {
  $square = $number * $number;
  printf "%5g %8g\n", $number, $square;
}
```

These solutions both involve loops, using the **for** and **foreach** statements. The body of the loops are identical, because for both solutions, the value of **$number** proceeds from 0 to 32 on each iteration.

The first solution uses a traditional C-like **for** statement. The three expressions respectively: set **$number** to 0, test to see if **$number** is less than 32, and increment **$number** on each iteration.

The second solution uses a **foreach** statement. A list of 33 elements (0 to 32) is created, using the list contructor. The variable **$number** is then set to each element in turn.

Chapter 5, Hashes

1. Here is one way to do it:

```
%map = qw(red apple green leaves blue ocean);
print "A string please: "; chomp($some_string = <STDIN>);
print "The value for $some_string is $map{$some_string}\n";
```

The first line creates the hash, giving it the desired key-value pairs. The second line fetches a string, removing the pesky newline. The third line prints the entered value, and its mapped value.

You can also create the hash through a series of separate assignments, like so:

```
$map{'red'} = 'apple';
$map{'green'} = 'leaves';
$map{'blue'} = 'ocean';
```

2. Here's one way to do it:

```
chomp(@words = <STDIN>); # read the words, minus newlines
foreach $word (@words) {
```

```
    $count{$word} = $count{$word} + 1; # or $count{$word}++
  }
  foreach $word (keys %count) {
    print "$word was seen $count{$word} times\n";
  }
```

The first line reads the lines into the @words array. Recall that this method will cause each line to end up as a separate element of the array, with the newline character still intact.

The next four lines step through the array, setting $word equal to each line in turn. The newline is discarded with chomp(), and then the magic comes. Each word is used as a key into a hash. The value of the element selected by the key (the word) is a count of the number of times we've seen that word so far. Initially, there are no elements in the hash, so if the word **wild** is seen on the first line, we have $count{"wild"}, which is undef. The undef value plus 1 turns out to be 0 plus 1, or one. (Recall that undef looks like a 0 if used as a number.) The next time through, we'll have 1 plus 1, or 2, and so on.

Another common way to write the increment is given in the comments. Fluent Perl programmers tend to be lazy (we call it "concise"), and would never go for writing the same hash reference on both sides of the assignment when a simple autoincrement will do.

After the words have been counted, the last few lines step through the hash by looking at each of its keys one at a time. The key and the corresponding value are printed after having been interpolated into the string.

The extra-challenge answer looks like this answer, with the **sort** operator inserted just before the word **keys** on the third-to-last line. Without the sorting, the resulting output is seemingly random and unpredictable. However, after being sorted, the output is predictable and consistent. (Personally, I rarely use the **keys** operator without also adding a sort immediately in front of it—this method ensures that reruns over the same or similar data generate comparable results.)

Chapter 6, Basic I/O

1. Here's one way to do it:

```
    print reverse <>;
```

You may be surprised at the brevity of this answer, but this answer will get the job done. Here's what is happening, from the inside out:

First, the **reverse** operator is looking for a list for its arguments. Accordingly, the diamond operator (<>) is being evaluated in a list context. Thus, all of the lines of the files named by command-line arguments (or standard input, if none are named) are read in, and then massaged into a list with one line per element.

Next, the **reverse** operator reverses the list end-for-end.

Finally, the **print** operator takes the resulting list, and displays it.

2. Here's one way to do it:

```
@ARGV = reverse @ARGV;
print reverse <>;
```

The first line just takes any filename arguments and reverses them. That way if the user called this script with command line arguments "camel gecko alpaca", **@ARGV** would then contain "alpaca gecko camel" instead. The second line reads in all the lines in all the files in **@ARGV**, flips them end on end, and prints them. If no arguments were passed to the program, then as before, <> works on STDIN instead.

3. Here's one way to do it:

```
print "List of strings:\n";
chomp(@strings = <STDIN>);
foreach (@strings) {
  printf "%20s\n", $_;
}
```

The first line prompts for a list of strings.

The next line reads all of the strings into one array, and gets rid of the newlines at the end of each line.

The **foreach** loop steps through this array, giving $_ the value of each line.

The **printf** operator gets two arguments: the first argument defines the format—**%20s\n** means a 20-character right-justified column, followed by a newline.

4. Here's one way to do it:

```
print "Field width: ";
chomp($width = <STDIN>);
print "List of strings:\n";
chomp(@strings = <STDIN>);
foreach (@strings) {
  printf "%${width}s\n", $_;
}
```

To the previous exercise's answer, we've added a prompt and response for the field width.

The other change is that the **printf** format string now contains a variable reference. The value of $width is included into the string before **printf** considers the format. Note that we cannot write this string as:

```
printf "%$widths\n", $_; # WRONG
```

because then Perl would be looking for a variable named $widths, not a variable named $width to which we attach an s. Another way to write this is:

```
printf "%$width"."s\n", $_; # RIGHT
```

because the termination of the string also terminates the variable name, protecting the following character from being sucked up into the name.

Chapter 7, Regular Expressions

1. Here are some possible answers:

    a. /a+b*/

    b. /***/ (Remember that the backslash cancels the meaning of the special character following.)

    c. /($whatever){3}/ (You must have the parentheses, or else the multiplier applies only to the last character of $whatever; this solution also fails if $whatever has special characters.)

    d. /[\000-\377]{5}/ or /(.|\n){5}/ (You can't use dot alone here, because dot doesn't match newline.)

    e. /(^|\s)(\S+)(\s+\2)+(\s|$)/ (\S is non-whitespace, and \2 is a reference to whatever the "word" is; the caret or whitespace alternative ensures that the \S+ begins at a whitespace boundary.)

2. a. One way to do this is:

    ```
    while (<STDIN>) {
      if (/a/i && /e/i && /i/i && /o/i && /u/i) {
        print;
      }
    }
    ```

    Here, we have an expression consisting of five match operators. These operators are all looking at the contents of the $_ variable, which is where the control expression of the while loop is putting each line. The match operator expression will be true only when all five vowels are found.

    Note that as soon as any of the five vowels are not found, the remainder of the expression is skipped, because the && operator doesn't evaluate its right argument if the left argument is false.

    b. Another way to do this is:

    ```
    while (<STDIN>) {
      if (/a.*e.*i.*o.*u/i) {
        print;
      }
    }
    ```

This answer turns out to be easier than the other part of this exercise. Here we have a simple regular expression, that looks for the five vowels in sequence, separated by any number of characters.

c. A third way to do this is:

```
while (<STDIN>) {
  if (/^[eiou]*a[^iou]*e[^aou]*i[^aeu]*o[^aei]*u[^aeio]*$/i) {
    print;
  }
}
```

This solution is ugly, but it works. To construct this solution, just think "What can go between the beginning of the line, and the first a?" Then, think "What can go between the first a and the first e?" Eventually, everything works out, with a little assistance from you.

Chapter 8, Functions

1. Here's one way to do it:

```
sub card {
  my %card_map;
  @card_map{1..9} = qw(
    one two three four five six seven eight nine
  );

  my($num) = @_;
  if ($card_map{$num}) {
    $card_map{$num}; # return value
  } else {
    $num; # return value
  }
}
# driver routine:
while (<>) {
  chomp;
  print "card of $_ is ", &card($_), "\n";
}
```

The &card subroutine (so named because it returns a *cardinal* name for a given value) begins by initializing a constant hash called %card_map. This array has values such that $card_map{6} is six; consequently, the mapping is easy.

The if statement determines if the value is in range by looking the number up in the hash—if there's a corresponding hash element, the test is true, so that array element is returned. If there's no corresponding element (such as when $num is 11 or -4, the value returned from the hash lookup is undef, so the else-branch of the if statement is executed, returning the original number. You can also replace that entire `if` statement with the single expression:

```
$card_map{$num} || $num;
```

If the value on the left of the `||` is true, it's the value for the entire expression, which then gets returned. If it's false (such as when `$num` is out of range), the right side of the `||` operator is evaluated, returning `$num` as the return value.

The driver routine takes successive lines, chomping off their newlines, and hands them one at a time to the `&card` routine, printing the result.

2. Here's one way to do it:

```
sub card { ...; } # from previous problem
print "Enter first number: ";
chomp($first = <STDIN>);
print "Enter second number: ";
chomp($second = <STDIN>);
$message = &card($first) . " plus " .
  &card($second) . " equals " .
  &card($first+$second) . ".\n";
print "\u$message";
```

The first two `print` statements prompt for two numbers, with the immediately following statements reading the values into `$first` and `$second`.

A string called `$message` is then built up by calling `&card` three times, once for each value, and once for the sum.

After the message is constructed, its first character is uppercased by the case-shifting backslash operator `\u`. The message is then printed.

3. Here's one way to do it:

```
sub card {
  my %card_map;
  @card_map{0..9} = qw(
    zero one two three four five six seven eight nine
  );

  my($num) = @_;
  my($negative);
  if ($num < 0) {
    $negative = "negative ";
    $num = - $num;
  }
  if ($card_map{$num}) {
    $negative . $card_map{$num}; # return value
  } else {
    $negative . $num; # return value
  }
}
```

Here, we've given the `%card_map` array a name for 0.

The first `if` statement inverts the sign of $num, and sets `$negative` to the word negative, if the number is found to be less than 0. After this `if` statement, the value of $num is always non-negative, but we will have an appropriate prefix string in `$negative`.

The second `if` statement determines if the (now positive) $num is within the hash. If so, the resulting hash value is appended to the prefix within `$negative`, and returned. If not, the value within `$negative` is attached to the original number.

That last `if` statement can be replaced with the expression:

```
$negative . ($card_map{$num} || $num);
```

Chapter 9, Miscellaneous Control Structures

1. Here's one way to do it:

```
sub card {} # from previous exercise

while () { ## NEW ##
  print "Enter first number: ";
  chomp($first = <STDIN>);
  last if $first eq "end"; ## NEW ##

  print "Enter second number: ";
  chomp($second = <STDIN>);
  last if $second eq "end"; ## NEW ##

  $message = &card($first) . " plus " .
    &card($second) . " equals " .
    &card($first+$second) . ".\n";
  print "\u$message";
} ## NEW ##
```

Note the addition of the **while** loop, and the two **last** operators. That's it!

2. Here's one way to do it:

```
{
  print "Enter a number (999 to quit): ";
  chomp($n = <STDIN>);
  last if $n == 999;
  $sum += $n;
  redo;
}

print "the sum is $sum\n";
```

We're using a naked block with a **redo** and a **last** to get things done this time. We start by printing the prompt and grabbing the number. If it's 999, we exit the block with **last** and print out the sum on exit. Otherwise, we add to our running total and use **redo** to execute the block again.

Chapter 10, Filehandles and File Tests

1. Here's one way to do it:

```
print "What file? ";
chomp($filename = <STDIN>);
open(THATFILE, "$filename") ||
  die "cannot open $filename: $!";
while (<THATFILE>) {
  print "$filename: $_"; # presume $_ ends in \n
}
```

The first two lines prompt for a filename, which is then opened with the file-handle THATFILE. The contents of the file are read using the filehandle, and printed to STDOUT.

2. Here's one way to do it:

```
print "Input file name: ";
chomp($infilename = <STDIN>);
print "Output file name: ";
chomp($outfilename = <STDIN>);
print "Search string: ";
chomp($search = <STDIN>);
print "Replacement string: ";
chomp($replace = <STDIN>);
open(IN,$infilename) ||
  die "cannot open $infilename for reading: $!";
## optional test for overwrite...
die "will not overwrite $outfilename" if -e $outfilename;
open(OUT,">$outfilename") ||
  die "cannot create $outfilename: $!";
while (<IN>) { # read a line from file IN into $_
  s/$search/$replace/g; # change the lines
  print OUT $_; # print that line to file OUT
}
close(IN);
close(OUT);
```

This program is based on the file-copying program presented earlier in the chapter. New features here include the prompts for the strings, the substitute command in the middle of the while loop, and the test for overwriting a file. Note that backreferences in the regular expression do work, but references to memory in the replacement string do not.

3. Here's one way to do it:

```
while (<>) {
  chomp; # eliminate the newline
  print "$_ is readable\n" if -r;
  print "$_ is writable\n" if -w;
  print "$_ is executable\n" if -x;
  print "$_ does not exist\n" unless -e;
}
```

This while loop reads a filename each time through. After discarding the newline, the series of statements tests the file for the various permissions.

4. Here's one way to do it:

```
while (<>) {
  chomp;
  $age = -M;
  if ($oldest_age < $age) {
    $oldest_name = $_;
    $oldest_age = $age;
  }
}
print "The oldest file is $oldest_name ",
  "and is $oldest_age days old.\n";
```

First, we loop on each filename being read in. The newline is discarded, and then the age (in days) gets computed with the **-M** operator. If the age for this file exceeds the oldest file we've seen so far, we remember the filename and its corresponding age. Initially, $oldest_age will be zero, so we're counting on there being at least one file that is more than zero days old.

The final **print** statement generates the report when we're done.

Chapter 11, Formats

1. Here's one way to do it:

```
$file = shift || die "usage: $0 filename";
open(F, $file) || die "open: $!";
while (<F>) {
  ($user, $company, $email) = split /:/;
  write;
}
format STDOUT =
@<<<<<<<<<<<<< @<<<<<<<<<<<<<<<<<<<<<<< @<<<<<<<<<<<<<<<<<
$user,        $company,               $email
.
```

The second line opens the file. The **while** loop processes the file line-by-line. Each line is torn apart (with colon delimiters), which loads up the scalar variables. The final statement of the **while** loop invokes write to display all of the data.

The format for the **STDOUT** filehandle defines a simple line with three fields. The values come from the three scalar variables that are given values in the **while** loop.

2. Here's one way to do it:

```
# append to program from the first problem...
format STDOUT_TOP =
User            Company                  Real Name
==============  ======================   =================
.
```

All you need to get page headers for the previous program is to add a top-of-page format. Here, we put column headers on the columns.

To get the columns to line up, we copied the text of format STDOUT and used overstrike mode in our text editor to replace @<<< fields with ==== bars. That's the nice thing about the one-character-to-one-character correspondence between a format and the resulting display.

3. Here's one way to do it:

```
# append to program from the first problem...
format STDOUT_TOP =
Page @<<<
$%

User            Company                   Real Name
==============  ========================  =================
.
```

Well, here again, to get stuff at the top of the page, we've added a top-of-page format. This format also contains a reference to $%, which gives us a page number automatically.

Chapter 12, Directory Access

1. Here's one way to do it:

```
print "Where to? ";
chomp($newdir = <STDIN>);
chdir($newdir) || die "Cannot chdir to $newdir: $!";
foreach (<*>) {
  print "$_\n";
}
```

The first two lines prompt for and read the name of the directory.

The third line attempts to change the directory to the given name, aborting if this isn't possible.

The foreach loop steps through a list. But what's the list? It's the glob in a list context, which expands to a list of all of the filenames that match the pattern (here, *).

2. Here's one way to do it, with a directory handle:

```
print "Where to? ";
chomp($newdir = <STDIN>);
chdir($newdir) ||
  die "Cannot chdir to $newdir: $!";
opendir(DOT,".") ||
  die "Cannot opendir . (serious dainbramage): $!";
foreach (sort readdir(DOT)) {
    print "$_\n";
  }
closedir(DOT);
```

Just as with the previous program, we prompt and read a new directory. After we've `chdir`'ed there, we open the directory creating a directory handle named DOT. In the `foreach` loop, the list returned by `readdir` (in a list context) is sorted, then stepped through, assigning each element to $_ in turn.

And here's how to do it with a glob instead:

```
print "Where to? ";
chomp($newdir = <STDIN>);
chdir($newdir) || die "Cannot chdir to $newdir: $!";
foreach (sort <* .*>) {
    print "$_\n";
}
```

Yes, this solution is basically the other program from the previous exercise, but I've added a `sort` operator in front of the glob, and I also added `.*` to the glob to pick up the files that begin with dot. We need the `sort` because a file named `!fred` belongs before the dot files, and `barney` belongs after them. In addition, an easy glob pattern that can get them all in the proper sequence does not exist.

Chapter 13, File and Directory Manipulation

1. Here's one way to do it:

   ```
   unlink @ARGV;
   ```

   Yup, that's it. The @ARGV array is a list of names to be removed. The `unlink` operator takes a list of names, so we just marry the two, and we're done.

   Of course, this solution doesn't handle error reporting, or the -f or -i options, or anything like that, but those things are just gravy. If your solution addressed these things, good!

2. Here's one way to do it:

   ```
   ($old, $new) = @ARGV; # name them
   if (-d $new) { # new name is a directory, need to patch it up
     ($basename = $old) =~ s#.*\\##s; # get basename of $old
     $new .= "\\$basename"; # and append it to new name
   }
   rename($old,$new) || die "Cannot rename $old to $new: $!";
   ```

   The workhorse in this program is the last line, but the remainder of the program is necessary for the case in which the name we are renaming to is a directory.

   First, we give understandable names to the two elements of @ARGV. Then, if the $new name is a directory, we need to patch it by adding the basename of the $old name to the end of the new name. Finally, after the basename is patched up, we're home free, with a `rename` invocation.

Chapter 14, Process Management

1. Here's one way to do it:

```
my ($src, $trg) = @ARGV;
die "$src isn't a directory" unless -d $src;
die "$trg isn't a directory" unless -d $trg;
`xcopy /s /e $src $trg`;
```

We check to make sure both arguments are really directories, then we invoke *xcopy* to do the dirty work. We could have also used:

```
system("xcopy /s /e $src $trg");
```

2. Here's one way to do it:

```
@hosts = `net view`;
foreach (@hosts) {
  next unless m#\\\\#;
  chop;
  s/^(\S+).*/$1/;
  push @sorted, $_;
}
print join("\n", sort @sorted);
```

We run the command *net view* and capture the output as a list of lines. We then go through each line looking for hostnames (they start with \\), chop off newlines and comments, and add the matches to another list. We then sort the second list and print it.

Chapter 15, Other Data Transformation

1. Here's one way to do it:

```
while (<>) {
  chomp;
  $slash = rindex($_,"/");
  if ($slash > -1) {
    $head = substr($_,0,$slash);
    $tail = substr($_,$slash+1);
  } else {
    ($head,$tail) = ("", $_);
  }
  print "head = '$head', tail = '$tail'\n";
}
```

Each line read by the diamond operator is first chomped (tossing the newline). Next we look for the rightmost slash in the line, using rindex(). The next two lines break the string apart using substr(). If no slash exists, the result of the rindex is -1, so we hack around that. The final line within the loop prints the results.

2. Here's one way to do it:

```
chomp(@nums = <STDIN>); # note special use of chomp
@nums = sort { $a <=> $b } @nums;
foreach (@nums) {
  printf "%30g\n", $_;
}
```

The first line grabs all of the numbers into the @nums array. The second line sorts the array numerically, using an inline definition for a sorting order. The foreach loop prints the results.

3. Here's one way to do it:

```
while (<>) {
  substr($_,0,1) =~ tr/a-z/A-Z/;
  substr($_,1) =~ tr/A-Z/a-z/;
  print;
}
```

For each line read by the diamond operator, we use two tr operators, each on a different portion of the string. The first tr operator uppercases the first character of the line, and the second tr operator lowercases the remainder. The result is printed.

Another way to do this, using only double-quoted string operators, is:

```
while (<>) {
  print "\u\L$_";
}
```

Give yourself an extra five points if you thought of that method instead.

Chapter 16, System Information

1. Here's one way to do it.

```
foreach $host (@ARGV) {
  ($name, $aliases, $addrtype, $length, @addrs) =
gethostbyname($host);
  print "$host:\n";

  foreach $a (@addrs) {
    print join(".", unpack("C4", $a)), "\n";
  }
}
```

This code just takes a list of machine names, iterates over them, calling get-hostbyname() for each one. We then enumerate each of the addresses, printing them out in dotted decimal notation.

2. Here's one way to do it:

```
use Win32::Registry;
$p = shift || die "usage: $0 path";
# strip leading backslashes
```

```
$p =~ s#^\\##;
$main::HKEY_LOCAL_MACHINE->Open($p, $key) ||
        die "Open: $!";
$key->GetValues(\%vals); # get values -hash ref
foreach $k (keys %vals) {
    $key = $vals{$k};
    print "$$key[0] = $$key[2]\n";
}
```

This code takes a path relative to HKEY_LOCAL_MACHINE (something like *SOFTWARE\ActiveWare\Perl5*) and strips beginning backslashes, if there are any. It opens the key using the precreated HKEY_LOCAL_MACHINE key. It then calls GetValues (passing it a reference to a hash; see Chapter 18, *CGI Programming*, for more on references). The code then enumerates over the keys of the hash, printing them. Each value consists of a reference to a list with three items, so we assign the list reference to $key. We then have to dereference $key in order to access its values; we do so with the $$key[0] construct.

3. Here's one way to do it:

```
sub CreateKeyPath {
  my ($subtree, $path) = @_;
  # break it into components
  # strip initial path separator, if there is one
  $path =~ s#^\\##;
  my (@klist) = split(/\\/, $path);
  my $key;
  my $regkey = $subtree;
  foreach $key (@klist) {
    $regkey->Create($key, $regkey) ||
      die "Can't create key $key: $!";
  }
  return $regkey;
}
```

We first strip the leading backslash out of the path, then break it into a series of keys. We then iterate over each key, creating the key (remember, create opens it if it already exists) and return the deepest key. We're assuming that we have passed in an open key as the first argument.

4. Here's one way to do it:

```
sub print_dword_key {
    my ($dw) = @_;
    printf ("0x%x", unpack("l", $dw));
}
```

This subroutine takes a scalar value that's assumed to be a four-byte integer value and unpacks it using the long format l (which unpacks a four-byte integer). The subroutine then uses printf and its hexidecimal specifier (%x) prefixed with 0x to print out the value.

Chapter 17, Database Manipulation

1. Here's one way to do it:

```
# program 1:
dbmopen(%WORDS,"words",0644);
while (<>) {
  foreach $word (split(/\W+/)) {
    $WORDS{$word}++;
  }
}
dbmclose(%WORDS);
```

The first program (the writer) opens a DBM in the current directory called words, creating files named *words.dir* and *words.pag*. The `while` loop grabs each line using the diamond operator. This line is split apart using the `split` operator, with a delimiter of `/\W+/`, meaning nonword characters. Each word is then counted into the DBM array, using the `foreach` statement to step through the words.

```
# program 2:
dbmopen(%WORDS,"words",undef);
foreach $word (sort { $WORDS{$b} <=> $WORDS{$a} } keys %WORDS) {
  print "$word $WORDS{$word}\n";
}
dbmclose(%WORDS);
```

The second program opens a DBM in the current directory called *words*. That complicated looking `foreach` line does most of the dirty work. The value of $word each time through the loop will be the next element of a list. The list is the sorted keys from %WORDS, sorted by their values (the count) in descending order. For each word in the list, we print the word and the number of times the word has occurred.

Chapter 18, CGI Programming

1. Here's one way to do it:

```
use strict;
use CGI qw(:standard);
print header(), start_html("Add Me");
print h1("Add Me");
if(param()) {
  my $n1 = param('field1');
  my $n2 = param('field2');
  my $n3 = $n2 + $n1;
  print p("$n1 + $n2 = <strong>$n3</strong>\n");
} else {
  print hr(), start_form();
  print p("First Number:", textfield("field1"));
  print p("Second Number:", textfield("field2"));
```

```
      print p(submit("add"), reset("clear"));
      print end_form(), hr();
   }
   print end_html();
```

We simply generate a form if there's no input with two textfields (using the
`textfield()` method). If there is input, we simply add the two fields
together and print the result.

2. Here's one way to do it

```
use strict;
use CGI qw(:standard);
print header(), start_html("Browser Detective");
print h1("Browser Detective"), hr();
my $browser = $ENV{'HTTP_USER_AGENT'};
$_ = $browser;
if (/msie/) {
  msie($_);
} elsif (/mozilla/i) {
  netscape($_);
} elsif (/lynx/i) {
  lynx($_);
} else {
  default($_);
}

print end_html();
sub msie{
  print p("Internet Explorer: @_.  Good Choice\n");
}
sub netscape {
  print p("Netscape: @_.  Good Choice\n");
}
sub lynx {
  print p("Lynx: @_.  Shudder...");
}
sub default {
  print p("What the heck is a @_?");
}
```

The key here is checking the environment for the HTTP_USER_AGENT variable (line 5). Although this step isn't implemented by every server, many of
them do set the variable. This method is a good way to generate content
geared at the features of a particular browser. Note that we're just doing some
basic string matching (case insensitive) to see what they're using (nothing too
fancy). Experienced Perl programmers would probably prefer to write the
string-matching section more along these lines:

```
BROWSER:{
  /msie/i    and do { msie($_), last BROWSER; };
  /mozilla/i and do { netscape($_), last BROWSER; };
  /lynx/i    and do { lynx($_), last BROWSER; };
  default($_);
}
```

However we haven't talked about this construct in this book. If you're interested, see Chapter 2 of *Programming Perl* for several other ways to emulate a switch construct.

Chapter 19, OLE Automation

1. Here are a couple of ways to do it with *Internet Explorer 3.x*:

   Here's one for the ActiveState distribution (5.003, build 306):

   ```
   use OLE;
   $ie = CreateObject OLE "InternetExplorer.Application.1" ||
     die "CreateObject: $!";
   $ie->{Visible} = 1;
   $ie->Navigate("http://www.ora.com/publishing/perl/");
   ```

   And here's one for the Perl 5.004 distribution using *libwin32*:

   ```
   use Win32::OLE;
   Win32::OLE::CreateObject("InternetExplorer.Application.1",
   $ie) || die "CreateObject: $!";
   $ie->{Visible} = 1;
   $ie->Navigate("http://www.ora.com/publishing/perl/");
   ```

2. Here are some ways to solve this exercise (this example uses Microsoft Excel 97—other versions may have slightly different automation objects):

   a. One solution for the ActiveState distribution is:

      ```
      use OLE;
      # grab the numbers
      @numbers = <STDIN>;
      # create the automation object
      $xl = CreateObject OLE "Excel.Application" ||
              die "CreateObject: $!";
      # show it and add a new workbook
      $xl->{Visible} = 1;
      $xl->Workbooks->Add();
      # start at the top left
      $col = "A"; $row = 1;
      foreach $num (@numbers) {
          chomp($num);
          $cell = sprintf("%s%d", $col, $row++);
          # add it to Excel
          $xl->Range($cell)->{Value}  = $num;
      }
      ```

   b. One solution for the Perl 5.004 distribution using *libwin32* is:

      ```
      use Win32::OLE;
      # grab the numbers
      @numbers = <STDIN>;
      # create the automation object
      Win32::OLE::CreateObject("Excel.Application", $xl) ||
              die "CreateObject: $!";
      # show it and add a new workbook
      ```

```
$xl->{Visible} = 1;
$xl->Workbooks->Add();
# start at the top left
$col = "A"; $row = 1;
foreach $num (@numbers) {
    chomp($num);
    $cell = sprintf("%s%d", $col, $row++);
    # add it to Excel
    $xl->Range($cell)->{Value}  = $num;
}
```

The first task is to grab our list of numbers (you'll need to enter CTRL-Z to terminate the input). After that, we create an Excel application object, make it visible by setting the {Visible} property, and then add a new workbook. Then, we iterate over our array of numbers and add them to Excel, incrementing the row counter as we go. Note that we could have saved this workbook using the Save method, and then terminated Excel using the Quit method, but we chose not to, so that we could see what was going on more easily.

B

Libraries and Modules

For simple programs, you can easily write your own Perl routines and subroutines. As the tasks to which you apply Perl become more difficult, however, sometimes you'll find yourself thinking, "someone must have done this already." You are probably more right than you imagine.

For most common tasks, other people have already written the code. Moreover, they've placed it either in the standard Perl distribution or in the freely downloadable CPAN archive. To use this existing code (and save yourself some time), you'll have to understand how to make use of a Perl library. This task was briefly discussed in Chapter 18, *CGI Programming*.

One advantage in using modules from the standard distribution is that you can then share your program with others without having to take any special steps. This statement is true because the same standard library is available to Perl programs almost everywhere.

You'll save yourself time in the long run if you get to know the standard library. No one benefits from reinventing the wheel. You should be aware, however, that the library contains a wide range of material. While some modules may be extremely helpful, others may be completely ·irrelevant to your needs. For example, some modules are useful only if you are creating extensions to Perl.

To read the documentation for a standard module, use the *perldoc* program (if you have the standard distribution), or perhaps your web browser on HTML versions of the documentation. If all else fails, just look in the module itself; the documentation is contained within each module in pod format. To locate the module on your system, try executing this Perl program from the command line:

```
perl -e "print \"@INC\n\""
```

You should find the module in one of the directories listed by this command.

Library Terminology

Before we list the standard modules, let's untangle some terminology:

Package

A package is a simple namespace management device, which allows two different parts of a Perl program to each have a (different) variable named `$fred`. These namespaces are managed with the `package` declaration, described in Chapter 5 of *Programming Perl*.

Library

A library is a set of subroutines for a particular purpose. Often the library declares itself a separate package so that related variables and subroutines can be kept together, and so that they won't interfere with other variables in your program. Generally, an old-style library used to be placed in a separate file, often with a name ending in *.pl*. The library routines were then pulled into the main program via the `require` function. More recently this older approach has been replaced by the use of *modules* (see next paragraph), and the term *library* often refers to the entire system of modules that come with Perl.

Module

A module is a library that conforms to specific conventions, allowing the library routines to be brought into your program with the `use` directive at compile time. Module filenames end in *.pm*, because the `use` directive insists on that convention. Chapter 5 of *Programming Perl* describes Perl modules in greater detail.

Extension

An extension is a combination of a module written in Perl and a library written in C (or C++). On Win32 systems, these extensions are implemented as dynamic-link libraries and have a *.pll* file extension. Extension modules are used just like modules—with the `use` directive at compile time. The case is important here: it doesn't necessarily need to match the filename that the package is stored in, but should match the case used in the package declaration.

Pragma

A pragma is a module that affects the compilation phase of your program as well as the execution phase. Think of it as something that contains hints to the compiler. Unlike other modules, pragmas often (but not always) limit the scope of their effects to the innermost enclosing block of your program (that is, the block enclosing the pragma invocation). The names of pragmas are by convention all lowercase.

Standard Modules

The following is a list of all Perl pragmas and modules included with the current Perl distribution (version 5.004). Modules new to 5.004 are *italicized*. The classification of the modules is admittedly arbitrary, and not all of them are applicable to Windows NT systems.

General Programming: Miscellaneous

autouse
   Defers loading of a module until it's used

constant
   Creates compile-time constants

Benchmark
   Checks and compares running times of code

Config
   Accesses Perl configuration information

Env
   Imports environment variables

English
   Uses English or *awk* names for punctuation variables

FindBin
   Finds path of currently executing program

Getopt::Long
   Provides extended processing of command-line options

Getopt::Std
   Processes single-character switches with switch clustering

lib
   Manipulates @INC at compile time

Shell
   Runs shell commands transparently within Perl

strict
   Restricts unsafe constructs

Symbol
   Generates anonymous globs; qualifies variable names

subs
   Predeclares subroutine names

vars
   Predeclares global variable names

General Programming: Error Handling and Logging

Carp
> Generates error messages

diagnostics
> Forces verbose warning diagnostics

sigtrap
> Enables stack backtrace on unexpected signals

Sys::Syslog
> Provides Perl interface to UNIX *syslog*(3) calls

General Programming: File Access and Handling

Cwd
> Gets pathname of current working directory

DirHandle
> Supplies object methods for directory handles

Fcntl
> Loads the C *Fcntl.h* defines

File::Basename
> Parses file specifications

File::CheckTree
> Runs many tests on a collection of files

File::Copy
> Copies files or filehandles

File::Find
> Traverses a file tree

File::Path
> Creates or removes a series of directories

FileCache
> Keeps more files open than the system permits

FileHandle
> Supplies object methods for filehandles

SelectSaver
> Saves and restores selected filehandles

General Programming: Classes for I/O Operations

IO

Top-level interface to IO::* classes

IO::File

Object methods for filehandles

IO::Handle

Object methods for I/O handles

IO::Pipe

Object methods for pipes

IO::Seekable

Seek-based methods for I/O objects

IO::Select

Object interface to select

IO::Socket

Object interface to sockets

General Programming: Text Processing and Screen Interfaces

locale

Uses POSIX locales for built-in operations

Pod::HTML

Converts POD data to HTML

Pod::Text

Converts POD data to formatted ASCII text

Search::Dict

Searches for key in dictionary file

Term::Cap

Interfaces termcap

Term::Complete

Word-completion module

Text::Abbrev

Creates an abbreviation table from a list

Text::ParseWords

Parses text into an array of tokens

Text::Soundex

Implements the Soundex Algorithm described by Knuth

Text::Tabs
> Expands and unexpands tabs

Text::Wrap
> Wraps text into a paragraph

Database Interfaces

AnyDBM_File
> Provides framework for multiple DBMs

DB_File
> Provides access to Berkeley DB

GDBM_File
> Provides tied access to GDBM library

NDBM_File
> Provides tied access to NDBM files

ODBM_File
> Provides tied access to ODBM files

SDBM_File
> Provides tied access to SDBM files

Mathematics

Integer
> Does integer arithmetic instead of double precision

Math::BigFloat
> Provides arbitrary-length, floating-point math package

Math::BigInt
> Provides arbitrary-length integer math package

Math::Complex
> Provides complex numbers package

The World Wide Web

CGI
> Interfaces web server (Common Gateway Interface)

CGI::Apache
> Supports Apache's Perl module

CGI::Carp
> Details log server errors with helpful context

CGI::Fast

Supports FastCGI (persistent server process)

CGI::Push

Supports server push

CGI::Switch

Provides simple interface for multiple server types

Networking and Interprocess Communication

IPC::Open2

Opens a process for both reading and writing

IPC::Open3

Opens a process for reading, writing, and error handling

Net::Ping

Checks whether a host is online

Socket

Loads the C *socket.h* defines and structure manipulators

Sys::Hostname

Tries every conceivable way to get hostname

Automated Access to the Comprehensive Perl Archive Network

CPAN

Provides simple interface to CPAN

CPAN::FirstTime

Provides utility for creating CPAN configuration file

CPAN::Nox

Runs CPAN while avoiding compiled extensions

Time and Locale

Time::Local

Efficiently computes time from local and GMT time

I18N::Collate

Compares 8-bit scalar data according to the current locale

Object Interfaces to Built-in Functions

Class::Struct

Declares struct-like datatypes as Perl classes

File::stat

Provides object interface to `stat` function

Net::hostent

Provides object interface to `gethost*` functions

Net::netent

Provides object interface to `getnet*` functions

Net::protoent

Provides object interface to `getproto*` functions

Net::servent

Provides object interface to `getserv*` functions

Time::gmtime

Provides object interface to `gmtime` function

Time::localtime

Provides object interface to `localtime` function

Time::tm

Provides internal object for `Time::{gm,local}time`

User::grent

Provides object interface to `getgr*` functions

User::pwent

Provides object interface to `getpw*` functions

For Developers: Autoloading and Dynamic Loading

AutoLoader

Loads functions only on demand

AutoSplit

Splits a package for autoloading

Devel::SelfStubber

Generates stubs for a `SelfLoading` module

DynaLoader

Provides automatic dynamic loading of Perl modules

SelfLoader

Loads functions only on demand

For Developers: Language Extensions and Platform Development Support

blib

Finds *blib* directory structure during module builds

ExtUtils::Embed

Provides utilities for embedding Perl in C programs

ExtUtils::Install

Installs files from here to there

ExtUtils::Liblist

Determines libraries to use and how to use them

ExtUtils::MakeMaker

Creates a *Makefile* for a Perl extension

ExtUtils::Manifest

Provides utilities to write and check a *MANIFEST* file

ExtUtils::Miniperl

Writes the C code for *perlmain.c*

ExtUtils::Mkbootstrap

Makes a bootstrap file for use by DynaLoader

ExtUtils::Mksymlists

Writes linker-option files for dynamic extension

ExtUtils::MM_OS2

Provides methods to override UNIX behavior in `ExtUtils::MakeMaker`

ExtUtils::MM_Unix

Provides methods used by `ExtUtils::MakeMaker`

ExtUtils::MM_VMS

Provides methods to override UNIX behavior in `ExtUtils::MakeMaker`

ExtUtils::testlib

Fixes @INC to use just-built extension

Opcode

Disables opcodes when compiling Perl code

ops

Provides pragma for use with Opcode module

POSIX

Interfaces to IEEE Std 1003.1

Safe

Creates safe namespaces for evaluating Perl code

Test::Harness
    Runs Perl standard test scripts with statistics

vmsish
    Enables VMS-specific features

For Developers: Object-Oriented Programming Support

Exporter
    Provides default import method for modules

overload
    Overloads Perl's mathematical operations

Tie::RefHash
    Provides base-class definitions for tied hashes with references as keys

Tie::Hash
    Provides base-class definitions for tied hashes

Tie::Scalar
    Provides base-class definitions for tied scalars

Tie::StdHash
    Provides base-class definitions for tied hashes

Tie::StdScalar
    Provides base-class definitions for tied scalars

Tie::SubstrHash
    Provides fixed-table-size, fixed-key-length hashing

UNIVERSAL
    Provides base-class definitions for all classes

CPAN: Beyond the Standard Library

If you don't find an entry in the standard library that fits your needs, someone still may have written code that will be useful to you. Many superb library modules exist that are not included in the standard distribution, for various practical, political, and pathetic reasons. To find out what is available, you can look at the Comprehensive Perl Archive Network (CPAN). See the discussion of CPAN in Chapter 1, *Introduction*.

Here are the major categories of modules available from CPAN:

- Module listing format

- Perl core modules, Perl language extensions, and documentation tools

- Development support

- Operating system interfaces

- Networking, device control (modems), and interprocess communication

- Data types and data type utilities

- Database interfaces

- User interfaces

- Interfaces to or emulations of other programming languages

- Filenames, filesystems, and file locking (see also filehandles)

- String processing, language text processing, parsing, and searching

- Option, argument, parameter, and configuration-file processing

- Internationalization and locale

- Authentication, security, and encryption

- World Wide Web, HTML, HTTP, CGI, and MIME

- Server and daemon utilities

- Archiving, compression, and conversion

- Images, pixmap and bitmap manipulation, drawing and graphing

- Mail and Usenet news

- Control-flow utilities (callbacks and exceptions)

- Filehandle, directory handle, and input/output stream utilities

- Microsoft Windows modules

- Miscellaneous modules

Win32 Extensions

We've said that extensions consist of a module written in Perl, and a library written in C or C++. Win32 extensions are valuable tools because they provide Windows-specific functionality that otherwise wouldn't be present in the base language. The following list details the extensions included with the ActiveState distribution (these are also available for the standard distribution via the *libwin32* distribution, available from CPAN).

OLE (Win32::OLE in the **libwin32** distribution)
　　Access to OLE automation and OLE variants

Win32::Process
　　Access to extended Win32 process creation and management; includes methods to kill, suspend, resume, and set the priorities of processes

Win32::Semaphore

Provides access to Win32 semaphores and synchronization

Win32::IPC

Provides sychronization for objects of type Semaphore, Mutex, Process, or ChangeNotify

Win32::Mutex

Provides access to Win32 mutex objects

Win32::ChangeNotify

Provides access to Win32 change-notification objects, letting you do things like monitor changes to directory trees

Win32::EventLog

Provides access to the Windows NT event log

Win32::Registry

Provides access to the Windows NT registry

Win32::NetAdmin

Lets you manipulate users and groups

Win32::File

Lets you get and set file attributes

Win32::Service

Provides a service control interface: lets you start, pause, resume, and stop services

Win32::NetResource

Lets you work with shares, both as a client and a server

Win32::FileSecurity

Lets you work with file permissions on NTFS

Win32::Error

Provides an interface to the system error codes and messages

The following Win32 extensions are not included in (but are readily available for) the ActiveState distribution, and are included with the *libwin32* distribution.

Win32::Internet

Provides an interface to HTTP and FTP

Win32::ODBC

Provides an interface to ODBC data sources

Win32::Shortcut

Lets you create Explorer (shell) shortcuts

Win32::Sound

Plays *.wav* files or uses system sounds

Win32::AdminMisc

Provides an extension of `Win32::NetAdmin` that adds user impersonation, password manipulation, and DNS administration

Win32::Clipboard

Accesses the Windows NT clipboard

Win32::Console

Interfaces to console screen drawing; lets you do colors, boxes, etc.

Win32::Pipe

Provides access to named pipes on Windows NT

In addition to these extensions, a Win32 extension is included with the ActiveState distribution, and is available as part of *libwin32*. The Win32 extension provides the following list functions (we've given a brief code snippet to illustrate how you might code each one):

Win32::GetLastError

Returns the last error value generated by a call to a Win32 API function:

```
use Win32;
$err = Win32::GetLastError();
```

Win32::BuildNumber

Returns the build number of Perl for Win32:

```
use Win32:
$build = Win32::BuildNumber(); # $build has 306 (or whatever it is)
```

Win32::LoginName

Returns the username of the owner of the current perl process:

```
use Win32;
$user = Win32::LoginName();   # $user has eriko (account name of
    current user)
```

Win32::NodeName

Returns the Microsoft Network node name of the current machine:

```
use Win32;
$node = Win32::NodeName(); # $node has machine name
```

Win32::DomainName

Returns the name of the Microsoft Network domain that the owner of the current perl process is logged into:

```
use Win32;
$domain = Win32::Domain();  # $domain has network domain name (not
    TCP/IP domain name)
```

Win32::FsType

Returns a string naming the filesystem type of the currently active drive:

```
use Win32;
$fs = Win32::FsType();        # $fs contains fs type, like NTFS or FAT
```

Win32::GetCwd

Returns the current active drive and directory; this function does not return a UNC path:

```
use Win32;
$cwd = Win32::GetCwd();        # $cwd has current working directory
```

Win32::SetCwd NEW_DIRECTORY

Sets the current active drive and directory; this function does not work with UNC paths:

```
use Win32;
Win32::SetCwd("c:/temp") || die "SetCwd: $!";
```

Win32::GetOSVersion

Returns an array ($string, $major, $minor, $build, and $id). $string is a descriptive string, $major is the major version of the operating system, $minor is the minor version of the operating system, $build is the build number of the OS, and $id is a digit that denotes the operating system variety (zero for Win32s, one for Windows 95, and two for Windows NT):

```
use Win32;
($string, $major, $minor, $build, $id) = Win32::GetOSVersion();
@os = qw(Win32s, Win95, WinNT);
print "$os[$id] $major\.$minor $string (Build $build)\n";
```

The output on a Windows NT 4.0 system is:

```
WinNT 4.0 Service Pack 3 (Build 1381)
```

Win32::FormatMessage ERROR_CODE

Converts the supplied Win32 error bitmap (returned by GetLastError) to a descriptive string:

```
use Win32;
use Win32::WinError;   # for error constants
$msg = Win32::FormatMessage(ERROR_INTERNAL_ERROR);
# $msg contains the string: There is not enough space on disk
```

Win32::Spawn COMMAND, ARGS, PID

Spawns a new process using the supplied COMMAND, passing in arguments in the string ARGS; the pid of the new process is stored in PID:

```
use Win32;
Win32::Spawn('c:/nt/system32/notepad.exe', undef, $pid); # $pid has
    new pid of notepad
```

Win32::LookupAccountName SYSTEM, ACCOUNT, DOMAIN, SID, SIDTYPE

Looks up `ACCOUNT` on `SYSTEM` and returns the domain name, `SID`, and `SID` type

Win32::LookupAccountSID SYSTEM, SID, ACCOUNT, DOMAIN, SIDTYPE

Looks up `SID` (Security ID) on `SYSTEM` and returns the account name, domain name, and `SID` type:

```
use Win32;
Win32::LookupAccountSID(undef, $some_sid, $acct, $domain,
$sidtype);
```

Win32::InitiateSystemShutdown MACHINE, MESSAGE, TIMEOUT, FORCECLOSE, REBOOT

Shuts down the specified `MACHINE` (`undef` means local machine), notifying users with the supplied `MESSAGE`, within the specified `TIMEOUT` (in seconds) interval. Forces closing of all documents without prompting the user if `FORCECLOSE` is true, and reboots the machine if `REBOOT` is true (be careful experimenting with this one):

```
use Win32;
Win32::InitiateSystemShutdown(undef, "Bye",  15, undef, 1);
# try to shut down local machine
```

Win32::AbortSystemShutdown MACHINE

Aborts a shutdown on the specified `MACHINE`:

```
use Win32;
Win32::AbortSystemShutdown(undef);
# stop a shutdown on local machine
```

Win32::GetTickCount

Returns the Win32 tick count, which is the number of milliseconds that have elasped since the system started:

```
use Win32;
$tick = Win32::GetTickCount();
# tick has number of milliseconds since system start
```

Win32::IsWinNT

Returns nonzero if the operating system is Windows NT:

```
use Win32;
$winnt = Win32::IsWinNT();  # true if running on Windows NT
```

Win32::IsWin95

Returns nonzero if the operating system is Windows 95:

```
use Win32;
$win95 = Win32::IsWin95(); # true if running on Windows 95
```

Win32::ExpandEnvironmentStrings STRING

Takes the `STRING` and builds a return string that has environment-variable strings replaced with their defined values:

```
use Win32;
$path = Win32::ExpandEnvironmentStrings('%PATH%'); # $path
contains expanded PATH
```

Win32::GetShortPathName LONGPATHNAME

Returns the short (8.3) pathname for `LONGPATHNAME`:

```
use Win32;
$short = Win32::GetShortPathName('words.secret');   # $short now
has 8.3 name (WORDS~1.SEC)
```

Win32::GetNextAvailDrive

Returns a string in the form of `<d>:\` where `<d>` is the first available drive letter:

```
use Win32;
$drive = Win32::GetNextAvailDrive();  # $drive has first drive
(e.g,. B:)
```

C

Networking Clients

Few computers (or computer users, for that matter) are content to remain isolated from the rest of the world. Networking, once mostly limited to government research labs and computer science departments at major universities, is now available to virtually everyone, even home computer users with a modem and dial-up SLIP or PPP service. More than ever, networking is now used daily by organizations and individuals from every walk of life. They use networking to exchange email, schedule meetings, manage distributed databases, access company information, grab weather reports, pull down today's news, chat with someone in a different hemisphere, or advertise their company on the Web.

These diverse applications all share one thing in common: they use TCP networking, the fundamental protocol that links the Net together.* And we don't just mean the Internet, either. Firewalls aside, the underlying technology is the same whether you're connecting far across the Internet, between your corporate offices, or from your kitchen down to your basement. As a result, you only have to learn one technology for all sorts of application areas.

How can you use networking to let an application on one machine talk to a different application, possibly on a totally different machine? With Perl, it's pretty easy, but first you should probably know a little bit about how the TCP networking model works.

Even if you've never touched a computer network before in your whole life, you already know another connection-based system: the telephone system. Don't let fancy words like "client-server programming" put you off. When you see the word "client," think "caller"; when you see the word "server," think "responder."

---

* Actually, IP (Internet Protocol) ties the Internet together, but TCP/IP is just a layer on top of IP.

If you ring someone up on the telephone, you are the client. Whoever picks up the phone at the other end is the server.

Programmers with a background in C programming may be familiar with *sockets*. A socket is the interface to the network in the same sense that a filehandle is the interface to files in the filesystem. In fact, for the simple stream-based clients we're going to demonstrate below, you can use a socket handle just as you would a filehandle.*

You can read from the socket, write to it, or both. That's because a socket is a special kind of bidirectional filehandle representing a network connection. Unlike normal files created via open, sockets are created using the low-level socket function.

Let's squeeze a little more mileage out of our telephone model. When you call into a big company's telephone switchboard, you can ask for a particular department by one name or another (such as Personnel or Human Resources), or by an exact number (like extension 213). Think of each service running on a computer as a department in a large corporation. Sometimes a particular service has several different names, such as both *http* and *www*, but only one number, such as 80. That number associated with a particular service name is its *port*. The Perl functions getservbyname and getservbyport can be used to look up a service name given its port number, or vice versa. Table C-1 lists some standard TCP services and their port numbers.

Table C-1. Standard TCP Services and Their Port Numbers

Service	Port	Purpose
echo	7	Accepts all input and echoes it back
discard	9	Accepts anything but does nothing with it
daytime	13	Returns the current date and time in local format
ftp	21	Server for file-transfer requests
telnet	23	Server for interactive telnet sessions
smtp	25	Simple mail transfer protocol; the mailer daemon
time	37	Return number of seconds since 1900 (in binary)
http	80	The World Wide Web server
nntp	119	The news server

Although sockets were originally developed for Berkeley UNIX, the overwhelming popularity of the Internet has induced virtually all operating-systems vendors to include socket support for client-server programming. For this book,

---

* Well, almost; you can't seek on a socket.

directly using the **socket** function is a bit low level. We recommend that you use the more user-friendly IO::Socket module,* which we'll use in all our sample code. Consequently, we'll also be employing some of Perl's object-oriented constructs. For a brief introduction to these constructs, see Chapter 18, *CGI Programming*. The *perltoot* documentation (starting with Perl 5.004) and Chapter 5 of *Programming Perl* offer a more complete introduction to object-oriented programming in Perl.

We don't have the space in this book to provide a full TCP/IP tutorial, but we can at least present a few simple clients. For servers, which are a bit more complicated, see Chapter 6 of *Programming Perl*. Generally speaking, writing servers in Perl on Windows NT is a difficult task because Perl doesn't currently offer support for threads, and there's no easy way to implement support for multiple simultaneous clients. This may change in the future, so stay tuned for future Perl releases.

A Simple Client

For our simplest client, we'll choose a rather boring service, called "daytime." The daytime server sends a connecting client one line of data containing the time of day on that remote server, then closes the connection.

Here's the client:

```
use IO::Socket;
$remote = IO::Socket::INET->new(
 Proto => "tcp",
 PeerAddr => "localhost",
 PeerPort => "daytime(13)",
 )
 or die "cannot connect to daytime port at localhost";
while ( <$remote> ) { print }
```

When you run this program, you should get something back that looks like this:

```
Thu May 8 11:57:15 1997
```

Here are what those parameters to the **new** constructor mean:

Proto

> The protocol to use. In this case, the socket handle returned will be connected to a TCP socket, because we want a stream-oriented connection, that is, one that acts pretty much like a plain old file. Not all sockets are of this type. For example, the UDP protocol can be used to make a datagram socket, used for message-passing.

---

* IO::Socket is included as part of the standard Perl distribution as of the 5.004 release and the current ActiveState at the time of this writing. If you're running an earlier version of Perl, just fetch IO::Socket from CPAN.

PeerAddr

> The name or Internet address of the remote host the server is running on. We could have specified a longer name like *www.perl.com*, or an address like *204.148.40.9*. For demonstration purposes, we've used the special hostname `localhost`, which should always mean the current machine you're running on. The corresponding Internet address for localhost is *127.0.0.1*, if you'd rather use that.

PeerPort

> This is the service name or port number we'd like to connect to. We could have gotten away with using just `daytime` on systems with a well-configured system services file,* but just in case, we've specified the port number (13) in parentheses. Using just the number would also have worked, but numbers as constants make careful programmers nervous.

Notice how the return value from the **new** constructor is used as a filehandle in the **while** loop? That example is an indirect filehandle, which is a scalar variable containing a filehandle. You can use this filehandle as you would a normal filehandle. For example, you can read one line from it this way:

```
$line = <$handle>;
```

Or all remaining lines from it this way:

```
@lines = <$handle>;
```

And send a line of data to it this way:

```
print $handle "some data\n";
```

A Webget Client

Here's a simple client that contacts a remote server and fetches a list of documents from it. This is a more interesting client than the previous one because it sends a line of data to the server before fetching that server's response.

```
use IO::Socket;
unless (@ARGV > 1) { die "usage: $0 host document ..." }
$host = shift(@ARGV);
foreach $document ( @ARGV ) {
 $remote = IO::Socket::INET->new( Proto => "tcp",
 PeerAddr => $host,
 PeerPort => "http(80)",
 );
 unless ($remote) { die "cannot connect to http daemon on $host" }
 $remote->autoflush(1);
 print $remote "GET $document HTTP/1.0\n\n";
```

---

* The system services file is in *%windir%/system32/drivers/etc/services* under Windows NT.

```
    while ( <$remote> ) { print }
    close $remote;
}
```

The web server handling the *http* service is assumed to be at its standard port, number 80. If the server you're trying to connect to is at a different port (say, 8080), you should give `PeerPort => 8080` as the third argument to `new()`. The `autoflush` method is used on the socket because otherwise the system would buffer up the output we sent.

Connecting to the server is only the first part of the process: after you have the connection, you have to use the server's language. Each server on the network has its own little command language that it expects as input. The string that we send to the server starting with GET is in HTTP syntax. In this case, we simply request each specified document. Yes, we really are making a new connection for each document, even though it's the same host. That's the way it works with HTTP. (Recent versions of web browsers may request that the remote server leave the connection open a little while, but the server doesn't have to honor such a request.)

We'll call our program *webget.plx*. Here's how it might execute:

```
command_prompt> perl webget.plx www.perl.com /guanaco.html
HTTP/1.1 404 File Not Found
Date: Thu, 08 May 1997 18:02:32 GMT
Server: Apache/1.2b6
Connection: close
Content-type: text/html
<HEAD><TITLE>404 File Not Found</TITLE></HEAD>
<BODY><H1>File Not Found</H1>
The requested URL /guanaco.html was not found on this server.<P>
</BODY>
```

OK, so the program is not very interesting, because it didn't find that particular document. But a long response wouldn't have fit on this page.

For a more full-featured version of this program, you should look for the *lwp-request* program included with the LWP modules from CPAN.

You might also want to investigate the `Win32::Internet` extension module that provides easy access to the `HTTP` and `FTP` protocols. `Win32::Internet` is bundled with *libwin32*, or is available separately for those using the ActiveState distribution.

D

Topics We Didn't Mention

Yes, it's amazing. A book this long, and some things still weren't covered. The footnotes contain additional helpful information.

The purpose of this section is not to teach you about the things listed here, but merely to provide a list. You'll need to go to *Programming Perl*, the *perl* documentation, the Perl FAQ, the Perl for Win32 FAQ, the HTML documents in CPAN's *doc* directory, the Usenet support groups, or the Perl mailing lists to get further information.

Full Interprocess Communications

Yes, Perl can do networking. Beyond the TCP/IP stream sockets discussed in Appendix C, *Networking Clients*, Perl also supports UDP-based message passing, named and anonymous pipes, semaphores, mutexes, process control, IPC, signal handling, and more. See Chapter 6 of *Programming Perl* or the *perlipc* documentation for standard modules, and the networking section of the CPAN modules directory for third-party modules.

The Debugger

Perl has a wonderful source-level debugger, which the *perldebug* documentation will tell you all about.

The Command Line

The Perl interpreter has a plethora of command-line switches. Check out the *perlrun* documentation for information.

Other Operators

The comma operator, for one. And there are the bit manipulation operators &, |, ^, and ~, the ternary ?\ : operator, and the .\|. and .\|.\|. flip-flop operators, just to name a few.

And there are some variations on operators, like using the g modifier on match. For this and more, see *perlop*.

Many, Many More Functions

Yes, Perl has a lot of functions. We're not going to list them here, because the fastest way to find out about them is to read through the function section of *Programming Perl* or the *perlfunc* documentation and look at anything you don't recognize that sounds interesting. Here are a few of the more interesting ones.

grep and map

The grep function selects elements from its argument list, based upon the result of an expression that's repeatedly evaluated for its truth value, with the $_ variable successively set to each element in the list. For example:

```
@bigpowers = grep $_ > 6, 1, 2, 4, 8, 16; # gets (8, 16)
@b_names = grep /^b/, qw(fred barney betty wilma);
@textfiles = grep -T, <*>;
```

The map operator is similar, but instead of selecting or rejecting items, it merely collects the results of the expression (evaluated in a list context):

```
@more = map $_ + 3, 3, 5, 7; # gets 6, 8, 10
@squares = map $_ * $_, 1..10; # first 10 squares
@that = map "$_\n", @this; # like "unchop"
@triangle = map 1..$_, 1..5; # 1,1,2,1,2,3,1,2,3,4,1,2,3,4,5
%sizes = map { $_, -s } <*>; # hash of files and sizes
```

The eval Operator (and s///e)

Yes, you can construct a piece of code at runtime and then eval it. This process forces a dynamic compilation of the code inside the eval. This compilation is actually rather useful, because you can get some compile-time optimizations (like a compiled regular expression) at runtime. You can also use it to trap otherwise fatal errors in a section of code: a fatal error inside the eval merely exits the eval and gives you an error status.

For example, here's a program that reads a line of Perl code from the user and then executes it as if it were part of the Perl program:

```
print "code line: ";
```

```
chop($code = <STDIN>);
eval $code; die "eval: $@" if $@;
```

You can put Perl code inside the replacement string of a substitute operator with the **e** flag. This is handy if you want to construct something complicated for the replacement string, such as calling a subroutine that returns the results of a database lookup. Here's a loop that increments the value of the first column of a series of lines:

```
while (<>) {
  s/^(\S+)/$1+1/e; # $1+1 is Perl code, not a string
  print;
}
```

Another use of **eval** is as an error-trapping mechanism:

```
eval {
  &some_hairy_routine_that_might_die(@args);
};
if ($@) {
  print "oops... some_hairy died with $@";
}
```

Here, **$@** will be empty as long as the **eval** block worked; otherwise, it will have the text of the die message.

Many, Many Predefined Variables

You've seen a few predefined variables, like **$_**. Well, a lot more exist. Pretty much every punctuation character has been pressed into service. The *perlvar* documentation will be of help here. Also, see the **English** module in *perlmod*.

Symbol Table Manipulation With *FRED

You can make **b** an alias for **a** with ***b = *a**. This statement means that **$a** and **$b** refer to the same variable, as do **@a** and **@b**, and even filehandles and formats **a** and **b**. You can also localize ***b** inside a block with **local(*b)**, letting you have local filehandles, formats, and other things. Pretty fancy stuff, but useful when you need it.

Additional Regular Expression Features

Regular expressions can contain *extended* syntax (where whitespace is optional, so a regular expression can be split over multiple lines, and can contain regular Perl comments), and can have positive and negative *lookahead*. The syntax is a bit ugly, so rather than scare you off here, go look in *Programming Perl*, or see the *perlre* documentation. Jeffrey Friedl's book, *Mastering Regular Expressions* (published by O'Reilly & Associates), explains all of this and much more.

Packages

When multiple people work on a project, or if you're slighly schizophrenic, you can carve up the variable namespace using packages. A package is just a hidden prefix put in front of most variables (except variables created with the my operator). By changing the prefix, you get different variables. Here's a brief example:

```
$a = 123;               # this is really $main::a
$main::a++;             # same variable, now 124
package fred;           # now the prefix is "fred"
$a = 456;               # this is $fred::a
print $a - $main::a;    # prints 456-124
package main;           # back to original default
print $a + $fred::a;    # prints 124+456
```

So, any name with an explicit package name is used as is, but all other names get packaged into the current default package. Packages are local to the current file or block, and you always start out in package main at the top of a file. For details, the *perlsub* documentation will help here.

Embeddible, Extensible

The guts of Perl is defined well enough that it becomes a relatively straightforward task to embed the Perl compiler/interpreter inside another application, or to extend Perl by connecting it with arbitrary code written in C/C++ (or having a C-like interface). In fact, about a third of the on-line documentation for Perl is specifically devoted to embedding and extending Perl. The *perlembed*, *perlapi*, *perlxs*, *perlxstut*, *perlguts*, and *perlcall* documenation pages cover these topics in depth.

And because Perl is freely reusable, you can write your proprietary spreadsheet application, using an embedded Perl to evaluate the expressions in your spreadsheet cells, and not have to pay one cent in royalties for all that power. Joy.

Security Matters

Perl was designed with security in mind. See Chapter 6 of *Programming Perl* or the *perlsec* documentation about taint checking. This is the kind of security where you trust the writer of the program, but not the person running it, such as is often the case with server-launched programs. The Safe module, covered in the Safe documentation and Chapter 7 of *Programming Perl*, provides something else entirely: the kind of security necessary when executing (as with eval) unchecked code.

Switch or Case Statements

No, Perl doesn't *really* have these statements, but you can easily make them by using more basic constructs. See Chapter 2 of *Programming Perl* or the *perlsyn* documentation.

Direct I/O: sysopen, sysread, syswrite, and sysseek

Sometimes Perl's high-level I/O is a bit too high-level for what you need to do. Chapter 3 of *Programming Perl* and the *perlfunc* documentation cover direct access to the raw system calls for I/O.

The Perl Compiler

Although we speak of Perl as compiling your code before executing it, this compiled form is not native object code. Malcolm Beatie's Perl compiler project can produce standalone byte code or compilable C code out of your Perl script. The 5.005 release of Perl is expected to have native code generation included as part of the standard release. See the material in the *perlfaq3* documentation about this.

Database Support

Yes, Perl can interface directly with your commercial database servers, including Oracle, Sybase, Informix, and ODBC, just to name a few. See the database section in the CPAN modules directory for the relevant extension modules.

Complex Data Structures

Using references, you can build data structures of arbitrary complexity. These are discussed in Chapter 4 of *Programming Perl*, and in the *perllol*, *perldsc*, and *perlref* documentation. If you prefer an object-oriented data structure, see Chapter 5 of *Programming Perl*, or the *perltoot* and *perlobj* documentation.

Function Pointers

Perl can store and pass pointers to functions via the `\&funcname` notation, and call them indirectly via `&$funcptr($args)`. You can even write functions that create and return new anonymous functions, just as you could in languages like Lisp or Scheme. Such anonymous functions are often called *closures*. See Chapter 2 of *Programming Perl* and the *perlsub* and *perlfaq7* documentation for details.

And Other Stuff

Perl just keeps getting more powerful and more useful, and it's quite an effort to keep the documentation up to date. (Who knows? By the time this book hits the shelves, there could be a Visual Perl.) But in any case, thanks, Larry!

Index

Symbols

&& operator as control structure, 114

**= operator, 49

@*, in formats, 131

@_, 103
  introduced, 22
  scope of, 103

! (logical not) operator, 23

!= operator, 44

!/usr/bin/perl line, 9

, (comma) operator, 265

$& (match string), 96

$` (before-match string), 96

$^ variable, 136

$^I variable, 181

$^T variable, 123

$: variable, 132

$= variable, 137

$#fred (index of last element of @fred), 60

$- variable, 137

$% (special variable), example of, 32

$' (after-match string), 96

$/ variable, 79

$~ variable, 136

$_
  $_[0], distinct from, 103
  file tests default, 123
  foreach statement and, 71
  implicit assignment to when reading, 80
  regular expression matching default, 85
  selecting other than with =~
      operator, 93

split( ) default, 97

stat( ), lstat( ) default, 124

tr( ) default target, 164

unlink( ) default, 145

$1, $2, ... in regular expressions, 95

$a, $b variables, in sort comparison
      routine, 161

.. operator, as list constructor operator, 56

.= operator, 49

== operator, 44

=~ operator
  defined, 93
  example of, 20
  substitution and, 97
  tr( ) and, 165

-= operator, 131

-- operator, 50

<, <= operators, 44

<=> (see spaceship operator), 162

<> (see diamond operator), 80, 181

+ (plus sign)
  open( ) and, 180
  in regular expressions, 88

+= operator
  defined, 48
  example of, 224

++ operator
  defined, 49
  example of, 151

?: operator, as control structure, 115

>, >= operators, 44

\1, in regular expressions, 89

About the Authors

Randal L. Schwartz is an eclectic tradesman and entrepreneur, making his living through software design, technical writing and training, system administration, security consultation, and video production. He is known internationally for his prolific, humorous, and occasionally incorrect spatterings on Usenet—especially his "Just another Perl hacker" signoffs in *comp.lang.perl*.

Randal honed his many crafts through seven years of employment at Tektronix, ServioLogic, and Sequent. Since 1985, he has owned and operated Stonehenge Consulting Services in his home town of Portland, Oregon. Randal is not new to O'Reilly. He is author of *Learning Perl* and co-author of *Programming Perl*, which he wrote with Tom Christiansen and Larry Wall, the creator of Perl.

Erik Olson is a renegade linguist who makes a living developing software for Win32 platforms. Since 1994, Erik has been director of advanced technologies for Axiom Technologies, LC, a software outsourcing shop. Erik delivers developer training, system administration, and program/concept development for a number of large-scale horizontal and vertical applications.

Working as a program developer since 1986, Erik has implemented a variety of systems ranging from point-of-sales systems to horizontal PIM products to real-time financial market applications. Although much of his work is done in C++, he has particular interests in interpreted languages and ActiveX scripting. Erik earned a B.A. in linguistics from the University of Utah and pursued graduate studies in Arabic linguistics there and at the University of Washington.

Tom Christiansen is a freelance consultant specializing in Perl training and writing. After working for several years for TSR Hobbies (of Dungeons and Dragons fame), he set off for college where he spent a year in Spain and five in America dabbling in music, linguistics, programming, and some half-dozen spoken languages. Tom finally escaped UW-Madison with B.A.s in Spanish and computer science and an M.S. in computer science.

He then spent five years at Convex as a jack-of-all-trades, working on everything from system administration to utility and kernel development, with customer support and training thrown in for good measure. Tom also served two terms on the USENIX Association Board of Directors. With over fifteen year's experience in UNIX system administration and programming, Tom presents seminars internationally. Living in the foothills above Boulder, Colorado, surrounded by mule deer, skunks, and the occasional mountain lion and black bear, Tom takes summers off for hiking, hacking, birding, music making, and gaming

Colophon

The animal on the cover of *Learning Perl on Win32 Systems* is a wall gecko. Geckos are a very large and diverse family of lizards, with approximately 670 species. The wall gecko is found in North Africa, southern parts of Spain, France, and Italy, the Canary Islands, and some South Pacific islands. Their wide distribution is largely due to geckos stowing away aboard cargo ships. Wall geckos regularly live among humans, making their homes in the crevices of houses.

As their name implies, wall geckos can climb walls with ease, a skill they share with other geckos. Contrary to long-held opinion, they do not have suction cup–like fingers and toes. Instead, they have microscopic, hooked cells covering their digits. The cells hook into any tiny crevice or irregularity in a surface, even glass.

Geckos are the only reptiles that make extensive use of their voices. They communicate danger, attract mates, and mark territory using a range of chirps, squeaks, and barks. If caught, a gecko can break off a section of its tail using muscular contraction, which severs a tail vertebra. The tail will regenerate, but can never again be broken off at that particular site.

Wall geckos, which are nocturnal, have excellent vision. They have no eyelids, just a transparent scale covering the eye surface. Like cats' eyes, the gecko's pupil closes to a slit to restrict light, and opens to fill the iris at night.

Edie Freedman designed this cover and the entire UNIX bestiary that appears on other Nutshell Handbooks. The beasts themselves are adapted from 19th-century engravings from the Dover Pictorial Archive. The cover layout was produced with Quark XPress 3.32 using ITC Garamond from Adobe. Whenever possible, our books use RepKover™, a durable and flexible lay-flat binding. If the page count exceeds RepKover's limit, perfect binding is used.

The inside layout was designed by Nancy Priest and formatted in FrameMaker 5.0 by Mike Sierra using ITC Garamond Light and ITC Garamond Book fonts. This colophon was written by Clairemarie Fisher O'Leary.

More Titles from O'Reilly

Perl

Perl Resource Kit—UNIX Edition

By Larry Wall, Clay Irving, Nate Patwardhan,
Ellen Siever & Brian Jepson
1st Edition November 1997 (est.)
1700 pages (est.)
ISBN 1-56592-370-7

The *Perl Resource Kit* is the most compre-
hesive collection of documentation and
commercially enhanced software tools yet
published for Perl programmers. The
UNIX edition, the first in a series, is the definitive Perl distribution for webmasters, programmers, and system administrators.

Software tools on the Kit's CD include:

- A Java/Perl back-end to the Perl compiler, written by Larry Wall,
  creator of Perl

- Snapshot of the freeware Perl archives on CPAN, with an Install
  program and a web-aware interface for identifying more recent
  online CPAN tools

This new Java/Perl tool allows programmers to write Java classes
with Perl implementations (innards), and run the code through a
compiler back-end to produce Java byte-code. Using this new
tool, programmers can exploit Java's wide availability on the
browser (as well as on the server), while using Perl for the
things that it does better than Java (such as string processing).

The Kit also includes four tutorial and reference books that contain systematic documentation for the most important Perl extension modules, as well as documentation for the commercially
enhanced and supported tools on the CD. The books in the Kit
are not available elsewhere or separatelyand include:

- *Perl Module Programmer's Guide*, by Clay Irving and Nate
  Patwardhan.

- *Perl Module Reference Manual* (two volumes), compiled and
  edited by Ellen Siever and David Futato.

- *Perl Utilities*, by Brian Jepson.

The *Perl Resource Kit* is the first comprehensive tutorialand reference documentation for hundreds of essential third-party Perl
extension modules used for creating CGI applications and more.
It features commercially enhanced Perl utilities specially developed for the Kit by Perl's creator, Larry Wall. And, it is all
brought to you by the premier publisher of Perl and UNIX books
and documentation, O'Reilly & Associates.

Programming Perl, 2nd Edition

By Larry Wall, Tom Christiansen &
Randal L. Schwartz
2nd Edition September 1996
670 pages, ISBN 1-56592-149-6

Programming Perl, second edition, is the
authoritative guide to Perl version 5, the
scripting utility that has established itself
as the programming tool of choice for the
World Wide Web, UNIX system administra-
tion, and a vast range of other applications. Version 5 of Perl
includes object-oriented programming facilities. The book is
coauthored by Larry Wall, the creator of Perl.

Perl is a language for easily manipulating text, files, and processes. It provides a more concise and readable way to do many jobs
that were formerly accomplished (with difficulty) by programming with C or one of the shells. Perl is likely to be available
wherever you choose to work.And if it isn't, you can get it and
install it easily and free of charge.

This heavily revised second edition of *Programming Perl* contains a full explanation of the features in Perl version 5.003.
Contents include:

- An introduction to Perl

- Explanations of the language and its syntax

- Perl functions

- Perl library modules

- The use of references in Perl

- How to use Perl's object-oriented features

- Invocation options for Perl itself, and also for the utilities that
  come with Perl

Perl 5 Desktop Reference

By Johan Vromans
1st Edition February 1996
46 pages, ISBN 1-56592-187-9

This is the standard quick-reference guide for
the Perl programming language. It provides a
complete overview of the language, from variables to input and output, from flow control to
regular expressions, from functions to document formats—all packed into a convenient,
carry-around booklet. Updated to cover Perl version 5.003.

O'REILLY™

TO ORDER: **800-998-9938** • *order@oreilly.com* • *http://www.oreilly.com/*

OUR PRODUCTS ARE AVAILABLE AT A BOOKSTORE OR SOFTWARE STORE NEAR YOU.

FOR INFORMATION: **800-998-9938** • **707-829-0515** • *info@oreilly.com*

Perl *continued*

Learning Perl, 2nd Edition

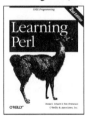

By Randal L. Schwartz & Tom Christiansen,
Foreword by Larry Wall
2nd Edition July 1997
302 pages, ISBN 1-56592-284-0

In this update of a bestseller, two leading Perl trainers teach you to use the most universal scripting language in the age of the World Wide Web. With a foreword by Larry Wall, the creator of Perl, this smooth, carefully paced book is the "official" guide for both formal (classroom) and informal learning. It is now current for Perl version 5.004.

Learning Perl is a hands-on tutorial designed to get you writing useful Perl scripts as quickly as possible. Exercises (with complete solutions) accompany each chapter. A lengthy, new chapter in this edition introduces you to CGI programming, while touching also on the use of library modules, references, and Perl's object-oriented constructs.

Perl is a language for easily manipulating text, files, and processes. It comes standard on most UNIX platforms and is available free of charge on all other important operating systems. Perl technical support is informally available—often within minutes—from a pool of experts who monitor a USENET newsgroup *(comp.lang.perl.misc)* with tens

of thousands of readers.

Contents include:

- A quick tutorial stroll through Perl basics
- Systematic, topic-by-topic coverage of Perl's broad capabilities
- Lots of brief code examples
- Programming exercises for each topic, with fully worked-out answers
- How to execute system commands from your Perl program
- How to manage DBM databases using Perl
- An introduction to CGI programming for the Web

Advanced Perl Programming

By Sriram Srinivasan
1st Edition August 1997
434 pages, ISBN 1-56592-220-4

This book covers complex techniques for managing production-ready Perl programs and explains methods for manipulating data and objects that may have looked like magic before. It gives you necessary background for dealing with networks, databases, and GUIs, and includes a discussion of internals to help you program more efficiently and embed Perl within C or C within Perl.

Learning Perl on Win32 Systems

By Randal L. Schwartz, Erik Olson &
Tom Christiansen
1st Edition August 1997
306 pages, ISBN 1-56592-324-3

In this carefully paced course, leading Perl trainers and a Windows NT practitioner teach you to program in the language that promises to emerge as the scripting language of choice on NT. Based on the "llama" book, this book features tips for PC users and new, NT-specific examples, along with a foreword by Larry Wall, the creator of Perl, and Dick Hardt, the creator of Perl for Win32.

Mastering Regular Expressions

By Jeffrey E. F. Friedl
1st Edition January 1997
368 pages, ISBN 1-56592-257-3

Regular expressions, a powerful tool for manipulating text and data, are found in scripting languages, editors, programming environments, and specialized tools. In this book, author Jeffrey Friedl leads you through the steps of crafting a regular expression that gets the job done. He examines a variety of tools and uses them in an extensive array of examples, with a major focus on Perl.

Windows

Developing Windows Error Messages

By Ben Ezzell
1st Edition November 1997 (est.)
300 pages (est.), Includes diskette
ISBN 1-56592-356-1

This book teaches C, C++, and Visual Basic programmers how to write effective error messages that notify the user of an error, clearly explain the error, and most importantly offer a solution to the error.

Win32 Multithreaded Programming

By Aaron Cohen & Mike Woodring
1st Edition November 1997 (est.), 700 pages (est.), Includes diskette, ISBN 1-56592-296-4

This book clearly explains the concepts of multithreaded programs and shows developers how to construct efficient and complex applications. An important book for any developer, it illustrates all aspects of Win32 multithreaded programming, including what has previously been undocumented or poorly explained.

Windows NT File System Internals

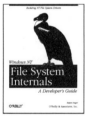

By Rajeev Nagar
1st Edition September 1997, 794 pages, Includes diskette, ISBN 1-56592-249-2

Windows NT File System Internals presents the details of the NT I/O Manager, the Cache Manager, and the Memory Manager from the perspective of a software developer writing a file system driver or implementing a kernel-mode filter driver. The book provides numerous code examples included on diskette, as well as the source for a complete, usable filter driver.

Access Database Design & Programming

By Steven Roman
1st Edition June 1997, 270 pages, ISBN 1-56592-297-2

This book provides experienced Access users who are novice programers with frequently overlooked concepts and techniques necessary to create effective database applications. It focuses on designing effective tables in a multi-table application; using the Access interface or Access SQL to construct queries; and programming using the Data Access Object (DAO) and Microsoft Access object models.

Inside the Windows 95 File System

By Stan Mitchell
1st Edition May 1997
378 pages, Includes diskette
ISBN 1-56592-200-X

In this book, Stan Mitchell describes the Windows 95 File System, as well as the new opportunities and challenges it brings for developers. Its "hands-on" approach will help developers become better equipped to make design decisions using the new Win95 File System features. Includes a diskette containing MULTIMON, a general-purpose monitor for examining Windows internals.

Dictionary of PC Hardware and Data Communications Terms

By Mitchell Shnier
1st Edition April 1996
532 pages, ISBN 1-56592-158-5

This comprehensive dictionary provides complete descriptions of complex terms in two of the most volatile and interesting areas of computer development: personal computers and networks. It contains up-to-date information about everything from a common item like "batteries" to an obscure font technology called "Speedo." Also available online. See *http://www.ora.com/reference/dictionary/* for details.

Inside the Windows 95 Registry

By Ron Petrusha
1st Edition August 1996
594 pages, ISBN 1-56592-170-4

An in-depth examination of remote registry access, differences between the Win95 and NT registries, registry backup, undocumented registry services, and the role the registry plays in OLE. Shows programmers how to access the Win95 registry from Win32, Win16, and DOS programs in C and Visual Basic. VxD sample code is also included. Includes diskette.

How to stay in touch with O'Reilly

1. Visit Our Award-Winning Web Site

http://www.oreilly.com/

★"Top 100 Sites on the Web" —*PC Magazine*
★"Top 5% Web sites" —*Point Communications*
★"3-Star site" —*The McKinley Group*

Our web site contains a library of comprehensiveproduct information (including book excerpts and tables of contents), downloadable software, background articles, interviews with technology leaders, links to relevant sites, book cover art, and more. File us in your Bookmarks or Hotlist!

2. Join Our Email Mailing Lists

New Product Releases

To receive automatic email with brief descriptions of all new O'Reilly products as they are released, send email to: **listproc@online.oreilly.com**
Put the following information in the first line of your message (*not* in the Subject field):
subscribe oreilly-news "Your Name" of "Your Organization" (for example: subscribe oreilly-news Kris Webber of Fine Enterprises)

O'Reilly Events

If you'd also like us to send information about trade show events, special promotions, and other O'Reilly events, send email to: **listproc@online.oreilly.com**
Put the following information in the first line of your message (*not* in the Subject field):
subscribe oreilly-events "Your Name" of "Your Organization"

3. Get Examples from Our Books via FTP

There are two ways to access an archive of example files from our books:

Regular FTP

• ftp to:
  ftp.oreilly.com
  (login: anonymous
  password: your email address)
• Point your web browser to:
  ftp://ftp.oreilly.com/

FTPMAIL

• Send an email message to:
  ftpmail@online.oreilly.com
  (Write "help" in the message body)

4. Visit Our Gopher Site

• Connect your gopher to:
  gopher.oreilly.com

• Point your web browser to:
  gopher://gopher.oreilly.com/

• Telnet to:
  gopher.oreilly.com
  login: gopher

5. Contact Us via Email

order@oreilly.com
To place a book or software order online. Good for North American and international customers.

subscriptions@oreilly.com
To place an order for any of our newsletters or periodicals.

books@oreilly.com
General questions about any of our books.

software@oreilly.com
For general questions and product information about our software. Check out O'Reilly Software Online at **http://software.oreilly.com/** for software and technical support information. Registered O'Reilly software users send your questions to: **website-support@oreilly.com**

cs@oreilly.com
For answers to problems regarding your order or our products.

booktech@oreilly.com
For book content technical questions or corrections.

proposals@oreilly.com
To submit new book or software proposals to our editors and product managers.

international@oreilly.com
For information about our international distributors or translation queries. For a list of our distributors outside of North America check out:
http://www.oreilly.com/www/order/country.html

O'Reilly & Associates, Inc.
101 Morris Street, Sebastopol, CA 95472 USA
TEL   707-829-0515 or 800-998-9938
            (6am to 5pm PST)
FAX   707-829-0104

O'REILLY™

Titles from O'Reilly

Please note that upcoming titles are displayed in italic.

WEB PROGRAMMING

Apache: The Definitive Guide
Building Your Own Web
 Conferences
Building Your Own Website
CGI Programming for the World
 Wide Web
Designing for the Web
HTML: The Definitive Guide,
 2nd Ed.
JavaScript: The Definitive Guide,
 2nd Ed.
Learning Perl
Programming Perl, 2nd Ed.
Mastering Regular Expressions
WebMaster in a Nutshell
Web Security & Commerce
Web Client Programming with
 Perl
World Wide Web Journal

USING THE INTERNET

Smileys
The Future Does Not Compute
The Whole Internet User's Guide
 & Catalog
The Whole Internet for Win 95
Using Email Effectively
Bandits on the Information
 Superhighway

JAVA SERIES

Exploring Java
Java AWT Reference
Java Fundamental Classes
 Reference
Java in a Nutshell
*Java Language Reference, 2nd
 Edition*
Java Network Programming
Java Threads
Java Virtual Machine

SOFTWARE

WebSite™ 1.1
WebSite Professional™
Building Your Own Web
 Conferences
WebBoard™
PolyForm™
Statisphere™

SONGLINE GUIDES

NetActivism   NetResearch
Net Law   NetSuccess
NetLearning   NetTravel
Net Lessons

SYSTEM ADMINISTRATION

Building Internet Firewalls
Computer Crime: A
 Crimefighter's Handbook
Computer Security Basics
DNS and BIND, 2nd Ed.
Essential System Administration,
 2nd Ed.
Getting Connected: The Internet
 at 56K and Up
Linux Network Administrator's
 Guide
Managing Internet Information
 Services
Managing NFS and NIS
Networking Personal Computers
 with TCP/IP
Practical UNIX & Internet
 Security, 2nd Ed.
PGP: Pretty Good Privacy
sendmail, 2nd Ed.
sendmail Desktop Reference
System Performance Tuning
TCP/IP Network Administration
termcap & terminfo
Using & Managing UUCP
Volume 8: X Window System
 Administrator's Guide
Web Security & Commerce

UNIX

Exploring Expect
Learning VBScript
Learning GNU Emacs, 2nd Ed.
Learning the bash Shell
Learning the Korn Shell
Learning the UNIX Operating
 System
Learning the vi Editor
Linux in a Nutshell
Making TeX Work
Linux Multimedia Guide
Running Linux, 2nd Ed.
SCO UNIX in a Nutshell
sed & awk, 2nd Edition
Tcl/Tk Tools
UNIX in a Nutshell: System V
 Edition
UNIX Power Tools
Using csh & tsch
When You Can't Find Your UNIX
 System Administrator
Writing GNU Emacs Extensions

WEB REVIEW STUDIO SERIES

Gif Animation Studio
Shockwave Studio

WINDOWS

Dictionary of PC Hardware and
 Data Communications Terms
Inside the Windows 95 Registry
Inside the Windows 95 File
 System
Windows Annoyances
*Windows NT File System
 Internals*
Windows NT in a Nutshell

PROGRAMMING

Advanced Oracle PL/SQL
 Programming
Applying RCS and SCCS
C++: The Core Language
Checking C Programs with lint
DCE Security Programming
Distributing Applications Across
 DCE & Windows NT
Encyclopedia of Graphics File
 Formats, 2nd Ed.
Guide to Writing DCE
 Applications
lex & yacc
Managing Projects with make
Mastering Oracle Power Objects
Oracle Design: The Definitive
 Guide
Oracle Performance Tuning, 2nd
 Ed.
Oracle PL/SQL Programming
Porting UNIX Software
POSIX Programmer's Guide
POSIX.4: Programming for the
 Real World
Power Programming with RPC
Practical C Programming
Practical C++ Programming
Programming Python
Programming with curses
Programming with GNU Software
Pthreads Programming
Software Portability with imake,
 2nd Ed.
Understanding DCE
Understanding Japanese
 Information Processing
UNIX Systems Programming for
 SVR4

BERKELEY 4.4 SOFTWARE DISTRIBUTION

4.4BSD System Manager's
 Manual
4.4BSD User's Reference Manual
4.4BSD User's Supplementary
 Documents
4.4BSD Programmer's Reference
 Manual
4.4BSD Programmer's
 Supplementary Documents
X Programming
Vol. 0: X Protocol Reference
 Manual
Vol. 1: Xlib Programming Manual
Vol. 2: Xlib Reference Manual
Vol. 3M: X Window System User's
 Guide, Motif Edition
Vol. 4M: X Toolkit Intrinsics
 Programming Manual, Motif
 Edition
Vol. 5: X Toolkit Intrinsics
 Reference Manual
Vol. 6A: Motif Programming
 Manual
Vol. 6B: Motif Reference Manual
Vol. 6C: Motif Tools
Vol. 8 : X Window System
 Administrator's Guide
Programmer's Supplement for
 Release 6
X User Tools
The X Window System in a
 Nutshell

CAREER & BUSINESS

Building a Successful Software
 Business
The Computer User's Survival
 Guide
Love Your Job!
Electronic Publishing on CD-
 ROM

TRAVEL

Travelers' Tales: Brazil
Travelers' Tales: Food
Travelers' Tales: France
Travelers' Tales: Gutsy Women
Travelers' Tales: India
Travelers' Tales: Mexico
Travelers' Tales: Paris
Travelers' Tales: San Francisco
Travelers' Tales: Spain
Travelers' Tales: Thailand
Travelers' Tales: A Woman's
 World

O'REILLY™

TO ORDER: **800-998-9938** • *order@oreilly.com* • *http://www.oreilly.com/*
OUR PRODUCTS ARE AVAILABLE AT A BOOKSTORE OR SOFTWARE STORE NEAR YOU.
FOR INFORMATION: **800-998-9938** • **707-829-0515** • *info@oreilly.com*

International Distributors

UK, Europe, Middle East and Northern Africa (except France, Germany, Switzerland, & Austria)

INQUIRIES
International Thomson Publishing Europe
Berkshire House
168-173 High Holborn
London WC1V 7AA, United Kingdom
Telephone: 44-171-497-1422
Fax: 44-171-497-1426
Email: itpint@itps.co.uk

ORDERS
International Thomson Publishing Services, Ltd.
Cheriton House, North Way
Andover, Hampshire SP10 5BE,
United Kingdom
Telephone: 44-264-342-832
  (UK orders)
Telephone: 44-264-342-806
  (outside UK)
Fax: 44-264-364418 (UK orders)
Fax: 44-264-342761 (outside UK)
UK & Eire orders: itpuk@itps.co.uk
International orders: itpint@itps.co.uk

France

Editions Eyrolles
61 bd Saint-Germain
75240 Paris Cedex 05
France
Fax: 33-01-44-41-11-44

FRENCH LANGUAGE BOOKS
All countries except Canada
Phone: 33-01-44-41-46-16
Email: geodif@eyrolles.com

ENGLISH LANGUAGE BOOKS
Phone: 33-01-44-41-11-87
Email: distribution@eyrolles.com

Australia

WoodsLane Pty. Ltd.
7/5 Vuko Place, Warriewood NSW 2102
P.O. Box 935, Mona Vale NSW 2103
Australia
Telephone: 61-2-9970-5111
Fax: 61-2-9970-5002
Email: info@woodslane.com.au

Germany, Switzerland, and Austria

INQUIRIES
O'Reilly Verlag
Balthasarstr. 81
D-50670 Köln
Germany
Telephone: 49-221-97-31-60-0
Fax: 49-221-97-31-60-8
Email: anfragen@oreilly.de

ORDERS
International Thomson Publishing
Königswinterer Straße 418
53227 Bonn, Germany
Telephone: 49-228-97024 0
Fax: 49-228-441342
Email: order@oreilly.de

Asia (except Japan & India)

INQUIRIES
International Thomson Publishing Asia
60 Albert Street #15-01
Albert Complex
Singapore 189969
Telephone: 65-336-6411
Fax: 65-336-7411

ORDERS
Telephone: 65-336-6411
Fax: 65-334-1617
thomson@signet.com.sg

New Zealand

WoodsLane New Zealand Ltd.
21 Cooks Street (P.O. Box 575)
Wanganui, New Zealand
Telephone: 64-6-347-6543
Fax: 64-6-345-4840
Email: info@woodslane.com.au

Japan

O'Reilly Japan, Inc.
Kiyoshige Building 2F
12-Banchi, Sanei-cho
Shinjuku-ku
Tokyo 160 Japan
Telephone: 81-3-3356-5227
Fax: 81-3-3356-5261
Email: kenji@oreilly.com

India

Computer Bookshop (India) PVT. LTD.
190 Dr. D.N. Road, Fort
Bombay 400 001
India
Telephone: 91-22-207-0989
Fax: 91-22-262-3551
Email: cbsbom@giasbm01.vsnl.net.in

The Americas

O'Reilly & Associates, Inc.
101 Morris Street
Sebastopol, CA 95472 U.S.A.
Telephone: 707-829-0515
Telephone: 800-998-9938 (U.S. & Canada)
Fax: 707-829-0104
Email: order@oreilly.com

Southern Africa

International Thomson Publishing Southern Africa
Building 18, Constantia Park
138 Sixteenth Road
P.O. Box 2459
Halfway House, 1685 South Africa
Telephone: 27-11-805-4819
Fax: 27-11-805-3648

O'Reilly & Associates, Inc.
101 Morris Street
Sebastopol, CA 95472-9902
1-800-998-9938

Visit us online at:
http://www.ora.com/
orders@ora.com

O'REILLY WOULD LIKE TO HEAR FROM YOU

Which book did this card come from?

_____

Where did you buy this book?
- ❏ Bookstore
- ❏ Direct from O'Reilly
- ❏ Bundled with hardware/software
- ❏ Other _____

What operating system do you use?
- ❏ UNIX
- ❏ Windows NT
- ❏ Other _____

- ❏ Computer Store
- ❏ Class/seminar

- ❏ Macintosh
- ❏ PC(Windows/DOS)

What is your job description?
- ❏ System Administrator
- ❏ Network Administrator
- ❏ Web Developer
- ❏ Other _____

- ❏ Programmer
- ❏ Educator/Teacher

- ❏ Please send me O'Reilly's catalog, containing a complete listing of O'Reilly books and software.

Name _____   Company/Organization _____

Address _____

City _____   State _____   Zip/Postal Code _____   Country _____

Telephone _____   Internet or other email address (specify network) _____

Nineteenth century wood engraving
of a bear from the O'Reilly &
Associates Nutshell Handbook®
Using & Managing UUCP.

BUSINESS REPLY MAIL
FIRST CLASS MAIL   PERMIT NO. 80   SEBASTOPOL, CA

Postage will be paid by addressee

O'Reilly & Associates, Inc.
101 Morris Street
Sebastopol, CA 95472-9902